Arkansas in Short Fiction

STORIES FROM 1841 TO 1984

This publication sanctioned by the
Arkansas Sesquicentennial Commission, Inc.

The Arkansas Sesquicentennial Commission
makes no judgment and assumes
no responsibility for the quality, value or
content of any sanctioned publication.

Arkansas in Short Fiction

STORIES FROM 1841 TO 1984

Edited by
William M. Baker
&
Ethel C. Simpson

AUGUST HOUSE / LITTLE ROCK

Printed in the United States of America

First Edition, 1986

10 9 8 7 6 5 4 3 2 1

LIBRARY OF CONGRESS CATALOGING-IN-PUBLICATION DATA

Arkansas in short fiction.

1. Short stories, American—Arkansas.
2. Arkansas—Fiction.
I. Baker, William M. (William McDowell), 1939–
II. Simpson, Ethel C., 1937–
PS558.A8A74   1986   813'.01'0832767   86-4506
ISBN 0-87483-007-9
ISBN 0-87483-006-0 (pbk.)

Cover illustration by Jacqueline Froelich
Production artwork by Ira Hocut
Design direction by Ted Parkhurst
Project direction by Liz Parkhurst
Typography by Arrow Connection

CONTENTS

FOREWORD

Almost as soon as Arkansas became a territory and state, it gained a place of its own in the popular and literary imagination. The folk play and tune of the Arkansaw Traveler, reinforced by thousands of prints inspired by Edward Payson Washburn's paintings, gave the name and a particular character of Arkansas a currency far out of proportion to its political importance. And the magazine contributions of Albert Pike and Charles Fenton Mercer Noland, especially Noland's "Pete Whetstone" letters to the *Spirit of the Times*, filled out the picture for a generation of male readers for whom Arkansas was a "creation state," where varmints and men wandered about in naive contempt of man's laws and civilization's demands. Thomas Bangs Thorpe's "The Big Bear of Arkansas" is the classic description of the Arkansas squatter as a shameless entertainer and practiced liar. This Arkansas stereotype was widely disseminated, in French and German as well as in English.

Thorpe's narrator is detached from "the Big Bear" almost to the point of total ironic disengagement. As such he is the most familiar character from nineteenth century literature, and we meet his counterparts in virtually every story in these pages, whether as the author or as the author's voice within a story. Arkansans have rarely been pleased with the depiction of Arkansas in commercial fiction; Opie Read and Thyra Samter Winslow paid especially high prices in social terms for their ironic treatment of Arkansas subject matter.

But, to redress the balances, that Arkansas connection amply rewarded many of these writers. Thorpe is best known for his "Big Bear." Opie Read, Alice French, and Ruth McEnery Stuart were all natives of other states, but though they practiced their arts on other locales, all achieved in their Arkansas stories their greatest artistic and commercial success. The same may be said of Thyra Samter Winslow in the twentieth century. As a group, their science of caricature is just, their eyes are true, their ears—and their hearts—are sound.

All the writers we have mentioned were professional in every sense. They produced a highly crafted—if sometimes overly standardized—fiction for appreciative editors and large attentive audiences in the cosmopolitan Northeast and Midwest. Dr. Charles E. Nash and George Rose together represent—in distinctive ways—another literary current, indigenous story-telling for a resident and native audience. Nash is better known today for his Civil War hagiographies, and is the author of the most curious book ever written by an Arkansan, the allegory of the bicycle ride to hell. Rose's usual manner, in contrast, was elevated and restrained. But both attest the presence of a mother lode of storytelling that underlies Arkansas fiction from the Pete Whetstone letters to Donald Harington's novels. This compulsion to story-telling, which includes an easy tolerance of the familiar and hackneyed, is what marks the Arkansas story throughout its history.

Thomas Bangs Thorpe (1815–1870) was a New Englander who went South for his health and became much at home there, though he spent his last years in New York. He was a painter, and his writing shows his talent for accurate and telling details of the pastimes of Southern frontier life, with all their grotesqueness and outrageous humor. His sketches were nationally popular, and some of his work was translated into French, Italian and German. Like Albert Pike and to a lesser extent Opie Read, Thorpe combined journalism and politics. He wrote for and edited a number of Whig papers in New Orleans and elsewhere.

"The Big Bear of Arkansas" first appeared in the *Spirit of the Times* in 1841. His stories were collected in two volumes, one *The Big Bear of Arkansas* (1845), edited by William T. Porter, from which it is reprinted here. The other anthology is entitled *Colonel Thorpe's Scenes in Arkansaw* (1858).

Opie Read (1852-1939) was born in Kentucky, but his association with newspapers and publishing in Little Rock was the basis of his best-known work. *The Arkansaw Traveler*, a "humorous and literary weekly," made its first appearance in 1882 and was widely distributed throughout the country. When he moved the paper to Chicago in 1887, he extended his range to other literary characters, but he is firmly identified with the hillbilly and the southern gentleman, two of the types frequently described in his pages. In addition to his journalistic writing, Read published more than fifty books. Like many popular writers of the time, he lectured widely on the Chautauqua circuit. His memoirs, *I Remember*, were published in 1930. The texts here are from the author's *Selected Stories* of 1891.

Octave Thanet is the pen name of Alice French (1850-1934). In the heyday of the American magazine, her short stories and articles appeared in *Harper's*, the *Atlantic Monthly*, *Scribner's*, and other major publications. Five volumes of her collected stories were published.

Thanet was a New Englander, transplanted to the Middle West, where her father made his fortune in lumber, railroads, and other enterprises. She acquired an interest in a Lawrence County, Arkansas, plantation in 1883 and began to use her experiences and observations there in her local color stories. She insisted on the realism of her portrayal of the Southern scene, which was frequently overlaid with her political and social views. She wrote about aristocrats, poor whites, including "white trash," and blacks. One story, "Trusty No. 49," is a satirical treatment of rural Arkansas justice and of the prison system.

"Sist' Chaney's Black Silk" is reprinted from *Otto the Knight, and Other Trans-Mississippi Stories* (1891). "Why Abbylonia Surrendered" is from *A Book of True Lovers* (1897).

Ruth McEnery Stuart (1852-1917) lived in Washington, Arkansas from 1879 to 1883, when her husband's death caused her to leave and to take up a career as a writer. She created an imaginary village, Simpkinsville, drawing on her experiences in Arkansas. Her stories enjoyed great popularity in the magazines of her day, and she was particularly associated with *Harper's Magazine*. Stuart was considered a master of Southern dialect, and she was a highly successful Chautauqua speaker.

By any modern standard, or even that of Thyra Samter Winslow, Stuart's stories are overly sentimental. The opinion of the old storyteller in "An Arkansas Prophet," that all stories should have a happy ending, is reflected in most of her work. But Stuart's stories abound in details of everyday life, and they are rich in humor.

Stuart published more than twenty books, including novels and verse. "The Woman's Exchange of Simpkinsville" is from the separate publication as a book in 1899.

George B. Rose (1860–1942) was a member of the Little Rock family who have participated for many years in the legal and judicial affairs of the state. He wrote numerous studies of Renaissance art, as well as reminiscences of Little Rock and literary works, including "Sebastian, a Dramatic Poem" (1894). His story "William Wilson" was privately printed c.1901, and is reprinted here from that text.

There are numerous differences between Rose's story and the one by Edgar Allan Poe with the same title, but both are saturated with Gothic atmosphere and supernatural events. The use of the railroad and the telephone give the Rose story a contemporary flavor, and it is rich in local details.

Charles J. Finger (1869–1941) wrote more than thirty-five books. An Englishman, he emigrated in 1890 to South America, where among other adventures, he worked as a guide to the Franco-Russian Ornithological Expedition in 1893. He went to the Klondike and to Texas, but later settled into a career with the Ohio River and Columbus Railway.

In 1916, he began writing for *Reedy's Mirror,* a literary magazine in St. Louis. He had just assumed the editorship of the *Mirror* when Mr. Reedy's death brought the magazine to an end.

The Fingers moved to Fayetteville, where they had a farm, Gayeta Lodge, replete with studio, outbuildings, livestock, and gardens. Gayeta became a focus of cultural and literary life in the community, and Finger started his own magazine *All's Well, or the Mirror Repolished.* He participated in the Arkansas Writers Project of the WPA. *Tales from Silver Lands* won a Newbery Medal in 1924. The story reprinted here, "Eric," is from *In Lawless Lands* (1924).

Thyra Samter Winslow (1885–1961) wrote stories for many of the popular magazines of her day, including the *Redbook, New Yorker,* and *Cosmopolitan.* She wrote more than a hundred for the *Smart Set* between 1915 and 1923, when H.L. Mencken and George Jean Nathan were its editors. The brittle sophistication and harsh satiric realism of that magazine were in large part due to her influence. Winslow's stories of small-town life contain many details of her early experiences in Fort Smith, regardless of their fictional names. These towns are mean places of seedy neighborhoods, cheap dance-halls, and the stuffy, overdone houses of the rich elite. Her stories depict the life of the common people, devoid of the sentimental aura of much magazine fiction. Indeed, one of her books about women is titled *The Sex Without Sentiment.* The story in the present volume is reprinted from *My Own My Native Land* (1935).

David Thibault (1892–1934) a native of Little Rock, was a plantation manager and agricultural writer and editor before he turned to fiction. In New York he supported himself in the promotion department of a publisher, while he wrote his own work in his spare time. He collaborated with Carl Liddle on a head-hunter novel, *Tunchi,* that was favorably received as a first novel.

Between 1928 and 1931 *Collier's Magazine* published eleven of Thibault's stories. He began a novel, *Salt for Mule,* drawing on his experiences in the Arkansas Delta. It was accepted in near-complete form by the John Day company in the summer of 1934. But Thibault died of meningitis, without ever reading the editor's letter, and the novel remained unpublished. *Harper's Magazine* published two chapters separately as short stories in 1937. "A Woman like Dilsie" was included in the *O. Henry Memorial Award Prize Stories of 1937,* from which the present text is printed.

Mary Elsie Robertson (b. 1937) was born at Charleston, Arkansas. She has degrees from the University of Arkansas and the University of Iowa. One of the stories in her first book, *Jordan's Stormy Banks* (1961), won a prize in the *Mademoiselle* Fiction contest. The stories here are reprinted from that collection.

She has written children's books and other novels as well as short fiction, and has received fellowships from the

MacDowell writers' colony and the Yaddo Corporation. Her latest work is a novel, *Speak Angel* (1983), whose characters are a family of displaced Ozarkers. Her Arkansas short stories sometimes contain elements of local folklore or custom, and their settings and characters reflect her experiences among rural and small-town people. But Robertson's voice is distinctive, much more somber and less sensational than many of her Arkansas contemporaries, and her humor is darker.

Donald Harington (b. 1935) has an MFA degree from the University of Arkansas, but it is in art, not writing. He taught art history at Wyndham College in Vermont, and after it closed its doors he returned to Arkansas and to full-time writing.

Harington's work has generally been mentioned favorably in the national press. *Some Other Place: The Right Place* (1972) was reviewed in the *Times Literary Supplement,* where the reviewer wrote: "There could not be a better illustration of the fact that novel-writing has no rules: you are allowed to do whatever you can get away with." His conclusion was that Harington had gotten away with it.

The town of Stay More was created in *Lightning Bug* (1970) from which the selection herein, "Beginning," is reprinted. Its rich and fascinating history is told in *The Architecture of the Arkansas Ozarks* (1975). It is a chronicle of six generations of the Ingledew family in Newton County, Arkansas. His most recent work, *Let Us Build Us a City* has been accepted for publication in 1986.

Lewis Nordan (b. 1939) came to Arkansas to study creative writing with Jim Whitehead at the University in Fayetteville. His stories have appeared in *Harper's, Redbook,* and smaller literary magazines like the *New Orleans Review.* Many of his stories are set in Arkansas, and he has a true ear for the language and rhythm of Arkansas storytelling. The story included here is reprinted from *Welcome to the Arrow-Catcher Fair* (1984). Like many Nordan stories, "Storyteller" draws from the Southern tradition of the comic grotesque. His works are peopled with midgets, cripples and vagrants, as well as with apparently normal Southern families. Many times the narrator is a young boy, as deadpan and garrulous as Huck Finn, but more respectable. In 1983, Nordan joined the creative writing faculty at the University of Pittsburgh.

It was not hard to fill a book with stories that use Arkansas as a literary setting; it was only difficult to sift the choicest within the limits of the chronological arrangement we have followed. The literary genre of the story, as we have surveyed it, was defined by the proliferation of popular and literary magazines in the decades that coincide very neatly with Arkansas' separate political identity. The body of short story literature produced in those years is so rich that there is probably no subject that would not permit the creation of a worthwhile anthology. We have limited our selection to the work of writers whose careers placed them in Arkansas for significant periods of creative activity. If we were to relax those restraints, we would find stories with credible Arkansas settings by O. Henry and Damon Runyan, as well as such a splendid piece as Bud Schulberg's "Your Arkansas Traveller."

Our own contemporaries are not heavily represented in this collection, for we hoped above all to remind Arkansas readers of their rich narrative heritage from the past. One might have expected that the decline of the popular magazine over the last thirty years would have prevented any continuation of the tradition. This does not appear to be the case, however. For one thing, the Creative Writing faculties at the University of Arkansas have attracted many young writers to the state, who have made some use of indigenous material with or without reference to an Arkansas narrative tradition. Moreover, both native and adopted writers continue as before to use Arkansas as a literary setting.

William McDowell Baker *Ethel C. Simpson*
Malvern Fayetteville

THE BIG BEAR OF ARKANSAS

Thomas Bangs Thorpe

A STEAMBOAT ON the Mississippi frequently, in making her regular trips, carries between places varying from one to two thousand miles apart; and as these boats advertise to land passengers and freight at "all intermediate landings," the heterogeneous character of the passengers of one of these up-country boats can scarcely be imagined by one who has never seen it with his own eyes. Starting from New Orleans in one of these boats, you will find yourself associated with men from every state in the Union, and from every portion of the globe; and a man of observation need not lack for amusement or instruction in such a crowd, if he will take the trouble to read the great book of character so favourably opened before him. Here may be seen jostling together the wealthy Southern planter, and the pedler of tin-ware from New England—the Northern merchant, and the Southern jockey—a venerable bishop, and a desperate gambler—the land speculator, and the honest farmer—professional men of all creeds and characters—Wolvereens, Suckers, Hoosiers, Buckeyes, and Corncrackers, beside a "plentiful sprinkling" of the half-horse and half-alligator species of men, who are peculiar to "old Mississippi," and who appear to gain a livelihood simply by going up and down the river. In the pursuit of pleasure or business, I have frequently found myself in such a crowd.

On one occasion when in New Orleans, I had occasion to take a trip of a few miles up the Mississippi, and I hurried on

15

board the well-known "high-pressure-and-beat-everything" steamboat "Invincible," just as the last note of the last bell was sounding; and when the confusion and bustle that is natural to a boat's getting under way had subsided, I discovered that I was associated in as heterogeneous a crowd as was ever got together. As my trip was to be of a few hours' duration only, I made no endeavors to become acquainted with my fellow passengers, most of whom would be together many days. Instead of this, I took out of my pocket the "latest paper," and more critically than usual examined its contents; my fellow passengers at the same time disposed of themselves in little groups. While I was thus busily employed in reading, and my companions were more busily still employed in discussing such subjects as suited their humours best, we were startled most unexpectedly by a loud Indian whoop, uttered in the "social hall," that part of the cabin fitted off for a bar; then was to be heard a loud crowing, which would not have continued to have interested us— such sounds being quite common in that *place of spirits*— had not the hero of these windy accomplishments stuck his head into the cabin and hallooed out, "Hurra for the Big Bar of Arkansaw!" and then might be heard a confused hum of voices, unintelligible, save in such broken sentences as "horse," "screamer," "lightning is slow," &c. As might have been expected, this continued interruption attracted the attention of every one in the cabin; all conversation dropped, and in the midst of this surprise the "Big Bar" walked into the cabin, took a chair, put his feet on the stove, and looking back over his shoulder, passed the general and familiar salute of "Strangers, how are you?" He then expressed himself as much at home as if he had been at "the Forks of Cypress," and "perhaps a little more so." Some of the company at this familiarity looked a little angry, and some astonished; but in a moment every face was wreathed in a smile. There was something about the intruder that won the heart on sight. He appeared to be a man enjoying perfect health and contentment: his eyes were as sparkling as diamonds, and good-natured to simplicity. Then his perfect confidence in himself was irresistibly droll. "Prehaps," said he, "gentlemen," running on without a person speaking, "prehaps you have been to New Orleans often; I never made *the first visit before*, and I don't intend to make another in a crow's life. I am thrown away in that ar place, and useless, that ar a fact. Some of the gentlemen thar called me *green*—well, prehaps I am, said I, *but I arn't so at home;* and if I aint off my trail much, the heads of them perlite chaps themselves wern't much the hardest; for according to my notion, they were *real know-nothings*, green as a pumpkin-vine—couldn't, in farming, I'll bet, raise a crop of turnips: and as for shooting, they'd miss a barn if the door was swinging, and that, too, with the best rifle in the country. And then they talked to me 'bout hunting, and laughed at my calling the principal game in Arkansaw poker, and high-low-jack. 'Prehaps,' said I, 'you prefer chickens and rolette;' at this they laughed harder than ever, and asked me if I lived in the woods, and didn't know what *game* was? At this I rather think I laughed. 'Yes,' I roared, and says, 'Strangers, if you'd asked me *how we got our meat* in Arkansaw, I'd a told you at once, and given you a list of varmints that would make a caravan, beginning with the bar, and ending off with the cat; that's *meat* though, not game.' Game, indeed, that's what city folks call it; and with them it means chippen-birds and shite-pokes; maybe such trash live in my diggins, but I arn't noticed them yet: a bird any way is too trifling. I never did shoot at but one, and I'd never forgiven myself for that, had it weighed less than forty pounds. I wouldn't draw a rifle on any thing less that that; and when I meet with another wild turkey of the same weight I will drap him."

"A wild turkey weighing forty pounds!" exclaimed twenty voices in the cabin at once.

"Yes, strangers, and wasn't it a whopper? You see, the thing was so fat that it couldn't fly far; and when he fell out of the tree, after I shot him, on striking the ground he bust open behind, and the way the pound gobs of tallow rolled out of the opening was perfectly beautiful."

"Where did all that happen?" asked a cynical-looking Hoosier.

"Happen! happened in Arkansaw: where else could it have happened, but in the creation state, the finishing-up country—a state where the *sile* runs down the centre of the 'arth, and the government gives you a title to every inch of it? Then its airs—just breathe them, and they will make you snort like a horse. It's a state without a fault, it is."

"Excepting mosquitoes," cried the Hoosier.

"Well, stranger, except them; for it ar a fact that they are rather *enormous*, and do push themselves in somewhat troublesome. But, stranger, they never stick twice in the same place; and give them a fair chance for a few months, and you will get as much above noticing them as an alligator. They can't hurt my feelings, for they lay under the skin; and I never knew but one case of injury resulting from them, and that was to a Yankee: and they take worse to foreigners, any how, than they do to natives. But the way they used that fellow up! first they punched him until he swelled up and busted; then he sup-per-a-ted, as the doctor called it, until he was as raw as beef; then he took the ager, owing to the warm weather, and finally he took a steamboat and left the country. He was the only man that ever took mosquitoes at heart that I know of. But mosquitoes is natur, and I never find fault with her. If they ar large, Arkansaw is large, her varmints ar large, her trees ar large, her rivers ar large, and a small mosquitoe would be of no more use in Arkansaw than preaching in a cane-brake."

This knock-down argument in favour of big mosquitoes used the Hoosier up, and the logician started on a new track, to explain how numerous bear were in his "diggins," where he represented them to be "about as plenty as blackberries, and a little plentifuler."

Upon the utterance of this assertion, a timid little man near me inquired if the bear in Arkansaw ever attacked the settlers in numbers.

"No," said our hero, warming with his subject, "no, stranger, for you see it ain't the natur of bar to go in droves; but the way they squander about in pairs and single ones is edifying. And then the way I hunt them—the old black rascals know the crack of my gun as well as they know a pig's squealing. They grow thin in our parts, it frightens them so, and they do take the noise dreadfully, poor things. That gun of mine is a perfect *epidemic among bar:* if not watched closely, it will go off as quick on a warm scent as my dog Bowie-knife will: and then that dog—whew! why the fellow thinks that the world is full of bar, he finds them so easy. It's lucky he don't talk as well as think; for with his natural modesty, if he should suddenly learn how much he is acknowledged to be ahead of all other dogs in the universe, he would be astonished to death in two minutes. Strangers, that dog knows a bar's way as well as a horse-jockey knows a woman's: he always barks at the right time, bites at the exact place, and whips without getting a scratch. I never could tell whether he was made expressly to hunt bar, or whether bar was made expressly for him to hunt: anyway, I believe they were ordained to go together as naturally as Squire Jones says a man and woman is, when he moralizes in marrying a couple. In fact, Jones once said, said he, 'Marriage according to law is a civil contract of divine origin; it's common to all countries as well as Arkansaw, and people take to it as naturally as Jim Doggett's Bowie-knife takes to bar.' "

"What season of the year do your hunts take place?" inquired a gentlemanly foreigner, who, from some peculiarities of his baggage, I suspected to be an Englishman, on some hunting expedition, probably at the foot of the Rocky Mountains.

"The season for bar hunting, stranger," said the man of Arkansaw, "is generally all the year round, and the hunts take place about as regular. I read in history that varmints have their fat season, and their lean season. That is not the case in Arkansaw, feeding as they do upon the *spontenacious* productions of the sile, they have one continued fat season the year round: though in winter things in this way is rather more greasy than in summer, I must admit. For that reason bar with us run in warm weather, but in winter they only waddle. Fat, fat! it's an enemy to speed; it tames every thing that has plenty of it. I have seen wild turkeys, from its influence, as gentle as chickens. Run a bar in this fat condition, and the way it improves the critter for eating is amazing; it sort of mixes the ile up with the meat, until you can't tell t'other from which. I've done this often. I recollect one perty morning in particular, of putting an old he fellow on the stretch, and considering the weight he carried, he run well. But the dogs soon tired him down, and when I came up with him wasn't he in a beautiful sweat—I might say fever; and then to see his tongue sticking out of his mouth a feet, and his sides sinking and opening like a bellows, and his cheeks so fat he couldn't look cross. In this fix I blazed at him, and pitch me naked into a briar patch if the steam didn't come out of the bullet-hole ten feet in a straight line. The fellow, I reckon, was made on the high-pressure system, and the lead sort of bust his biler."

"That column of steam was rather curious, or else the bear must have been *warm*," observed the foreigner, with a laugh.

"Stranger, as you observe, that bar was WARM, and the

blowing off of the steam show'd it, and also how hard the varmint had been run. I have no doubt if he had kept on two miles farther his insides would have been stewed; and I expect to meet with a varmint yet of extra bottom, who will run himself into a skinfull of bar's grease: it is possible; much onlikelier things have happened."

"Whereabouts are these bears so abundant?" inquired the foreigner, with increasing interest.

"Why, stranger, they inhabit the neighbourhood of my settlement, one of the prettiest places on old Mississippi—a perfect location, and no mistake; a place that had some defects until the river made the 'cut-off ' at 'Shirt-tail bend,' and that remedied the evil, as it brought my cabin on the edge of the river—a great advantage in wet weather, I assure you, as you can now roll a barrel of whiskey into my yard in high water from a boat, as easy as falling off a log. It's a great improvement, as toting it by land in a jug, as I used to do, *evaporated* it too fast, and it became expensive. Just stop with me, stranger, a month or two, or a year if you like, and you will appreciate my place. I can give you plenty to eat; for beside hog and hominy, you can have bar-ham, and bar-sausages, and a mattress of bar-skins to sleep on, and a wildcat-skin, pulled off hull, stuffed with corn-shucks, for a pillow. That bed would put you to sleep if you had the rheumatics in every joint in your body. I call that ar bed a *quietus*. Then look at my land—the government ain't got another such a piece to dispose of. Such timber, and such bottom land, why you can't preserve any thing natural you plant in it unless you pick it young, things thar will grow out of shape so quick. I once planted in those diggins a few potatoes and beets: they took a fine start, and after that an ox team couldn't have kept them from growing. About that time I went off to old Kentuck on bisiness, and did not hear from them things in three months, when I accidentally stumbled on a fellow who had stopped at my place, with an idea of buying me out. 'How did you like things?' said I. 'Pretty well,' said he; 'the cabin is convenient, and the timber land is good; but that bottom land ain't worth the first red cent.' 'Why?' said I. 'Cause,' said he. 'Cause what?' said I. 'Cause it's full of cedar stumps and Indian mounds,' said he, 'and *it can't be cleared.'* 'Lord,' said I, 'them ar "cedar stumps" is beets, and them ar "Indian mounds" ar tater hills.' As I expected, the crop was overgrown and useless: the sile is too rich, *and planting in Arkansaw is dangerous.* I had a good-sized sow killed in that same bottom land. The old thief stole an ear of corn, and took it down where she slept at night to eat. Well, she left a grain or two on the ground, and lay down on them: before morning the corn shot up, and the percussion killed her dead. I don't plant any more: natur intended Arkansaw for a hunting ground, and I go according to natur."

The questioner who thus elicited the description of our hero's settlement, seemed to be perfectly satisfied, and said no more; but the "Big Bar of Arkansaw" rambled on from one thing to another with a volubility perfectly astonishing, occasionally disputing with those around him, particularly with a "live Sucker" from Illinois who had the daring to say that our Arkansaw friend's stories "smelt rather tall."

In this manner the evening was spent; but conscious that my own association with so singular a personage would probably end before morning, I asked him if he would not give me a description of some particular bear hunt; adding, that I took great interest in such things, though I was no sportsman. The desire seemed to please him, and he squared himself round towards me saying, that he could give me an idea of a bar hunt that was never beat in this world, or in any other. His manner was so singular, that half of his story consisted in his excellent way of telling it, the great peculiarity of which was the happy manner he had of emphasizing the prominent parts of his conversation. As near as I can recollect, I have italicized them, and given the story in his own words.

"Stranger," said he, "in bar hunts *I am numerous,* and which particular one, as you say, I shall tell, puzzles me. There was the old she devil I shot at the Hurricane last fall—then there was the old hog thief I popped over at the Bloody Crossing, and then—Yes, I have it! I will give you an idea of a hunt, in which the greatest bar was killed that ever lived, *none excepted;* about an old fellow that I hunted, more or less, for two or three years; and if that ain't a *particular bar hunt,* I ain't got one to tell. But in the first place, stranger, let me say, I am pleased with you, because you ain't ashamed to gain information by asking, and listening, and that's what I say to Countess's pups every day when I'm home; and I have got great hopes of them ar pups, because they are continually *nosing* about; and though they stick it sometimes in the wrong place, they gain experience any how, and may learn something useful to boot. Well, as I was saying about this big bar, you see when I and some more first settled in our region, we were drivin to hunting naturally; we soon liked it, and after that we found it an easy matter to make the thing our business. One old chap who had pioneered 'afore us, gave us to understand that we had settled in the right place. He dwelt upon its merits until it was affecting, and showed us, to prove his assertions, more marks on the sassafras trees than I ever saw on a tavern door 'lection time. 'Who keeps that ar reckoning?' said I. 'The bar,' said he. 'What for?' said I. 'Can't tell,' said he; 'but so it is: the bar bite the bark and wood too, at the highest point from the ground they can reach, and you can tell, by the marks,' said he, 'the length of the bar to an inch.' 'Enough,' said I; 'I've learned something here a'ready, and I'll put it in practice.'

Well, stranger, just one month from that time I killed a bar, and told its exact length before I measured it, by those very marks; and when I did that, I swelled up considerable— I've been a prouder man ever since. So I went on, larning something every day, until I was reckoned a buster, and allowed to be decidedly the best bar hunter in my district; and that is a reputation as much harder to earn than to be reckoned first man in Congress, as an iron ramrod is harder than a toadstool. Did the varmints grow over-cunning by being fooled with by green-horn hunters, and by this means get troublesome, they send for me as a matter of course; and thus I do my own hunting, and most of my neighbors'. I walk into the varmints though, and it has become about as much the same to me as drinking. It is told in two sentences—a bar is started, and he is killed. The thing is somewhat monotonous now—I know just how much they will run, where they will tire, how much they will growl, and what a thundering time I will have in getting them home. I could give you this history of the chase with all the particulars at the commencement, I know the signs so well—*Stranger, I'm certain.* Once I met with a match though, and I will tell you about it; for a common hunt would not be worth relating.

"On a fine fall day, long time ago, I was trailing about for bar, and what should I see but fresh marks on the sassafras trees, about eight inches above any in the forests that I knew of. Says I, 'them marks is a hoax, or it indicates the d——t bar that was ever grown.' In fact, stranger, I couldn't believe it was real, and I went on. Again I saw the same marks, at the same height, and *I knew the thing lived.* That conviction came home to my soul like an earthquake. Says I, 'here is something a-purpose for me: that bar is mine, or I give up the hunting business.' The very next morning what should I see but a number of buzzards hovering over my corn-field. 'The rascal had been there,' said I, 'for that sign is certain:' and, sure enough, on examining, I found the bones of what had been as beautiful a hog the day before, as was ever raised by a Buckeye. Then I tracked the critter out of the field to the woods, and all the marks he left behind, showed me that he was *the bar.*

"Well, stranger, the first fair chase I ever had with that big critter, I saw him no less than three distinct times at a distance: the dogs run him over eighteen miles and broke down, my horse gave out, and I was as nearly used up as a man can be, made on *my* principle, *which is patent.* Before this adventure, such things were unknown to me as possible; but, strange as it was, that bar got me used to it before I was done with him; for he got so at last, that he would leave me on a long chase *quite easy.* How he did it, I never could understand. That a bar runs at all, is puzzling; but how this one could tire down and bust up a pack of hounds and a horse, that were used to overhauling everything they started after in no time, was past my understanding. Well, stranger, that bar finally got so sassy, that he used to help himself to a hog off my premises whenever he wanted one; the buzzards followed after what he left, and so, between *bar and buzzard,* I rather think I was *out of pork.*

"Well, missing that bar so often took hold of my vitals, and I wasted away. The thing had been carried too far, and it reduced me in flesh faster than an ager. I would see that bar in every thing I did: *he hunted me,* and that, too, like a devil, which I began to think he was. While in this fix, I made preparations to give him a last brush, and be done with it. Having completed every thing to my satisfaction, I started at sunrise, and to my great joy, I discovered from the way the dogs run, that they were near him; finding his trail was nothing, for that had become as plain to the pack as a turnpike road. On we went, and coming to an open country, what should I see but the bar very leisurely ascending a hill, and the dogs close at his heels, either a match for him this time in speed, or else he did not care to get out of their way—I don't know which. But wasn't he a beauty, though? I loved him like a brother.

"On he went, until he came to a tree, the limbs of which formed a crotch about six feet from the ground. Into this crotch he got and seated himself, the dogs yelling all around it; and there he sat eyeing them as quiet as a pond in low water. A green-horn friend of mind, in company, reached shooting distance before me, and blazed away, hitting the critter in the center of his forehead. The bar shook his head as the ball struck it, and then walked down from that tree as gently as a lady would from a carriage. 'Twas a beautiful sight to see him do that—he was in such a rage that he seemed to be as little afraid of the dogs as if they had been sucking pigs; and the dogs warn't slow in making a ring around him at a respectful distance, I tell you; even Bowie-knife, himself, stood off. Then the way his eyes flashed—why the fire of them would have singed a cat's hair; in fact that bar was in a *wrath all over.* Only one pup came near him, and he was brushed out so to tally with the bar's left paw, that he entirely disappeared; and that made the old dogs more cautious still. In the mean time, I came up, and taking deliberate aim as a man should do, at his side, just back of his foreleg' *if my gun did not snap,* call me a coward, and I won't take it personal. Yes, stranger, *it snapped,* and I could not find a cap about my person. While in this predicament, I turned around to my fool friend—says I, 'Bill,' says I, 'you're an ass—you're a fool—you might as well have tried to kill that bar by barking the tree under his belly, as to have done it by hitting him in the head. Your shot has made a tiger of him, and blast me, if a dog gets killed or wounded when they come to blows, I will stick my knife into your liver, I will——' my wrath was up. I had lost my caps, my gun had snapped, the fellow with me had fired at the bar's head, and I expected every moment to see him close in with the dogs, and kill a dozen of them at least. In this thing I was mistaken, for the bar leaped over the ring formed by the dogs, and giving a fierce growl, was off— the pack, of course, in full cry after him. The run this time was short, for coming to the edge of a lake the varmint jumped in, and swam to a little island in the lake, which it reached just a moment before the dogs. 'I'll have him now,' said I, for I had found my caps in the *lining of my coat*—so, rolling a log onto the lake, I paddled myself across to the island, just as the dogs had cornered the bar in a thicket. I rushed up and fired—at the same time the critter leaped over the dogs and came within three feet of me, running like mad; he jumped into the lake, and tried the mount the log I had just deserted, but every time he got half his body on it, it would roll over and send him under; the dogs, too, got around him, and pulled him about, and finally Bowie-knife clenched with him, and they sunk into the lake together. Stranger, about this time I was excited, and I stripped off my coat, drew my knife, and intended to have taken a part with Bowie-knife myself, when the bar rose to the surface. But the varmint staid under—Bowie-knife came up alone, more dead then alive, and with the pack came ashore. 'Thank God,' said I, 'the old villain has got his deserts at last.' Determined to have the body, I cut a grape-vine for a rope, and dove down where I could see the bar in the water, fastened my queer rope to his leg, and fished him, with great difficulty, ashore. Stranger, may I be chawed to death by young alligators, if the thing I looked at wasn't a *she-bar, and not the old critter after all.* The way matters got mixed on that island was onaccountably curious, and thinking of it made me more than ever convinced that I was hunting the devil himself. I went home that night and took to my bed—the thing killing me. The entire team of Arkansaw in bar-hunting, acknowledged himself used up, and the fact sunk into my feelings like a snagged boat will in the Mississippi. I grew as cross as a bar with two cubs and a sore tail. The thing got out 'mong my neighbours, and I was asked how come on that individ-u-al that never lost a bar when once started: and if that same individ-u-al didn't wear telescopes when he turned a she bar, of ordinary size, into an old he one, a little larger than a horse? 'Prehaps,' said I, 'friends'—getting wrathy—'prehaps you want to call somebody a liar.' 'Oh, no,' said they, 'we only heard such things as being *rather common* of late, but we don't believe one word of it; oh, no,'—and then they would ride off and laugh like so many hyenas over a dead nigger. It was too much, and I determined to catch that bar, go to Texas, or die,—and I had made my preparations accordin'. I had the pack shut up and rested. I took my rifle to pieces, and iled it. I put caps in every pocket about my person, *for fear of the lining.* I then told my neighbours, that on Monday morning—naming the day—I would start THAT BAR, and bring him home with me, or they might divide my settlement among them, the owner having disappeared.

Well, stranger, on the morning previous to the great day of my hunting expedition, I went into the woods near my house, taking my gun and Bowie-knife along, just *from habit*, and there sitting down also from habit, what should I see, getting over my fence but *the bar!* Yes, the old varmint was within a hundred yards of me, and the way he walked *over that fence*—stranger, he loomed up like a *black mist*, he seemed so large, and he walked right towards me. I raised myself, took deliberate aim, and fired. Instantly the varmint wheeled, gave a yell, and *walked through the fence* like a falling tree would through a cobweb. I started after, but was tripped up by my inexpressibles, which either from habit, or the excitement of the moment, were about my heels, and before I had really gathered myself up, I heard the old varmint groaning in a thicket near by, like a thousand sinners, and by the time I reached him he was a corpse. Stranger, it took five niggers and myself to put that carcase on a mule's back, and old long-ears waddled under his load, as if he was foundered in every leg of his body, and with a common whopper of a bar, he would have trotted off, and enjoyed himself. 'Twould astonish you to know how big he was: I made a *bed-spread of his skin*, and the way it used to cover my bar mattress, and leave several feet on each side to tuck up, would have delighted you. It was in fact a creation bar, and if it had lived in Samson's time, and had met him, in a fair fight, it would have licked him in the twinkling of a dice-box. But, stranger, I never liked the way I hunted him, *and missed him*. There is something curious about it, I could never understand,—and I never was satisfied at his giving in so *easy at last*. Prephaps, he had just heard of my preparations to hunt him the next day, so he jist come in, like Capt. Scott's coon, to save his wind to grunt with in dying; but that ain't likely. My private opinion is, that that bar was an *unhuntable bar, and died when his time come.*"

When the story was ended, our hero sat some minutes with his auditors in a grave silence; I saw there was a mystery to him connected with the bear whose death he had just related, that had evidently made a strong impression on his mind. It was also evident that there was some superstitious awe connected with the affair,—a feeling common with all "children of the wood," when they meet with any thing out of their everyday experience. He was the first one, however, to break the silence, and jumping up, he asked all present to "liquor" before going to bed,—a thing which he did, with a number of companions, evidently to his heart's content.

Long before day, I was put ashore at my place of destination, and I can only follow with the reader, in imagination, our Arkansas friend, in his adventures at the "Forks of Cypress" on the Mississippi.

AN ARKANSAS HANGING

Opie Read

SOME TIME AGO, while reporting on the Little Rock *Gazette*, I
was sent down to a place called Buck Snort to write up the
hanging of a negro who had been so unfortunate as to fall
within the clutches of the law. After going as far as I could by
rail, I hired a horse and started across the country, intending
to reach Buck Snort on the following day. Late in the
afternoon, just after rounding a bend in the road, I suddenly
came upon the residence of a typical planter. Tall turkeys
strutted in the yard, and an excited guinea hen was
declaiming her "pot rack, pot rack" epic to an audience of
ducks that quacked their applause or their derision. An old
man, the planter, sat on the long gallery, with his chair
tipped back against the wall; and a negro boy, half grinning
on the verge of a nod, was keeping the flies off him with a
broad mulberry branch. It was, surely, a lazily inviting place.
The cool morning-glory vines clung to strings stretched in a
sort of zigzag lattice-work along the gallery, and a
resplendent peony, the impudent bawd of flowers, tossed her
disdainful head at a modest white rose.

I dismounted at the gate, and, advancing into yard, called
the old gentleman and asked him if I might get a drink of
water from the well, a short distance away.

"Water!" he exclaimed, tipping his chair forward. "W'y,
dog my cats, what do you want with water? Come up, suh;
come up and have a seat."

"I have but a moment to stay," I answered, as I stepped upon the gallery.

"That's all right. Set down there," he added, pointing to a chair. "John, you son of a gun, bring a julep. Where is that infernal nigger? Ah, here he is. [The boy had not left the old man's elbow.] Fetch us a julep here—fetch two, or I'll hang yo' hide on the gatepost."

"You must really excuse me," I pleaded. "I don't care to drink anything but water, and hardly have time to drink that."

"Water!" he repeated, contemptuously. "Here you are." John brought the juleps. "Now, drink that."

"I tell you, sir, that I"——

"Drink it, or, by the Lord, there'll be trouble."

I drank it.

"Where you goin'?" the old fellow asked, when I had swallowed the liquor.

"Going over to Buck Snort to report the hanging of a negro."

"John—where is that son of a gun? If I don't hang that rascal's black hide on the fence, the devil never snorted. Here you are. Fetch us two juleps here, and that blamed quick. What are you standing there for?"

The boy was not standing, having instantly taken to his heels.

"My dear sir," I began to plead, "I can't drink anything more. I have an important"——

"Here he is," the old man broke in, as John reappeared. It seemed to me that he had a tub of julep made up, and that all he had to do was to dip it out. "Drink that. Confound it, suh, drink it."

I drank it.

"Where you goin'?"

"I told you that I was going over to Buck Snort to report the hanging of a negro."

"Damn the nigger. John—where is that scoundrel?"

"I's right yere, sah."

"Well, it's a blamed good thing, or the first thing you know you would wonder how yo' hide come on the fence. Fetch us two juleps."

"I can not drink any more," I declared, arising. "I must attend to my assignment or I shall be discharged."

"Set down there," he exclaimed, reaching over and laying

29

hands on my "gyarments." "You set there now till I get through talkin' to you. Powerful glad you come along. Was just a-settin' here, lookin' up an' down the road wishin' fur somebody. Wife's gone over to a sort of camp-meetin'. Don't know my wife, do you? Wall, suh, she beats any woman you ever saw—and shout! w'y, she can out-shout any woman you ever saw. Prides herself on it—it's her strong p'int. W'y, if she thought there was any woman in the country that could out-shout her, she would get up at midnight to see about it. She nearly drives me off the place sometimes when she's rehe'rsin'. Allus has to rehe'rse just befo' a camp-meetin'. A woman come into this community from Mississippi once, and give it out that she was the best shouter in the country. She was awful fat, an' hanged if she didn't look powerful promisin', but my wife wa'nt skeered at all, but set back and waited for the comin' of the camp-meetin'. Well, the time come, and at it they went. Fust one and then the other was on top, figertively speakin', and, nachully havin' a pride in the matter, I was a trifle oneasy till my wife raised her reserve whoop, and driv' the pretender outen the neighborhood. Where in the thunder is that boy? John, didn't I tell you to bring two juleps? Let me tell you," he said, shaking his fore-finger at the boy, "by the time the sun goes down yo' hide will be out there dryin' on the fence."

John brought the juleps. "Here, drink this."

I muttered a sort of protestation, but drank the liquor.

"Where are you goin', anyhow?"

"I told you that I was going over to Buck Snort to write up the hanging of a negro.

"Let it go and stay here with me, for I tell you that my wife has gone over to a sort of a camp-meetin'."

"I can't let it go. Our paper must have an account of the hanging, and I must report it."

"Well, you stay right where you are. I'll send a nigger to report it."

"You'll do what!" I exclaimed.

"Send a nigger to report it, I tell you."

"But a negro can't report it."

"Who can't? Do you mean that Felix can't? W'y, dang yo' hide, you don't know him like I do. Ah, you are just in time."

The last sentence was addressed to the boy, who anticipating the old man, had appeared with two more juleps. I did not protest.

"And you say Felix can't report the hangin' of a common, ordinary nigger? You don't know him. W'y, when I want a yoke of steers broke, who breaks 'em? Felix. When I want a sheep killed, who does it? Felix. Yander he is. Come here, Felix."

By that time I didn't care whether the negro was hanged or not. Felix came up to the edge of the gallery.

"Felix."

"Yas, sah."

"You know where Buck Snort is, don't you?"

"Yas, sah."

"Well, there's goin' to be a blamed nigger hung over there to-morrow, and I want you to ketch old Kit, and go over there, and come back as quick as you can and tell us all about it. Do you hear?"

"Yas, sah."

"Well, go on now."

Felix saddled old Kit and rode away, and the old man yelled something at the boy. I don't know what it was. I lost my recollection somewhere on the gallery, and did not find it until the next morning when I came down-stairs. There it lay, soiled and feverish. The old man came out bright and hearty, and insisted upon my drinking another julep, but I violently refused. My spirits had been weak, and now my heart was heavy. I had thrown away my assignment, and the voice of a crabid dismissal rang in my ears.

"Don't you fret," said the old man. "Felix will fix it all right. He'll be along after a while."

I did look forward to his coming with a sort of indefinable and groundless hope, and it seemed that he would never show himself upon the brow of the hill down the road. He came at last, and now the sight of him increased my nervousness. He turned old Kit into the stable lot, hung the saddle on the fence, in the spot, I fancied, where the planter intended to hang the boy's hide, and, slowly approaching the gallery, sat down amid an entanglement of morning-glory vines. He did not say a word—he did not look at us.

"Felix," said the old man.

"Yas, sah," he replied, looking up.

"Did you go over to Buck Snort?"

"Yas, sah."

"Did you see that blamed nigger hung?"

"Yas, sah."

"Tell us about it."

"Wall, sah," he began, getting up, "I got on ole Kit, I did, an' started off down de road, an' I ain't gone fur till yere's old Miz Jones' steer standin' right 'cross de road. Says I, 'Whoa, Kit,' an' Kit, she whoaed. Den says I, 'Steer, oh, steer.' De steer ain't sayin' nuthin'. Says I, 'Steer, you doan know who you foolin' wid, does you?'' De steer ain't sayin' nuthin'. He had er lump o' mud on de eend o' his tail, an' keep on er lashin' fust one side an' den de uder. Says I, 'Steer, oh, steer.' He ain't sayin' nuthin', but kep' on er lashin' hisse'f, fust one side an' den de uder. Says I, 'Steer, you doan know who you foolin' wid. Ef I had er cum 'long yere yestidy an' you hader stood dar datter way, it woulder been all right, an' ef I wuster come erlong yer ter-mor' an' you wuster do diser way it would be all right, but you doan know who you foolin' wid now, steer. You foolin' wid er man dat's er 'po'tin' fur er paper.'

"De ole steer flung his tail up in de a'r an' jumped ober in de paster. I went on down de road den, I did, an' I ain't gone fur till I come ter old man Bozel's houn' dog er standin' right in de middle o' de road, barkin' fitten ter kill hisse'f. Says I, 'Whoa, Kit,' an' Kit she whoaed. Den I says, 'Dog, oh, dog.' De dog ain't sayin' nuthin', but kep' on er barkin'. 'Dog, I mus' say dat you ain't up in de erfairs o' dis yere life. You ain't been edycated er tall.' De dog ain't sayin' word, but kep' on er barkin'. 'Dog,' says I, 'its almighty well fur you ter fool wid de common run o' folks, but now you is foolin' wid er pussun dat's 'po'tin' fer er paper.' Huh. De dog jumped ober de fence an' run under de house, an' he howled might'ly, he did, too.

"Den I rid on an' finally got inter de town. Neber seed de like o' folks. I rid up ter er rack an' turned de sheriff 's hoss loose an' hitched old Kit. De sheriff 's hoss didn't want ter go erway an' I boxed him side de jaw, an say, 'G'way frum yere. I's got no time ter fool wid you. I's 'po'tin' fur er paper.' De hoss he went erway, he did. Den I went ter de jail. Da had de man dar; oh, yas, da had him right dar. Says I, 'Folks, git outen de way. I's 'po'tin fur er paper.' An' de folks got outen de way. Da had de little ole nigger in er iron cage. Yas, da did, right in er iron cage. I nebber seed er pusson look ez bad ez he did. De skin wuz offen de wrist whar de hand'cuff dun rubbed him. Den I yere clank, clank, clank. Da wuz er cuttin' de iron rings offen his ankles. 'Oh, Lawd,' he moaned, 'sabe my po' soul!' Clank, clank, clank. 'Oh, Mars Jesus, look down on dis po' ole

nigger!' Clank, clank, clank. Off come de iron rings, an' den
de sheriff say, 'Come on wid me. I will be jes' ez tender wid
you ez I kin.' Tender wid him! Talk erbout bein' tender wid er
man when you gwine put er rope roun' his naik. W'y, I kain't
stan' er tight collar, an' I knows I couldn't stan' dat rope. Da
tuck de man out—da led him erlong like some po' dog dat da
wuz gwine kill caze he dun got too ole. Da led him up de steps
o' er flatfo'm dat da had built. Yas, da had dun built one, an'
says I ter myse'f, 'Whut da go ter so much 'spense fur, jest ter
kill one po' ole nigger?" When he stood up on de flatfo'm, he
look up, he did, an' say, 'Oh, Lawd!' Er ole 'oman ober in de
cornder o' de fence, she say, 'Oh, Lawd!' 'I's wid you, honey,'
says I. 'Oh, Lawd,' says her old man, ober in ernuder cornder.
'I's wid you, too,' says I. De sheriff he axed de ole nigger ef he
had anything ter say, an' he said no, but jest ez de sheriff had
put on de black cap, de nigger shuddered in de darkness, an'
says:

" 'Take off de cap jest er minit, Mr. Sheriff.'

"Mr. Sheriff he tuck it off; an' den de nigger looked up at
de sun an' didn't say nuthin' fer er little while. Den he says:
'Dar's dat sun gwine erlong up dar—gwine erlong—gwine
erlong. It has allus been gwine erlong, an' it always will be
gwine erlong, but whar will I be when dat sun is gwine erlong
termorrow? Dat sun wuz gwine erlong jest the same way
long time ergo, when I wuz er little boy, out in de fiel', settin'
up in the cornder o' de fence under de elder-bushes by de
water-jug, whar de dog lay er hittin' de groun' wid his tail
wheneber I spoke to him, an' it was gwing 'long jes' de same
when I wuz er plowin' in de fiel' atter I got big ernuff, an' I
uster wonder ef it wuz de gre't eye o' de Lawd er lookin' down
at me. One ebenin' when de gre't eye o' de Lawd dun gone
down behin' de hill, I stood at de do' o' de laug meetin'-house,
wipin' de tears outen my eyes. Suthin'—it mout er been de
gre't eye o' de Lawd—tole me dat I wuz er sinner man, an' I
knelt down at de mo'ners' bench an' de Speret had dun
whispered dat my sins wuz wiped out. Peace wuz in my soul,
an' I stood dar listenin' ter the glad shouts o' de folks inside
and ter de whipperwill down in de bottom. I went home wid
dat same peace in my soul, an' de next mawnin' when I went
out ter plow de gre't eye o' de Lawd looked brighter den it had
ever done, an' de dew-draps in de bud o' de young co'n 'peared
like specks o' de gre't eye dun drapped off down in dar. I wuz
er singin' er glad song when er man come out in de fiel' an'

'gunter talk ter me. I wuz so happy at fust dat I didn't know whut he wuz er sayin', but finally understood dat he 'cused me o' stealin' his money. De Lawd knows dat I neber did take er cent o' his money, but he kep' on 'cusin' me, an' at las' he grabbed er holt o' me, an' den ole Satan he entered in, an' I snatched up er hoe dat lay dar an' chopped him on de head wid it. Dead! He lay dar, dead, an' his blood run out aroun' er hill o' co'n, an' de gre't eye o' de Lawd drawed de blood up. I stood dar shakin' like er man wid er chill, an' I roamed roun', I doan know whar, till at las' Mr. Sheriff he come an' say he wanted me, an' now, yere I is, an' dar is de gre't eye o' de Lawd still gwine on. Put on de cap, Mr. Sheriff.'

"Den Mr. Sheriff he put on de cap, an' de fust thing I knowed—*flip.* De man wuz down dar, an' de fuzz stood out all up an' down de rope. 'Git outen de way, Folks,' says I; 'git outen de way, 'caze I's done 'po'tin' fur dis yere paper.' An' de folks got outen de way, an' I got on old Kit, I did, an I come on erway ez fast ez I could, an' dat wuz peart, 'caze old Kit didn't want ter 'po't fur dat paper no mo' nuther, an lemme tell you, Mars' John, I'll break de steers fur you, an' git de hogs out frum under de fence, an' mend de wagin tongue, an' all dat, but lemme tell you, I ain't gwine 'po't fur no mo' paper."

His report, just as he had given it to me, appeared in the *Gazette*, and I was not discharged.

BIG BILL AND LITTLE BILL

Opie Read

BIG BILL AND Little Bill were combined in the forming of a strong evidence that friendship, which is supposed to be based upon judgment, is sometimes as capricious as love, which, it is declared, has for its foundation a sort of impulsive fancy. Big Bill was almost a giant; Little Bill was almost a dwarf. They first met at a card table—or, rather, at a card cottonbale on the Mississippi River—and, as they expressed it, hankered at once for each other's society. They became so much attached to each other that they soon decided to settle down together, and, building a cabin in Chicot County, Arkansas, they began the business of "general merchants and dealers in plantation supplies."

The very oddity of the firm was a valuable advertisement, and it is well known that negroes rode at least ten miles, Saturday afternoons, to deal with the "long an' short o' it." The sign—which read as follows: "Big Bill & Little Bill"— conveyed the only intelligence that the community had ever received with regard to their names, but, as people who live in the Mississippi River bottoms are not curious with regard to the affairs of other men, no one showed those symptoms of uneasy concern which make life in a hill-side village the fit abode of Beelzebub.

Of course, some one would occasionally ask a question something like this: "Say, did you fellows lose your other names durin' the overflow?" But about the nearest to a satisfactory reply that was ever rendered was the following answer, sometimes delivered by the giant and sometimes by the dwarf:

"Yes; you see the water riz on us so fast that we didn't have time to git out but a few of our duds, and we 'lowed that it would be better to load the boat with the most necessary artickles. We did think fur a minit ur two that it would be better to leave our dogs an' finish loadin' with our names, but then, when we recollected what fine critters they was at treein' all sort uv varmints, we drapped our names an' gathered up the dogs."

At night the two partners would sit in a little cuddy-hole at the back end of the store, and, smoking cob pipes, would entertain each other until bedtime. Sometimes they sang songs of lively words but of most doleful tune, and sometimes they formed themselves into a sort of legislature and made speeches on the condition of the country.

Ten years at least were passed in this way, and not a difference of opinion sufficient to cause the slightest jar occurred between the partners. Some of their customers declared that so warm a friendship must come to an end; that so cheerful an agreement was against human nature; but the slow drag of time brought no jar.

One day while the two Bills were sitting in their store, waiting for customers, a woman drove up on a buckboard and asked for a drink of water; and, as rain began to fall at that very minute, she was invited into the store. She was rather good-looking, with long black hair and the snappy quality of black eyes so much admired by river-bottom people. She was not backward in speaking of herself.

"My name is Tildy Blake," said she, "and I have come here from East Tennessee to teach school over near Fetterson's saw-mill, but I don't reckon there's much to be teached over there, only readin', writin' and 'rithmetic, mebby, but it's no odds to me s'long as I get my money for it, for I am a widow woman with nobody to support but myself, it is true, but a person always likes to have plenty of this world's goods, for as my husband used to say before he died—and do you know that I have been thinkin' of him for the last hour?—for he popped into my head back yonder when a razor-back hog jumped up from behind a log and made off through the woods, for po' Dan was mighty partial to razor-back hogs, 'lowin' that their meat—if you ever got any on 'em—was sweeter than any other meat, but it allus took a powerful sight of co'n; but Dan—that was his name—allus had plenty, and he jest nachully tuck to the razor-backs; and when he died he left three that eat me bodatiously out of house an' home, an' then was so haungry that they broke into a neighbor's field an' caused me to be sued for slander—no, not for slander, but for damages—the slander suit come later on and finished breaking me up; so here I am, with nothin' but a few duds that air putty well worn, an' a hoss an' a buckboard. What's the name of this here firm?"

"Big Bill & Little Bill," one of the partners replied.

"What's your name?" addressing the giant.

"Big Bill."

"So I see, but what's your other name?"

"Wall, Madam, it's been so long since I used it that it's too much kivered with rust to be reco'nized now."

"You're a funny man; a funny man. Haven't you got a name?" addressing the dwarf.

"Yes'um, I'm pleased to say I have."

"What is it?"

"Little Bill."

"Your other name. Got one, ain't you?"

"Yes'um, but I aint washed it in so long that I am 'shamed to fetch it out."

"What was your dad's name?"

"Little Buck."

"Oh, you're a funny man; a funny man. Doin' pretty well with this sto', I reckon?"

"Yes, middlin'."

"Sold anything to-day?"

"Yes, some calico an' a couple uv plow p'ints."

"Who keeps your books?"

"Aint got none."

"How do you know how you stand?"

"By lookin' 'round when we git up."

"You're a peart leetle cretur, now, aint you? Which way is it to where I want to go?"

"Straight ahead."

"One of you or both go with me; you kaint sell nothin' mo' this evening."

"Well, I don't kere ef I do," said Big Bill.

"An' I'm agreeable," Little Bill remarked. "Will your bread tray hold us?"

"Bread tray? What do you mean? It's a buckboard."

"Oh, skuze me. Failin' to see its ho'ns, I tuck it fur er doe board."

"But that don't make it a bread tray," she replied.

"Yes, it does," said Little Bill, "fur you know a bread tray ain't nothin mo' than a dough board."

"My conshuns alive!" turning to Big Bill, "the child is gittin' pearter an' pearter. Wall, shet up yore contrapshun, an' le's go. The folks air expectin' me this month, an' I don't want 'em to wait supper."

That night, when the two partners were sitting in their cuddy-hole, Big Bill, getting up to stretch his long legs, said:

"Little Bill, she hits me as bein' a monstrous fine woman. How does she hit you?"

"Slaps me in the same way, Big Bill. When I look at them black eyes uv hern I feel like goin' out in the woods and dancin'."

"Little Bill, mebbe that's what killed her husband. Mout have danced himself to death."

"Didn't know but he mout have been cut in two by one of his razor-back hogs," Little Bill replied, "S'pose we go out Sunday an' shine 'round a little with her."

"I'll jine you."

They called on her the next Sunday, and it was so odd a thing for the two Bills to go calling that many of the neighbors came and looked in upon them. Many attentions were bestowed upon the Widow Blake, and especially so by a young fellow who owned a spavined horse and a buggy with red wheels; yet she seemed best pleased with the Bills. She invited them to go to church with her, which they did, and as she walked between them, no one, even the most observant-eyed old maid, could have decided upon her favorite.

That night, when the cob pipes had been lighted in the cuddy-hole, Big Bill said:

"She's gittin' better-lookin' all the time."

"Yes," replied the dwarf, "an' her eyes ain't losin' none uv their snap as you go along. Tell you what's a fact, Big Bill, I'll be hanged if I don't b'lieve I'm in love with her."

"Podner," replied Big Bill, "we are still in the same boat, fur I love her myself. Shake."

They arose and warmly shook hands.

They called on the widow again the following Sunday, and

again she walked between them to church. Just before parting that evening, the two Bills held her hands, changing about from right to left so that there might be no appearance of partiality.

"Never seed a woman git better an' better lookin' faster than she do," said Big Bill, when they reached home and lighted their pipes. "Puts me in min' uv a young deer runnin' toward you. Gits puttier as it comes near. Look here, Little Bill, tell you what I was thinkin' about. I was thinkin' that I would ax her to marry me."

"Blast me ef I wa'n't thinkin' 'bout doin' the very same caper myself."

"Say, Little Bill."

"Wall."

"We kain't both marry her."

"That's a fack," the dwarf replied, after a moment's reflection. "What air we goin' to do about it?"

"I'll be dinged if I hardly know," said the giant. "You've got mo' l'arnin' than I have, so make some suggestion."

"No, I hain't got mo' l'arnin'."

"W'y, you told me that you spelled 'way over in a book once."

"Yes, I did," replied Little Bill, "but I've dun forgot all I knowed about it."

"Wall, I never did know nuthin' about it, an' a man that has knowed an' has dun forgot still knows mo' than the man that never did know."

"S'pozen we leave it to her," said Little Bill. "We've been together too long to fall out even about a putty woman, an' we'll jest 'bide by what she says."

"That strikes me about right," the giant replied.

They called on the widow the following Sunday.

"Miz Blake," said Big Bill, "we've got something we want to say to you, so s'pozen we don't go to church, fur what we've got to say must be said airter all other folks have dun gone offen the place."

"I am allus ready to hear anything to my intrust," the widow replied. "My husband used to say that I was the patientest women to lissen he ever seed in his life, and he used to tell me that if I could only overcome my unnat'ral dislike for razor-back hogs an' take to helpin' a little mo' 'round the mourners' bench that I would be wuth my weight in shoats, an' I recollect jest as well as if it was yistidy that a few minits befo' his fatal pain struck him he eat a piece of ham an' 'lowed that it was the finest b'iled meat he ever eat in his life. The folks have all gone, so now what have you got to say?"

"Big Bill, wanter to do the talkin'?"

"No, Little Bill, I ain't a-hurtin'. You go ahead."

"Wall, Miz Blake, it's just this," said the dwarf. "Our firm is powerful in love with you an' wants to marry you, but, knowin' under the law as she now stands that a firm kain't very well git married to one woman, w'y, we have agreed to leave it to you which one uv us to take. Big Bill thar would make you a fine husband."

"No better than Little Bill thar, an' mebbe not half as good," replied the giant.

"Wall, now, this do place me in a strait," said the widow. "I like you both jist the same, an' I don't know which one to take. I am in putty much the same fix my po' husband was in when he had to decide which razor-back hog he oughter kill when he thought jist the same of all of 'em. Big Bill, you air stronger, but, Little Bill, you are pearter. I declare I don't know which one of you to take. It won't do to run a race, fur Little Bill is the fastest, an' it won't do to rassle, fur it's a short thing that Big Bill is the best man. How air you at poker?"

" 'Bout the same," said the giant.

"Ain't a whit's difference," the dwarf agreed.

"Wall," said the widow, "there is a deck of cards here summers, and s'pozen we settle it that way."

The two men agreed, and the woman produced the cards.

They sat down, without any visible emotion, and while they were playing the widow placidly rocked herself. After a while the two men reached over and shook hands.

"Who won?" the widow asked.

"You did," replied Big Bill.

"What do you mean by that?"

"I mean that you have got the best man—Little Bill."

"Oh, it don't make a bit of difference to me," she said. "Now, let me see. There was something I wanted to say. Oh, yes, I must know your other name, for it would be horrid to go by the name of Mrs. Little Bill."

"We won't argy about that," said the dwarf.

"Oh, yes," said the widow, "there is something else that must be settled. The firm must be broke up. No matter how friendly you all are now, there mout come a time when Big Bill, seein' how happy I am makin' you, would git dissatisfied; so one of you, it makes no difference which, must leave."

This idea met with approval, and another game of poker decided that Big Bill must leave. The next day a satisfactory settlement was made, and Big Bill, mounted on a reddish mule, rode away. His travels ceased when he reached a lonely region of Georgia, and there he settled down.

Several years elapsed, when, one evening as Big Bill was sitting on a stump by the side of a grass-grown road, a canvas-covered wagon came in sight, and, as it drew near, Bill saw the tow-heads of several children protruding from under the covering. He got up and was on the eve of turning away, when a man ran around from the other side of the wagon.

"W'y, hello, Little Bill!" the giant exclaimed.

"Stay where you air!" said the dwarf, "fur it's all I ken do to keep from shootin' you."

"W'y, what on the face o' the yeth is the matter, my old friend?"

"Jes' this: I b'lieve you let me win that woman on purpose."

" 'Tend to your business, Little Bill, an' don't talk to ever' ragtag and bobtail you meet, or I'll whale you agin. I should think two larrupin's a day is enough fur one man."

The giant, recognizing the voice said: "Podner, I'm sorry for you, an' I wanter say that I done my best at the cards."

"Do you want her now, Big Bill?"

"Wall, no. I'm obleeged to you. Good-by."

SIST' CHANEY'S BLACK SILK

Octave Thanet

LOW RED PARTITIONS separate the bath-rooms proper from the passageways of the bath-house. One morning early in November, when all the mountains about Hot Springs were still aglow with the red and yellow pigments spattered through the enduring pine green, three women sat outside, leaning back in their chairs after their baths. The bath-house was new and smart in all its appointments. The three women paid no attention to the medley of noises which poured through the partitions. A clatter of tongues and a continuous crack of slapping pierced—being of a shriller and higher quality—the monotonous fall and splash of water. So thin were the dividing walls between the two sides of the house that the conversation had rather a startling thread of masculine talk.

"Here, Polk, confound you!" "Yes, sah, yes, sah; in a minute." "Say Ben, what did you do with my crutch?" "Oh, yes, ma'am; I'm a heap better" (this in a Southern, feminine voice). "Viney, I'm all ready." "All right, darlin', jest set still, an' drink hot water an' sweat; I'm a comin'." "Well, I don't drink any more hot water, anyhow; I feel like a teakettle now." "All right, honey; I'm a-comin'."

"Oh, why are you waiting, my brother?"

It is the first line of a popular hymn; a rich tenor voice starts it, but the words are taken up by half a dozen bath-women, until the refrain, with its wailing minor, echoes through the room:

"Why not, why not, why not come to Him now?"

One of the singers has a beautiful contralto voice, possessed of that uncultivated, haunting sweetness one hears sometimes among the negro singers.

"Ain't that Dosier?" asked a woman waiting. She was a large woman, handsome and kindly looking, and while she mopped her face with a towel, she kept up a steady motion of her jaws. In fact, she was chewing gum. An extraordinary abandonment to "the gum habit" is a feature of Hot Springs. Every shop-counter seems to have a little tray of sticks in tinsel. One is told that the men buy it to help them through their deprivation of tobacco, Hot Springs doctors being very strict on this point. But why do the women use gum? They are Southern women usually, but not always. They have the dress, sometimes the manners and speech, of ladies, and they make not the slightest concealment of the practice. The large lady, as she spoke, offered a stick of "taffee tolu" to the person whom she addressed.

This was a thin, dark woman in a red wrapper, with large diamonds in her ears and at her throat. She waved the gum aside, remarking, severely, "No, I never chew; I haven't any bad habits."

The other, not at all abashed, answered: "Do you call chewing gum a bad habit? I don't. Gum is nice, clean, decent stuff. Now tobacco; there's some sense talking against that— chewing, I mean; I don't mind smoking no more than nothing; but chewing—Colonel Ponder used to chew till I couldn't keep a stove in the house decent. He did so. I hated terribly to take away his comfort, but finally I persuaded him to take up with gum instead. Never chewed a mite myself, before then, but I did it to keep him company, and now I like it 'most as well as him." Therewith she laughed,—a rollicking, tolerant laugh, having in its melody a note of something quite innocent and childlike.

The third woman, a delicate creature, whose maid had wrapped her carefully, looked up at the sound. "Weren't you speaking of Dosier?" she said. Her voice had distinctly Northern intonations; it was rather languid than faint. She had very large blue eyes, and a little wave to the brown hair brushed back from a low forehead. Her face was pretty, though so thin and colorless. She looked unhappy as well as ill. "Is Dosier your bath-woman?" she continued.

"Oh, yes, ma'am," said Mrs. Ponder, beaming upon her in a motherly fashion. ("Cayn't be more than twenty, and looks like she'd lost her last friend on earth," was the kind soul's inward comment.) "Why, Colonel wouldn't let me come to the Springs, I don't guess, if I couldn't have Dosier. Not that it would kill me"—she laughed her jolly laugh again—"if I didn't come: I never had a sick day since I was married and come to Arkansas. All I go here for is to reduce; I get ten pounds thinner every time I come, and last year I lost sixteen pounds in three weeks. Vapor baths. And Dosier's rubbings."

"She is very strong," said the invalid, with a sigh.

"Six feet tall," said Mrs. Ponder, "and can lift me. You'd hardly believe it, but she's done it. And the cleanest creature, and as gentle as gentle. She's a good woman if there ever was one."

"Yes," agreed the woman with diamonds, "I think Dosier is decent. Though"—lowering her voice—"she is the first negro woman I've seen in the South that I'd trust."

"Laws! I've seen a heap," said Mrs. Ponder. "I was born and raised among niggers; and they're very much like white folks—they're good and they're bad. You Northern people all 'lowed the niggers were angels during the war; and ayfter the war, when you come down here and found they weren't, you turn plumb round and think they're all trash. Fact is, they're just middling, like the rest of us. But Dosier is the best kind of a colored woman; and when they're good, you won't find anybody better, Mrs. Higgins."

Mrs. Higgins looked strong dissent, but all she said was: "What's become of that husband of hers?—the one that was in the penitentiary."

"Why, she never had but one husband, did she?" said the invalid.

"Well, that one. Two years ago she was spending all the money she had saved up to get him out. He killed somebody."

"He shot one of the worst gamblers and desperadoes ever in Hot Springs"—the stout lady now took up the conversation with decision—"and he hadn't ought to have had anything done to him. Anyway and anyhow, they pardoned him out ayfter Dosier had spent more than three hundred and seventy dollars on him."

"Well, what became of him?"

"Oh, he was all broke up in health, and he died."

"Poor Dosier!" said the little woman. "Has she any children?"

"No, ma'am; but she's got a helpless invalid sister, and a niece that's a widow, and two little boys of hers. I reckon Dosier looks out ayfter the whole of them. Well, Nettie, she does work about the bath-houses some, but she cayn't more than keep herself."

"The sister's a helpless kind of thing," said Mrs. Higgins; "paralyzed some way. She must be a burden."

Mrs. Ponder's face wore a new expression, a very gentle one. "I'm not so sure of that," said she; "sometimes it looks like folks weren't any comfort because they ain't any help about the house or earning money, and yet they may be a sight of company and comfort. I've heard Dosier say she wouldn't know how to get along without Chaney."

The young woman looked for a second at Mrs. Ponder. Mrs. Higgins gave a rapid glance downward at her own hands, crippled with rheumatism; then jumped up and began to pace the room. "Well, when I can't help myself I want to die," she muttered.

Mrs. Ponder changed the subject. "Chaney," she continued, in her soft, leisurely tones,—"Chaney gets the funniest notions. What do you think she's got into her head now?"

"I don't think she's got good sense," said Mrs. Higgins, acidly.

"Oh, yes, ma'am; she's got plenty of sense. But this is curious, for she doesn't go out of the house once a year. If you please, ladies, she's plumb crazy for a black silk gown. Ever since Dosier got hers, she's been craving one. Dosier wants right bad to get her one for a Christmas gift; but you see, Chaney is sick—gone into a dropsy, the doctor says—and Dosier can only work mornings, and there's the doctor's bills and all: I'm afraid they will use up all the money she's laid by."

"It's a piece of extravagance anyhow," said Mrs. Higgins. "Chaney ought not to ask such a thing, and Dosier ought to tell her flat she can't have it."

She might have freed her mind more fully had not a bath-room door opened and a tall black woman appeared, Dosier herself.

"Say, don't you all go out till you're right cool," she remarked, shaking her head good-humoredly as she passed. "Miss Maine, you make your gyril wrop ye up *tight*, ef ye go out."

She had, in speaking, the same rich, melodious, winning voice as in singing, and her broad smile and bright eyes made her strong, dark features attractive. Even Mrs. Higgins looked kindly after her as she passed.

She walked through the two "cooling-rooms," into the office, and so into the street. At that hour of the day the Hot Springs main street is a picturesque scene, a kaleidoscope of shifting figures, all tints of skin, all social ranks: uncouth countrymen on cotton wagons; negroes in carts drawn by oxen or skeleton mules with rope harness; pigs lifting their protesting noses out of some of the carts, fowls squawking in others; a dead deer flung over a horseman's saddle; modish-looking men and women walking; shining horses curveting before handsome carriages; cripples on crutches; deformed creatures hugging the sunny side of the street before the bath-houses; pale ghosts of human beings in wheeled chairs,—so the endless procession of wealth or poverty or disease or hope oscillates along the winding street between the mountains. The houses are as different as the people, squalor and roughness of a mining camp flung cheek by jowl against brick facades of the American renaissance, with terra-cotta ornaments and low arched windows. Booths innumerable lean out over the mud sidewalk; Hot Springs crystals glitter in jewelers' windows; gaudy garments swing from projecting stringers; poultry in coops, rabbits in cages, squirrels, opossums, possibly a young bear, increase the lively aspect of the exhibition space of the street, and very much curtail the footman's passageway. Every house that is not a hotel has a sign of "Rooms to Let." Visibly the town lives upon the stranger within its gates.

Dosier, to whom the sight was too familiar for notice, and who was, moreover, absorbed in painful thoughts of her own, moved rapidly along to a cross street.

Frequently she met acquaintances, black or white. They all greeted her with a degree of respect. The negroes said, "Good-mornin', Sist' Rogers!" or "Howdy, Mis' Rogers?" A few stopped to shake hands and inquire about her sister. Dosier's invariable reply was: "Well, she ain't no better. We all gwine have a conserlation dis mornin'. Free doctors."

46

Admiration evidently tinged the sympathy of the comments. The commonest was: "Is dat so? Well, you suttinly *is* doin' all you kin."

"I *aims* ter," said Dosier.

After awhile she left her friends behind and came to her own house, a neat brown cottage, standing on the side of the hill, in a large garden. Dosier, who was indefatigably industrious, had fine roses as well as a thrifty company of vegetables. A bush of La France roses brushed the window-pane with their pink, exquisitely crumpled petals. The bed was drawn close to the window. Chana loved to lie watching the long stems sway, and the green leaves tap the glass, and the light flicker in the pink bloom. She used to sit up, but of late she had lain all day, too weak or in too much pain to rise. Dosier looked quickly for the face on the big white pillows. It was turned away, and the hands were clutching at the forehead with an unmistakable gesture.

"My Lawd! Chaney's cryin'." gasped Dosier. There was a climbing pain in her throat that choked her. The tears swam in her eyes. "It ben bad, an' dat fool Nettie done tole 'er," she thought. "Yes, thar's them buggies," glancing down the road.

Two buggies, Dr. Green's and Dr. Le Verneau's, were drawn up close to the fence and the line of clover, still fresh and green. The horses were munching dry grass and juicy clover together.

Directly, the little red door of the house opened and three gentlemen appeared. They had the medical gravity of expression over a serious case. On the walk, the youngest man began to talk animatedly, but the others checked him, observing Dosier. Old Dr. Le Verneau raised his hat.

Dosier, even then, did not forget her old-fashioned manners, which prompted the hasty courtesy before she said, in an unsteady voice: "You all ain't no need to tell me, gentlemen. She cayn't get up no mo'. Dis yeah her last spell er sickness."

"You see it is this way, Aunt Dosier," said Dr. Green: it was a relief to him to plunge into medical details, knowing that Dosier, the best nurse in Hot Springs, could understand him. Strangely enough, it calmed her also, forcing her into the impartial professional scrutiny of "the patient" that becomes a nurse's second nature.

"I got to give up gwine t' de baths," she said, quietly, after he had outlined the condition of the sick woman and the best mode of treatment to alleviate her suffering; there was no hope of prolonging her life. Then she courtesied again and thanked the physicians, saying that she was sure that they would do all that could be done, and entered the house. She stopped a second outside the door to stiffen herself and fling out her hands. Then she shut the palms tight.

"Bracing up," muttered the youngest man. "She feels *bad.* Queer, too: the woman's always been a burden to her."

"That's all you know about it," said Dr. Le Verneau, irritably. "Don't you suppose she's fond of her kin? That poor soul there has lived with Dosier twenty years."

Dosier's fingers may have trembled a little on the latch, but there was no tremble in her voice as she greeted Nettie; she forced a kind of smile on her face. Ah! which of us is so happy as not to know that pitiful smile of the sick-room?

Nettie was a slender brown woman, never very wise. She "p'intedly did favor her paw," Dosier used to say, and the late Jacob Faury, Chana's husband was "trifling."

Nettie sat in the yellow rocking-chair rocking and sobbing, while she strained her youngest child so hard to her breast that he set up a wail on his own account.

Poor Chana was quietly weeping on the bed.

"My Lawd! Nettie," cried Dosier, with the irritation of suffering, "how come you let dat chile beller dat a way in yeah? 'Ain't you got no sense?" Then her voice dropping to its gentlest key, "Howdy, Chaney? Is you got de mis'ry back?"

No movement, no sound except the low sobbing from the bed.

"You needs some milk shake, dat's wat you does; an' I got some nice new w'iskey to putt in. An' den we'll count de stockin'."

Presently she came back, and gently took the hand down. She had an old yarn stocking hung over her arm.

"Oh, Doshy," sobbed Chana, "I'm gwine t' die, ayfter all. Ye needn't count de stockin'. I'll never w'ar no silk gownd."

Dosier, pillar of the church though she was, looked at the quivering face, and for a moment contemplated lying bravely—only for a moment; because something in Chana's eyes told her that a lie would be useless. Instead, she sank down on her knees by the bedside. "Chaney," she whispered, "you like me pray de Lawd holp you tuh bar it?"

"Naw, I doan't," said Chana.

48

A thunderbolt could hardly have cloven Dosier's sore heart like those words. Chana, after years of obdurate "stan'in' out agin de Spirit," had been hopefully converted only a month ago. The stumbling-block in the ways of God with men, in her case, had been her own undeserved misfortunes. Finally she had been brought to regard these as a means of grace, but now her faith failed her.

"Looks like I cud bar it better ef I done had my silk dress, an' ben out jes *oncet* in it," she said, after a pause, filled by poor Dosier with desperate mute supplication. "I doan' wanter die."

"Oh, Chaney, tink er de bright worl' above, an' de glori's w'ite ga'ment!"

"I'd heap ruther have a black silk," muttered Chana, and turned her face to the window.

All that day she hardly spoke. She could eat nothing. In vain Dosier went down town and returned with California grapes, which Chana used to like. Chana only shook her head, saying, "I'm too busy studyin' t' eat."

Dosier carefully put them away for a more propitious moment; but it never came. A black cloud of depression swathed poor Chana's soul. Every little act of kindness, every sign of affection from Dosier or her daughter, every one of the small pleasures which they tried so hard to give her, was like a hand drawing the gloom tighter, for it made life more desirable and death more hideous.

"She cayn't seem to get reconciled nohow," Dosier confided with tears to Mrs. Ponder. "She says now we all got so nicely fixed, an' she got her bed by the winder, an' kin see de roses, an' folks gwine by on de street, she doan' min' layin' in bed. Ye know we fetched a couple er w'ite figgers, imiges, fo' tuh putt on de bureau, an' a beaucherful picter tuh hang on de wall. Chaney she doan' git many presents, and she ben so pleased when she got dem she jes *cried*—she done so. An' now she says she hates fo' ter leave. An'—an' "—Dosier choked over the words—"she hates fo' tuh leave me an' Nettie an' de little tricks. She allus uster like tuh look down de road so she see me comin' nights, an' she laffed so when somebody give me a present. She say she won't have no good times in heaben, an' she cayn't git no satisfaction outer studyin' 'bout it. She won't pray no mo', neether. Po' chile, she cayn't git reconciled tuh de Lawd's ways, an' she faults *Him*. She takes on orful, an' says He mout of 'lowed 'er to live *one* year longer, an' 'j'y 'erself a bit—an' sich. Makes me feel turrible bad." She wiped away the tears that had been rolling down her cheeks before she continued: "Doan' you be 'maginin' dat I'm fearin' de Lawd lay dem bad feelin's er Chaney up agin her. He knows better. Naw, ma'am. But I cayn't b'ar havin' her go on so oneasy; I cayn't b'ar it noway, 'tall.

"Oh, hush, Dosier," said Mrs. Ponder, soothingly. "She'll get reconciled; they always do. Say, don't she want me to lend her my music-box? You can keep it ayfter I'm gone, long's she wants it. She used to like to hear the hymn-tunes. And there's 'Rainbow Polka' and 'Sweet Violets' beside."

But Dosier answered sadly that Chana no longer cared for hymns. "She jes lays an' studies," said she.

Mrs. Ponder, not a religious woman herself, cast about in vain through her scattering reminiscences of religious people for some comforting suggestion. The consequence of the interview was that she burst into tears herself, and sent Chana a large red-velvet pincushion, having a yellow and white bunch of flowers painted on it, which she had bought the day before at a church fair, and was treasuring for the place of honor in her guest-chamber.

She carried an uneasy sense of compassion with her to the bath-house and to her accustomed companions, Mrs. Higgins and Miss Maine. In the frank Southern fashion she shared her perplexities, at once. "And what would you say poor Dosier had ought to do?"

"What *can* she do?" added Miss Maine. "I dare say Chaney is crazy."

"I don't see what she's got to make such a fuss about," Mrs. Higgins grumbled. "A bed-ridden invalid, I should think she'd be willing and glad to go. Why don't they talk to her about heaven and such things?"

"Well, they have, a heap," said Mrs. Ponder; "but it looks like she cayn't get up an interest in heaven. You see really there ain't so *very* much we all know about heaven anyhow."

"Isn't her husband dead?" said Miss Maine. The girl spoke with a vibrating accent of emotion under her indifferent manner. To her, one presence filled all her imaginations of the mysteries beyond this life: it was that of the man whom she was to have married, and who had died a year ago, on the morning of their wedding day. How could any wife—But the instinctive cynical second thought of her class interrupted that first thrill of sympathy. Such people, of course, were different. How *did* they feel?

"Well," said Mrs. Ponder, impartially, "he's dead, that's true enough; but I don't guess he counts much. He was a trifling no-'count nigger, who wanted to wear his Sunday clothes every day, and sit in the store-doors and ogle the yellow girls. I reckon he wasn't any too kind to her, either, ayfter she got too sick to earn money for him to spend."

Miss Maine laughed a sharp, quick little laugh. "Then you have to fall back on Mrs. Higgins's panacea—she's not losing much."

Mrs. Ponder looked rather wistfully from the set young face to the worn older face, with its quiver of irritable pain. "There *don't* seem much we poor human beings can do for each other in trouble," she said.

"I hope, for her own sake and ours too," Mrs. Higgins continued, paying no attention to this, "that she won't have a lingering illness. That new bath-woman we've got isn't half as good as Dosier."

Miss Maine's eyebrows went up a little; she directed a side glance to Mrs. Ponder, who had taken out her gum, and was rocking and chewing with unusual vigor.

"She has no heart either," thought the girl, scornfully; "they are all coarse and disagreeable together."

Really, however, she did the worthy Arkansas woman injustice. Gum had become a sort of intellectual motor to Mrs. Ponder, who never felt her mind really working without a simultaneous action of her jaws.

But she said nothing to her companions. Indeed, the notion of comfort that she was revolving would have seemed heartless and ridiculous to one unacquainted with the African "ways." She went to see Dosier on purpose to tell her. "Did you ever think of telling Chaney 'bout the funeral?" said she. "I know you 'low to give her a nice one."

"I does so," said Dosier. She clapped her hands together, though the tears were in her eyes. "De Lawd bless you fo' dat t'ought, Miss Betty; I do reckon I got another myse'f by it, an' dat I cheer 'er up. Come an' see 'er, won't you, Miss Betty?"

The conversation had taken place outside the house, on the white sand walk. Now silently Mrs. Ponder followed Dosier into Chana's room.

The sick woman had turned her face away from the

humble and careful adorning of the walls to the greenery swinging against her window-pane; but her eyes saw the varying shadows on leaf and rose, and the lovely flush of color, as little as they did Dosier's chromos and plaster images. Absorbed in her ceaseless and impotent wrestle with her doom, she would lie thus for hours, hardly speaking. What visions of her thwarted, dim, pain-dogged life, what forlorn gropings among the eternal problems, what wild, half-savage, suffocating revolt against the Power that would not save her, were hidden behind that dull mask which her face had become! Her eyes looked out solemn and turbid with inarticulate thoughts and misery. Sometimes they would follow every movement of her sister, until Dosier would feel an intolerable pity. All her own personal grief and ache of loss was consumed by an overpowering longing to soothe Chana's torment. "Ef I cud only git 'er tuh go easy an' peaceful, I give 'er up. Oh, dear Lawd, holp 'er!" she moaned. "It's wusser dan de pain, kase de doctor kin give 'er opium fur *dat*." Now she walked up to the bed and gently took Chana's hand. It lay lead-like in hers. "Heah Mis' Betty Ponder, Chaney; she done come tuh see ye."

Chana did not move or turn her head, but her lips moved: "Tell 'er howdy. I cayn't talk."

Mrs. Ponder said a few hearty words, which passed over Chana's apathy like a breeze over a rock.

Then Dosier's mellow, tender voice struck the new note of thought. "I ben studyin' 'bout you, sist' Chaney. You 'ain't had much good times, has you?"

All the while she was softly stroking Chana's hand. There was no word or sign of response, but Dosier felt the faintest tremor under her fingers.

"Yes, honey, dat so; but ef you didn't have a good time, you shall have de bigges' an' de nices' burryin' of ary cullud pusson in Hot Springs."

Chana lifted her free hand. "Turn me over," said she. Whenever the poor woman would move, she must be helped. Dosier assisted her to change position.

"Go on," she said faintly. There was no dawning of interest in her face, but she listened while Dosier talked, and it was the first time since the doctors spoke their sentence that she had so much as listened. Dosier had no perception of anything grotesque or horrible in telling her sister about her funeral. The negroes all magnify funerals. She thought

52

simply that Chana might be "chirked up a bit" to know what a nice funeral she would have. Nor was she mistaken. Poor Chana had her meagre social ambitions; she wanted to be well thought of. Since her conversion she had regularly sent her quarter on Sunday for the preacher. Dosier had promised her fifty cents to give on the proud day when she should wear her new black silk to church. It may be that her bewildered soul saw a light of hope in this last chance of display. Death would not utterly crush her, if she might have a "gran' burryin'."

"Br'er Warner shill preach yo' funeral, sister," said Dosier. "You *shill* go ter church oncet mo' like you wanted tuh, an' you shill w'ar my bes' under-cloz, an'—an' my black silk dress."

There was no mistake now; the sick woman was listening. *"What!"* she cried hoarsely; *"you'*— Naw, I cayn't take hit, sist' Doshy; you onlies' good dress, and you spendin' sech er heap er money on me now. Tuh *burry* dat beaucherful dress! Why, 't wud be plumb wicked."

But there was a light in her eyes, a flickering, timid hope. Do not despise it; behind the barbarian greed for show was the human longing to be mourned by her kind; to touch them, move them somehow, leave some more vivid impression behind her than merely the image of a bed-ridden old black woman out of the way. Who knows that poor Chana's funeral was not to her that one enchanted moment which we all, in some wise—being mortal—must covet, the moment when we are the central figure of our world?

More and more did the hard pain soften as Dosier went on, taking no denial: "You shill w'ar my new ruche dat Mis' Higgins give me, an' de pin, an' be clothed in silk from head to toe. Oh, Chaney, honey, ye doan' know how willin' I gives it up, ef it on'y ease you' min'. I tanks de Lawd ever' night I *got* de money tuh spend on ye."

"An' me tinkin' ha'sh tings er de Lawd kase He call me 'way!" sobbed the now entirely overcome woman. "When *you* is so good tuh me, I give up, sist' Doshy; I reckon He does love me; I is willin' tuh go. Mabbe—mabbe He let me outer Heaven oncet in a w'ile, an' I kin git back an' see you all. Doshy, den I am tuh shake dat rosebush agin de winder. Den ye know it's *me."*

Miss Maine stood at her window in the hotel and watched the long procession of Chana's funeral creeping up the hill to the church. The last buggy had turned the corner, and still she stood, held motionless by the sombre reverie that was her usual state of mind—a dismal day-dream where the sorrows of others always were merged into her own grief.

Thus Mrs. Ponder found her, when she was ushered into the room, breathless with her rapid ascent of the stairs, and red in the face from a combination of weeping and fast walking.

"I've just come from Dosier's," she said, after the formal greeting, unaffectedly wiping her eyes, "I've cried so I'm not fit to be seen. Besides, it's a long walk."

"I thought I saw you in a carriage," said Miss Maine.

"Oh, I left the carriage for Dosier; and Mrs. Higgins sent a carriage too."

"Mrs. Higgins!" cried Miss Maine, surprise overcoming her reserve. "Why, I thought she—she said—I didn't suppose she would care."

"Oh, she's right kind-hearted," said Mrs. Ponder, easily; "only she hates to show. Why, she's gone up to Dosier's a heap of times. She and I. We were there the day she died. She'd just gone, and Dosier told us about it. She died just as peaceful! After Dosier had that talk about the funeral with her she didn't think of nothing else; saw the preacher, picked out all the hymns—her mind was just full of it; and the morning when she died she had Dosier lay out all her things on the bed, the black silk and all, and Dosier said she actually laughed, and said, 'Will I look nice in it, sister, clothed in silk from top to toe?' That's what Dosier had said to her, you know. And when Dosier replied, 'Yes, she would look beautiful,' she laughed again, and went to sleep holding Dosier's hand, and passed away in her sleep. There couldn't be anything more peaceful. And really, Miss Maine, it was a beautiful funeral—such quantities of flowers, and so many closed carriages, and she did look so nice and happy in the black silk! Poor Dosier did give her her best, that's a fact."

"What a pity Chana couldn't see her own funeral!" said Miss Maine, rather dryly.

"Well, I don't know; perhaps she did," said Mrs. Ponder.

WHY ABBYLONIA SURRENDERED

Octave Thanet

Love that hath us in his net,
Shall he pass and we forget?
* * * * * * *
Love is hurt by jar and fret,
Love becomes a vague regret,
Eyes with idle tears are wet,
Idle habit links us yet.
What is love, for we forget!
Ah no! no!

—Tennyson.

ABBYLONIA EDDINGS, wife to the Reverend Eli Eddings, was always tired of a Monday afternoon; but never had she been so exhausted, soul and body, as she was one Monday in March. She stood in a tired woman's attitude, her knuckles on her hips, and gazed wearily about the kitchen. "Just slicked up!" sighed Abbylonia. "Well, it's the best I can do, with *this* back."

Yet the ordinary eye would have reported the room miraculously neat, from the big dresser to the glistening kitchen stove. But the eye of Abbylonia Eddings was no ordinary eye. She had more ambition than health, and in spite of eking out the latter with that which the New

Englanders name "faculty," and we in Arkansas call by no special name, but admire as sincerely, she at times strained her nerves to the tearing point.

"Abby," her mother-in-law, the widow Eddings, once said to her—"Abby, you had ought to *pray* to be more trifling!"

"I'll die sooner," replied Abby, vehemently. "Do you want me to sink to the level of these people around me? I can work, whether I'm tired or rested. There wouldn't be much done if I only worked when I was rested."

"But you're working on your *nerves*, Abby," the widow ventured, "and they won't last forever."

"I reckon they'll last *my* time," said Abby.

The widow shook her head and wiped away an unobtrusive tear. She was a woman of a gentle and plaintive turn, who said little, but wept frequently and at length. Abby herself seldom wept. Perhaps it were better for her had she thus washed the bitterness out of her heart. She did not shed any tears to-day, although she was crushed under the leaden misery of her anxieties and her physical exhaustion. She looked, dry-eyed, out of the window—not to see the street, but simply because the window happened to be in front of her eyes—and caught a glimpse of her mother-in-law's black mohair skirts brushing past her gate. "There comes maw," she said, "because I don't feel like seeing a mortal creature! Well, I don't care. I'd like maw to remember me kindly." The last thought summoned a flicker of a smile to her face as she opened the door.

The widow Eddings lived down the street, in her own house, which her son Eli had bought for her. He had selected this little village because Hattie, Mrs. Eddings's daughter, lived there, being married to one of the best tempered and most unsuccessful business men in the state of Arkansas. Eli had loaned him money twice (although Abby knew it would be lost), and now had hit upon the expedient of yoking him to a shrewd partner, who should manage the business, while Bud Slater might entertain the customers.

The widow came in gingerly, on tip-toe. "Dreadful muddy," said she; "and I 'lowed 'twas only shoe-mouth deep, and come off without my rubbers. I had to come most of the crossing on the railroad; and I was scared to death lest a train should come up behind, kinder quiet like, whilst I ben so busy picking my way, and run over me——"

"I don't think there's much danger of a train of cyars being *quiet*, maw," said Abby, who was wiping off the widow's shoes.

"Well, they do make a heap of noise in the street. But I didn't aim to contrairy you, Abby; I reckon you know best, reading so many books as *you* do." The widow sighed. She had a long, fair, plaintive face and timid eyes. There was a scar over one eyebrow. She was always carefully neat in her dress, which was black, not so much because she still mourned the husband of her youth (who used to throw things at her) as because she esteemed black an economical and useful habit. She continued: "There's a dreadful sight of typhoid fever in town. I reckon it's the mud puddles. Do you know you got a reg'lar slash outside the gate? I seen Susy Nell playing outside; she looked kinder puny, I 'lowed. Maybe not."

Susy Nell was the Eddings's only child. Abby could have explained her looks, but she had no mind for talk. The widow dismally continued to unpack her budget: "Say, Abby—I reckon I best tell you, for you're sure to hear it—Eli ain't going to git the job of painting the church pews."

"They didn't give it to Hobson?"

"That's jest what they did. I met Mis' Hobson on the street, and she told me herself. Right spiteful of her, too, I call it. But 'tain't right to jedge. Jedge not, and you ain't going to be jedged, you know. She was with Sister Arnott."

"That's how Hobson got the job," said Abby. But she showed none of that indignation that the widow had expected. "She's always toadying Mrs. Arnott. And anything Brother Arnott says, you know——"

"Yes, the committee'll jest grease its head and swaller it whole," said the widow, sadly. "I expect she talked him over. What do you think she had in her hand, Abby?"

"I don't know, maw." Abby spoke listlessly.

"It was that dress pattern you told me you aimed to buy."

"The blue mixture with the red thread in it?"

"Yes, ma'am. That very piece. It was sticking out of the bundle. And I felt so bad 'bout you being disappointed of that dress that I went round to the store, thinking maybe Bud might have some come in or something, and that's how come they sold it, and thinkin' I'd git it for you, to make sure——"

"Maw, that was right sweet and kind of you," exclaimed

Abby; her heart smote her with the remembrance of many kindnesses from her dismal mother-in-law, dolefully rendered, but in all willingness of heart.

"I don't guess you need to be thankful, Abby; didn't come to nothing. I only found out that they didn't have nare 'nother bit. Bud had spoken to Mis' Arnott how you thought of taking the piece; but he said that only seemed to make her more wishful to have it, and he didn't like to mad her, she buys so much."

"Sister Arnott has been mean to us all ever since we came," said Abby; but, to the widow's surprise, she said it without violence. There was an absent look in her eye, dissipated for a second by the petty sting of the news, but returning at once. "I reckon the Arnotts would be glad to have us quit. Brother Arnott's got a nephew he thinks Elder would assign here."

"Oh laws, Abby! but he cayn't!" cried the widow, in dismay.

"Not unless Eli's willing; but—maw, Eli wants to leave the ministry!"

"Well, *sir!*" the widow gasped. She was not able to say more; her lips moved up and down like the gills of a fish out of water.

"It isn't like it was a question of support." Abby spoke doggedly. "Eli earns far more by his painting and papering than he does at preaching. You know what little places we've been at—making a crop and Eli preaching round. Yet we've laid by some money. I've slaved night and day, hoping we could leave the country and come to some civilized place. Eli's been away most of the time papering and painting, coming back to the circuit to preach Sundays. The conference made no objections, because he always did his full duty, and he was willing to take such little pay. It was lonesome for me, but I was willing to bear it, always hoping he would get a better circuit. And I was *so* happy when we moved here. But now Eli says he must quit. He has enough to buy a little farm if he cayn't open a shop here—maw, don't cry like that!"

The widow had taken out her handkerchief, and quietly, but in a thorough-going manner, with no attempt to gainstrive it, was abandoning herself to grief. Her first words were, "Reckon I got to ask you to give me another han'kercher, Abbylonia; I set out not knowing I'd have occasion to use it, excepting for ordinary purposes, and I picked up little Hattie's, and it's so small that I—I got to trouble you!"

She mopped her eyes patiently with the small cotton square until the fresh handkerchief appeared, when the deferred flood swept over the barriers of control and she wept aloud.

"Oh, he was a child of prayer!"—so articulate speech shaped itself in the chaos of woeful sounds. "When he wasn't more 'n twelve year old I told him I wanted him to be a preacher, and I begun reading of him sermons on a Sunday—and—he never *did* like 'em! He always wanted to paint and to chop things with the hatchet. He painted the hull wood shed different colors, to see how they'd look; and I used to pray over him and cry nights. I don't guess buckets on buckets would hole my tears; and at last you come to visit in the neighborhood, and he begun to wait on you, and you persuaded of him—oh, Lordy! how kin I bear it if he gives it up now! And this a heap the best place he ever did git!"

"The only decent place," said Abby.

"How come it, Abby? You taking in sech a heap of books and papers, they ain't led Eli astray, have they? That magazine on the table, are you sure it's sound religiously? The kiver is plumb worldly, to my mind. He ain't lost his faith?"

"He hates to preach, and he loves to paint. I reckon that's it, as near as I can ascertain."

The widow rocked to and fro, sobbing. There were no tears in Abby's eyes; her mouth was rigid.

"If he wasn't so obstinate," mourned the widow. "He always did be mule-headed, even as a little boy. He was mild as milk, but once get him to make up his mind, and there wasn't nare moving of him."

"We did move him once," said Abby; "he didn't ever want to be a minster."

"But look how well he's done—look at his sermons——" Her speech snapped off short; and both women colored. "Oh, Abby, I cayn't keep it from you no longer; I've known it all along!" the widow cried.

Abby smiled bitterly. "Well, maw, I reckon I'm glad. And you never told——"

"I never told a mortal soul. Not Hattie; not nobody."

"I'm sure you didn't, maw, or Bud would have had it all over town."

"Abby, is it *that!*"

"Yes, maw, it's that. He says he can't endure it any longer."

"I 'low you've always done it."

"Always. He never wrote a word himself. I wrote them, and he learned them, sometimes. More times he's read them off."

"It has been right hard on you, Abby."

Abby turned away her head; then she flung it back, and her eyes were glowing. "Yes, it has been hard, maw; but it's been a comfort in a way, too. You know how I always have hungered after books and papers. Maw, every cent of Eli's salary he's given me. He *would* do it. He's made a good living for us beside. And I've bought magazines and papers and books. I like having the money. But I like the——I don't know whether you'll understand me, but there's something in me that had to come out, and it came out in the sermons; and when I got so unhappy it was a strange kind of comfort to talk about troubles that were not like mine, yet, being troubles, made a suffering that *was* like mine."

"They always were powerful good sermons, Abby. But what were you unhappy about, daughter? Losing of the baby, of course, but anything else? Has this here you doing his work made a differ between you two?"

"Something has," said Abby; "he—he's kind as ever, but he tells me nothing. I know he's miserable. I've known it a long time, but he never has said a word until last week. Then, all at once, he told me he couldn't endure it any longer; he felt he was a fraud. As long as he was working round at little places, doing more pastoral work than preaching, it hadn't seemed so bad to him. I asked him what he was going to say, and he said, 'The truth!' He was going to get up in church and make confession before god and man——"

"Oh, laws, Abby, you mustn't let him do *that!*" cried the widow.

"I don't know if I can help it," said Abby, with a kind of groan. "Oh, maw, you don't understand." She bit her lips; even to her husband's mother the wife could not say: "You don't understand how little influence I have over him."

"Yes, I do, tew, Abby; he's powerful obstinate. And I reckon it's hard for a man to feel his wife's smarter 'n him!"

"I'm not, and I don't think it," said Abby; "but maw, you never told me—how did you find out?"

"Oh, easy," sighed the widow; "the sermons was like you and not like Eli, and one night I found some sheets of paper in the wood box. I couldn't help finding out—laws, Abby, there's Eli himself!"

"Abby! Is Abby here?" said a deep, mild voice. "Why, maw, is it you? Rest your bonnet on a chair and stay to supper with us."

Eli had opened the door and was before them, a tall figure, stooping a little, with a handsome face. The curly brown hair was wearing away on the temples. They were well shaped temples, and the forehead was a promising dome. The features beneath, too, were clear cut and manly, and the eyes were bright, but the whole countenance wore a deprecating expression that made one think of a dog expecting a blow, and for which there was no sufficient reason either in Eli Eddings's nature or prospects. He was a Methodist minister, who was known favorably among the brethren as one who asked for little from the conference, went willingly to the least desirable circuits, and preached impassioned sermons in an apathetic manner.

The widow kissed her son tearfully, but she could not be persuaded to stay, and he followed her voyage through the mud puddles with an anxious eye.

"Ain't maw been crying?" said he.

"You're right observing, Eli," said Abby, dryly. "Yes, she has."

"I hope it wasn't anything serious, Abby."

"That's as you look at it, Eli. She was crying about your leaving the ministry."

"I was 'fraid she would take it that way," said Eli. And he sighed.

"I don't know when I've seen your mother so worked up, Eli; it's going to be a most terrible thing to her if you do the way you said."

Eli's lips puckered with pain. He said nothing, and his silence and the very misery of his bearing pricked his wife's temper. She was exasperated and frightened at once. The thought darted to her, "He's fixing not to give in, no matter how it hurts him!" Her anger flashed out before she could ask herself was it wise to speak. "It's a cruel, unmanly thing you propose to do, Eli Eddings," she cried—"shaming your mother and me before all these strangers. You may have a right to confess your own sins, if you will call them that, but you've no right to confess *mine!*"

"But, Abby"—Eli found his voice—"you didn't do wrong; it was *me.* All the same, if you don't want it, I can jest say I didn't write the sermons. I won't speak your name."

Abby shivered. "I think," said she, slowly, in an emotionless voice, "that if you lived with me a hundred years you wouldn't understand me, Eli."

"Maybe not," Eli answered, patiently. "I expect I had better pack up some water for you, Abby, and fill the wood box." Therewith he was edging out of the room.

"Can't you see the box is full?" said Abby. "Johnny Hinds filled it. He was over here. Susy Nell fell in the cistern——" The father's face changed sharply before she could add, "Of course I pulled her out; I heard the splash and there she was, floundering——"

"And it's eight feet deep, and you cayn't swim! Oh Lord, Abby, what did you do?"

"Threw the clothes line to her, of course, and told her to catch on and hold on or I'd whip her! What else could I do? She'd have drowned before I could rummage up that ladder in the barn!"

"But how did you pull her up?"

"I called on Johnny Hinds, who was out in their yard, and *he* ran over. I made him get that long board you had for papering, and I had him put it down crossways in the cistern, and I hauled her to the board, and she climbed out enough for me to catch her."

"You—you weren't mad at her, Abby?" Eli spoke timidly, and Abbylonia's eyes turned to steel.

"Didn't I tell you she caught on to the rope as I told her? Do you suppose I'd punish her for minding of me? No; I boiled her some milk and gave Johnny and her some doughnuts. I had to change every stitch on her."

Eddings swallowed twice. "You're awful smart, Abby!" said he. Then he cleared his throat; but nothing came of the exercise, and presently he shuffled out of the room.

Abbylonia sank into a chair, leaned her head back, and laughed. "That's all the good it's done, my telling," she said to herself; "he's gone to hug and kiss *her;* he hasn't a thought left for *me.* He didn't even kiss me once. What do I care? When he does, it's only because he promised to love his wife. It's his duty. Well, I don't blame him. I'm ugly tempered and I'm homely; I'm worn to the bone working for him. Oh, Lord!

Oh, Lord! How can you make a woman like me, who can't make her husband love her, and can't stop loving him!" She walked to the little glass above the roller towel and gazed steadily on her image. The sunlight gave her every wrinkle. Mercilessly it painted the irregular sharp features, the straight black hair, the unquiet eyes, the lines scoring the brow between the eyebrows (like footprints of a frown), the set mouth, the crooked curve of the jaw. The attractions of the face, its clear soft tints, the brilliancy of the eyes, and the white teeth that showed in a flashing smile, the refinement of those irregular features, the vitality and changing intensity that informed the whole plain countenance—these, which were poor Abby's real charm, she could not see, and the picture was gallsome to her. She turned away with a groan. "He's a good man," she thought, "but nobody can be so cruel as good people. To get rest for his own conscience he's willing to send me to perdition! I'll die before I'll go back and live on a farm again, with Eli away half the time. And I wouldn't even have the sermons to write and the little money for my own." How much comfort she found in the spending of that pittance, without let or hindrance, on the books for which she hungered, is beyond the imagination of one who has not been a dependent step-daughter, filching a crude education from sleep, and picking cotton to earn the price of a print gown. "Yes," she repeated, "I'll die sooner!" Under all her physical and mental torture, even while she called herself hopeless, she had been hoping that Eli would be moved by the danger to the child and by her rescue, and that she could use his awakened tenderness to soften his purpose. The hope had failed.

"I'll give him one last chance," she said."I'll not be angry or bitter. I'll speak to him calmly and kindly. We'll talk it over, and at least he'll not be so cruel as to speak out; he can quit the ministry without making the town too hot to hold us."

Trying to blow the dead embers of her hope into life after this fashion, she went about preparing a better supper than usual for Eli. She was so footsore that every step hurt her, and there were shooting pains in her back, but she moved briskly. Whatever Abby lacked, it was not fortitude. Eli came in, laden with wood, and Susy Nell at his heels carried a basket of kindling.

"Susy Nell's been giving Johnny a beautiful knife," said Eli, in a cheerful high tone, "and papa's going to paint

Johnny's mamma's parlor for her to-morrow—to show how good we think he was to pull Susy Nell out of the mean, bad cistern. Now Susy's going to be mamma's little helpin' dirl, ain't she?"

Susy Nell, a chubby, smiling little creature of five, proffered the basket, and Abby kissed her, saying, "Now you run out and play." Susy Nell felt vaguely repulsed, but she took it in good part, and pattered away for the yard. She forgot the kisses which (as agreed outside) she was to give "dear mamma for pulling her out of the cistern." And Eli was too after-witted to remind her. He busied himself making the fire and cutting the meat.

"Maw told me you didn't get the painting of the pews."

Eli avoided her eye. "No, Abby; they gave it to Hobson. Maybe I hadn't ought to say it, but I'm afraid they'll make a botch of it, too. They don't understand fine work."

"They certainly don't," said Abby; "They painted Hattie's aunt's house, and the paint streaked dark streaks the very next summer."

"Put turpentine in it, and most likely used boiled linseed oil," said Eli, with a sudden air of interest. "Well, I would hate to have them spoil those pews. I wonder would they take it hard if I was to caution them against boiled oil, and ask 'em to put plenty of japan in the paint for the inside. They're going to varnish the pews, they say; and if they ain't careful and don't use the right kind of hard finish, which takes a heap of rubbing and goes on mighty slow like, there'll be trouble for sure."

"But why did Brother Arnott not get *you* to do it? you the minister, too, and having an interest——"

"Well, he said that was the very reason—said ministers of the Gospel had no right to be engaged in secular callings. I reckon he's partly right, too."

"Are you of the same mind still, Eli?"

"If I'd thought of changing, how *could* I ayfter the Lord's dealing with me this day?"

"Do you think the Lord pulled her out of the cistern? or maybe you think He pushed her *in*," said Abby. She had turned around. Her face was flushed, and her eyes glittered, and she spoke in an unfamiliar voice.

Eli's sluggish wits could not rally under her vehemence. "I—I reckon we better not talk about it till you feel cammer, Abby," he stammered. Which was about the most irritating thing that he could have said.

Abby had begun the interview determined not to grow angry; but poor Abby, with her raw nerves and the canker-fret of jealousy in her heart, was not in a condition to discuss the merits of baking powder, safely. The passion that she had tried to smother, blazed up at Eli's words. She flung out her arms wildly, crying: "It's now or never, Eli Eddings. For the last time, and mighty near the first time too, I'm going to ask you to consider *me*. It is folly of you to imagine we can live on here ayfter your getting up and making that confession. I couldn't show my face among the ladies here. *I* have a little sense of shame, if you haven't."

Eli hung his head. "We could go into the country and rent and make a crop——"

"I *hate* the country! I hate the country people!"

"You didn't hate the folks at Sycamore Hurd when they were so kind to us, when little Eli died, and put up a stone to his grave, and Sister Mitchell picked all the geraniums she was saving for Rosy's wedding—you don't hate *them*, Abby?" said Eli, sorrowfully. And his patience, instead of quelling Abby's wrath, only made it mount the higher; it seemed to put her in the wrong, who was really in the right.

Except for the goading of her fury she could never have answered him so cruelly; but nothing seems cruel to an angry wife who has disputed with her husband. She said: "If we hadn't been out in Sycamore Hurd, if you'd taken the other circuit they offered, and been in town near a doctor, perhaps baby wouldn't have died!"

Eli recoiled, and his face went white. Abby was not looking at him; she had whisked back to her frying pan on the stove; when the hot grease spattered on her wrist she smiled savagely at the pain. Her husband's voice came after a long pause:

"I don't guess there's much use our talking, Abby; if there ain't anything I can do to help you 'bout supper I reckon I'll go out in the yard with Susy Nell."

"Eli, are you going to speak out next Sunday?"

"We won't talk 'bout it now, Abby. You—you pray, too, and then we'll talk."

"Eli, no prayer will change this to me. And I tell you now, you'll be sorrier than you ever were in your life if you do speak."

Eli made no reply at all. He left the house. He carried away a deep wound of his own; and pain always made him silent. But again his silence infuriated his wife. At supper she told him that Susy Nell was coughing, and she had best stay with her that night.

"Don't you think we'd ought to have the doctor step in?" said Eli, anxiously, "Is your throat sore, honey lamb?"

He made no slightest objection. Abby staid with Susy Nell every night that week. The cold had disappeared—if there ever had been a cold—but Eli did not speak of a change.

"He's glad to be rid of me," thought the miserable wife; "all he cares for is Susy Nell," and her anger changed into something deadly and still. At times she was conscious that her torment of soul was overmuch for anything that Eli had done. Then she would tell herself that she had lost her husband's love, and she would have to grow old and haggard in the slavery of a farm, and gradually, as her health failed, that she would sink into the like of the slatternly drudges that she despised. She felt her strength failing. She could not do half the work that she used to do unless she lashed herself through the last part of her tasks. Years of overtaxed days and robbed nights were having their revenge. The creeping paralysis of estrangement had aided them, and the shock of Eli's decision dealt the last blow. Abby's nervous system simply collapsed. She did not suspect it, but she was not a responsible creature.

There was a strange sensation in her head all the time. It seemed to her that she was conscious of the physical working of her thoughts, and that as they passed from one chamber of her brain to another, she felt the passage. Once this notion had fastened on her mind, she could not pluck it away, and the wearisome disquietude of it, it is impossible to suggest. Unreal noises began to vex her ears. She would hear her dead baby cry; wailing voices would rise and sink, which, no sooner did she hearken, would cease or change into the clamor of the poultry yard. At first the ghastly path of escape from her trouble had been only the mental elaboration of her angry phrase, "I'll die sooner!"

Then she did not mean to die; but inch by inch the tide of despair submerged the nervous woman's reason. The fancy became a possibility; at last it was a desire.

"I'm growing crazy, I expect." said Abby. "Well, it don't matter, if I can die in time!"

It may be asked, had Abby no religious scruples regarding

the sin that she meditated? Not any. It is the besetting temptation of the handler of religious things to lose his reverence in the familiarity of habit. Every clergyman knows the deadening effect of the constant use of religious phraseology. And Abby had no protection of religious zeal. She was not a pious woman. She wrote her sermons not to save souls, but to help the Reverend Eli Eddings. From indifference she had slipped into doubt.

"If there is a God, He knows I cayn't bear it!" she said.

Thus it came to pass that she no longer watched Eli's face for signs of relenting. She withdrew into the shadow of her distempered dreams. Here was a way to punish Eli, all the dearer because it would make her suffer as well as him. A woman always likes to strike the man that she loves through her own heart.

So the soul of Eli's wife walked apart among formless hopes and fears, or beat against that *impasse,* a realization of the next step beyond the gate. Yet to outward seeming she was not changed, except that she was a trifle absent minded. Until Friday she had a faint—was it hope or fear?—that Eli might give up his purpose to his mother's pleadings if not to hers. Friday, the widow paid her a visit. After thanking Abby for certain gifts of preserves sent in during the week, she took out her handkerchief.

"You always have ben a good daughter to me, Abbylonia," she said; and the ready tears welled in her eyes. "I cayn't say how I feel, I feel so for you in this hour of trial. I've made it a subjec' of prayer, and studied and studied on it till my hand'cher wasn't enough and I had to take my apron! And this here is how I look at it. Abby, honey, there ain't no good comes of fighting agin the will of the Lord. I knew Eli hadn't no call to be a minister. He knew it too, and he tried to beg off; but I kept a-pecking at him and a-worrying of him until he gave up, wore out. And now looks like it is a judgment on me that he is going to quit in the sight of men. I've talked with him, and he's spoke his mind; and, Abby, I cayn't oppose him, though it'll mortify me so I reckon I'll be obliged to leave town."

Abby laid her sewing down. The widow shielded herself behind her handkerchief and sobbed. Had Abby scolded her, she would have sobbed the louder. But Abby answered, in a quiet, mild, voice: "I expect you have aimed to do right, maw. I don't want you to think I blamed you. It's between Eli and me. Don't cry. Look at this dress of Susy Nell's. Do you reckon she will like it?"

The widow sniffed gratefully, and was sure Susy Nell would like such a beautiful frock. She did not adventure any return to the perilous theme, and soon fared forth, equally bewildered and relieved.

Then Abby, in her neat street gown, her smooth hair shining, and every pin on her in place, walked down the broad, sunny village street, where bluets were sprinkling the green sod on either side the wooden walk, to Bud Slater's store, and bought a box of rat poison, with a lying jest. That night, for the first time in a week, she slept all night. All day Saturday her manner was exceedingly gentle. Eli was moved by her soft, unusual ways, but did not know how to show his feeling, beyond constant attention to the wood boxes and buying her a copper wash boiler. The strange diffidence that often stands between those in the closest relations, locked his tongue while he longed to speak. Abby no longer cared to talk. The desire for expression was all burned out by the constant thought of that one tremendous expression on which she was resolved.

Sunday morning dawned bright and beautiful, as March mornings often dawn in Arkansas. Abby bathed and dressed herself with unusual care. Then she made Susy Nell ready for church. She wondered at herself that she shouldn't feel more—this last time she would ever dress the child. She kissed her, but there was neither grief nor passion in the kiss. That was because grief belonged to the left lobes of the brain, and somehow it had become misplaced, and was on the right side; she couldn't suffer on the right side. "Or else I'm a wicked woman who doesn't love her children," thought Abby. "I'll let her go to Bessie Moon's for dinner. Better for her. I'd like to see her once more, but it doesn't matter about me; I'm a wicked woman. The hill women used to love their children best, better than their husbands, but I always loved Eli best—better than baby, even. Baby, what are you crying out in the barn for? Oh, he bruised his little pale cheek! Oh, baby, baby! the bruise was there in his coffin! And Mrs. Mitchell fetched all her flowers. She came over in that calico that was so short in front—I wish I'd helped her cut that dress instead of just lending her the pattern—she came over in all the rain. I hated to have it rain, and I cried that night to have it raining on his little grave, and to have him out in it all alone. I wish I could cry now."

But she did not cry; after all, why should she, when she would soon be out of all the worry, and wouldn't need to feel her thoughts beating through her brain?

It was a little difficult to remember about the cooking; nevertheless, she did remember, and it was a better breakfast than common that she set before Eli. He ate very little of it. She said to herself that a few weeks ago she would have thought how handsome and manly he looked in his new black suit. Now she merely wondered would he have it for his wedding suit when he married again? Even that stab fluttered her heart but a second; then she was back working those weary thoughts through her brain.

Eli started when she came into the room ready for church. "It's awful kind of you, Abby," he faltered, "but you don't need to go. Maw is going to stay home."

"I rather go, Eli," said Abby, untenderly but gently.

They walked down the street together, little Susy Nell tripping ahead in the sunshine. The town was prosperous, and there were two or three new brick buildings with wooden trimmings smart with paint. Here and there over the plain a mansion rose a story or two above the pointed roofs; but for the most part the houses were modest southern cottages, not too finical about the back yards. The church bells were ringing, and the street was full of little groups of people wending their way churchward in sedate cheerfulness. The children's white frocks and a few lawn gowns lent a brightsome air to the simple toilettes.

Abby gazed quite carelessly about her. To-morrow—to-morrow—where would she be? She wondered why she did not suffer. "I'm going to die to-night, and I don't care," she said to herself, dully. "I reckon I'm past it." She didn't want to think, because it was such heavy work pushing the thoughts through the cells of her brain; and something seemed to be loose in the machinery within her head, and to be rattling about; but she kept remembering how after baby died Eli was in the same kind of daze. She, in her own passionate anguish, had called him stupid of heart. Perhaps she had misjudged him. It was then that the misunderstanding, the alienation, began between them. She had written a sermon about the death of children—a sermon that she seemed to write with the very blood of her heart—and Eli refused to preach it. He said: "I cayn't do it!" and when she pressed for a reason he answered, "I don't want to; it makes me feel too bad."

Her vanity was hurt. Without a word she wrote him another sermon, instead of the old one which he proposed to preach. She never mentioned the sermon afterward. Neither did he. Nor did she see it again; but she found some charred sheets of paper in the embers on the hearth next morning, and concluded (without examining) that Eli had burned the sermon overnight. And it hurt her. But now that it was too late, now that everything was too late, she wondered whether she had not been rash and hard. They were passing Colonel O'Neil's house, where the few Episcopalians of the village gathered Sundays to listen to the service read by one of their number. The music of their hymn rose in an air plaintive and intense. Passing the open window, Abby could hear every word:

> *"In the hour of trial,*
> *Jesus, plead for me!*
> *Lest by base denial*
> *I depart from Thee."*

She stole a glance at Eli. Was that the way *he* felt? A new apprehension of his motives was struggling into her confused mind. She drew a step nearer to him. Eli turned his eyes on her.

"I expect the folks are anxious to see the new paint," said he. "I spoke to Hobson and warned him, but he said he reckoned he knew his own business; and I'm nigh certain he hasn't used hard finish. Don't you sit down without feeling, Abby!"

Abby laughed a hard little laugh, and said that she wouldn't. She did not speak again. She had wondered what was passing through his mind. Well, she knew now—in this supreme day of his life he was worrying about paint! No, she hadn't done him injustice.

Eli parted with her at the church door. "Abby," he began— "Abby"—and could get no further; but he put out his rough workingman's hand and touched her sleeve with a lingering fall. Then he smiled feebly, and ended, "Mind you look out for the paint."

She did not understand that he was yearning to express his own suffering and his sympathy for her, that he longed to touch her, as a child in pain longs to touch its mother. And she parted from him with a mortal ache in her heart. Yet his words followed her, trivial as they were, and automatically she obeyed them. She touched the seat of the pew, which, truly enough, was sticky; and before Susy Nell and she sat down, she covered back and seat with one of the Sunday school papers which were scattered among the pews. Then she seated herself, and sank into a dreary reverie, imageless and numb. When she glanced up the pews were full, and Sister Arnott, in all the pomp of her new gown, was stiffly inclining her shoulders as she sat down in the front pew. The indestructible respect of a woman for a pretty gown was stronger than any ill will that she might bear to the wearer. Hastily she arrested the descent of those rustling sleeves. "Don't!" she whispered; "the varnish is all sticky; you'll spoil your dress!" And she picked up a paper and spread it out herself. At the same moment she nodded a warning to three women who were entering the seat, behind. "Perhaps the other seats stick too," she said. But Sister Arnott, with dignity, replied that these seats were varnished last; the others would surely be dry. And Abby, caring little, sank back into her thoughts.

Eli was on his feet announcing the hymn. "We will sing the one hundred and fortieth hymn, on page twenty-five— No. 140, page 25. 'God moves in a mysterious way His wonders to perform.'" The words rolled back into the minister's throat. He could see the whole church. And decidedly it was a spectacle to be seen, for all over the church men and women were struggling to rise, and squirming helplessly, wrathfully, on their seats.

The climax came when a wailing childish voice pealed out: "Mamma! mamma! I' *stuck!*" Then the emotions that decorum had gagged burst forth. There was a rending sound, a buzz of voices. The children especially were in great power, little girls whimpering and little boys giggling, and Sister Wayling's baby bawling with fright. Men wrestled and women writhed, but the varnish held stanchly, and the scene became a wild one. Brother Arnott, who came a few minutes late, stood horror-stricken in the middle of the aisle. The minister hurried to the aid of his imprisoned flock. Sister Arnott, Abby, a few fortunate tardy sheep, the three women in the seat behind Abby, and perhaps half a dozen provident ones whose custom was to look before they sat as well as before they leaped, helped Brother Arnott and Eli to pull and twist and wrench the people free, although at a sad cost to their Sunday clothes. At last all except Sister Moon and Brother Tredith were rescued from the snare of the spoiler, and the congregation gathered about these captives. Sister Moon was a woman of weight in every sense, the richest personage in the town, with a rich vein of obstinacy running through a pious and kindly nature, who had long since ceased to tempt the scales. Brother Tredith was a man of substance and great stature, and (as he carefully explained) he had sat down "kinder sky west and crooked," hence there was the more of him to stick.

As for Sister Moon she announced piteously to her audience: "It ain't that I'm so powerful heavy, but I always did set down hard! And, oh laws! this seat sticks like fly paper! I'll never have another sheet in my house, now I know how it feels! It's awful! Brother Eddings, nev' mind if you do tear my dress; I got plenty on underneath to be decent, and I never *was* proud! Pull away! Bless you, Sister Eddings, I really felt it give a mite then. Cayn't some more ketch holt on me? Brother Eddings, it's all we-all's own fault, for you done told us, and told them to put on different varnish; I know if you'd 'a' painted this church we'd be standing free praising the Lord this minnit!"

And Brother Tredith's tolling base chimed in: "That's right! There ain't a better painter in Arkansas, whatever you call him for a preacher! Now most like we'll have to be soaked off with alcohol, and all Hobson's fool work!"

The tide thus started ran high against Hobson, at which no one could wonder who had what might be called an all-round view of the unfortunate congregation. By this time a charitable commercial traveler was trying the effect of whisky on varnish, under Brother Tredith's direction, and those around Sister Moon were weak with laughter. Eli himself gave the last pull which freed her, and was in time to peel off Brother Tredith's long legs. Then Abby reached him, and whispered him to dismiss the congregation, which he did in a single sentence, "I reckon we all better go home now."

Abby lingered a little time behind the others; she was detained by Sister Arnott. Sister Arnott had never liked Abby, but now she took her hand, saying, heartily, "Sister Eddings, I am ashamed I got this dress when I more than half suspected you wanted it; and I think you showed a right Christian spirit saving it for me; and if I can ever do anything for you, count on *me!*"

Abby smiled, and said something in reply, she hardly knew what. She had the sensation of a criminal who receives a reprieve on his journey to the gallows. Moreover, the whole drift of her mind was diverted violently by the farce of the paint. It seemed ridiculous to think of suicide when she was still laughing over the picture of Sister Moon! Almost unconsciously she found herself laughing at it with Eli. "I believe maw would have had to laugh too," she cried. "I wish she had been there."

"It was awful good of you to come this morning," said Eli, with a grateful look; "and maw told me 'bout that dress, how you wanted it, and I sent to St. Louis for one for you. I think it was right sweet of you saving it for Sister Arnott that way."

"She looked so pretty in it, and it is such a nice dress——"

Eli opened his mouth, gasping vainly; it seemed to him a very lame speech that he made, but perhaps it served his purpose with Abby quite as well as eloquence. He said: "You're a heap prettier than her, Abby!"

Abby stood still in the road to look at him; but no suspicion could endure before his simple-hearted gaze. She reddened and smiled in spite of herself. "You haven't said that much to me, Eli, for—years!"

"But you knew I thought it!"

"No, I didn't. Susy Nell, run ahead; Bessie Moon's signaling to you over yonder! I reckon I am mean, Eli, but it's mighty hard to have your husband think so——"

"I never did think so, as God hears me, honey. But you were so much smarter'n me, and wrote such beautiful sermons, I 'lowed you looked down on a uneducated man like me——"

"Eli"—his wife interrupted him in strong agitation—"Eli, I believed you despised *me* because—because I wrote the sermons for you!"

He was in front of the puddle which had disturbed the widow; in his excitement he splashed into the worst of it. "I ain't such a pusillanimous, ornery, trifling tyke as that," he cried. "Abby, forgive me; I am pulling you into the mud!"

"You can pull me through all the mud in Hickory Ridge, Eli Eddings, and I won't say one word!"

He swung around. His eyes kindled. He caught the little figure up in his arms and carried her across the puddle to the firm ground. As he put her down he made a shamefaced apology: "Abby, I was just naturally *obliged* to get hold of you and hug you, and I didn't see no other way, out in the street as we are!"

Abby only made a kind of gurgle in her throat, and ran swiftly through their gate down the walk to the house. But when he overtook her, in their little parlor, simple as he was in woman's moods, he understood that his wife was not angry with him.

He sat down, he drew his wife on his knee in the fashion of his early married life, and kissed her. "Abby," said he, "I feel now like I could tell you all about it. You know how come I went into the ministry. I hadn't no more call to it than our caff! I went to please maw and you. And I staid because *you* wanted me! Oh, Abby"—his voice melted, and she hid her face—"*you* know what I felt about you! Why, your very clothes were so much nicer than the other girls', and the way you wore your hair, and it's white on your neck where the hair grows, and when I was near you I felt like I was walking in the woods with the wild honeyseckles! Abby! Abby! you little thing that I could crush, you're just like a flower yourself, honey, dearie. Don't cry, honey; I cayn't go on and do what I had ought to do if you cry; I'll *have* to give in to you, I love you so!"

And Abby? She forgot the nightmare of the last week, she forgot how she hated to live in the country, she forgot everything except that her husband loved her, and she sobbed, "Oh, Eli, I'll go anywhere and I'll live anyhow if you only will love me like that!"

"I love you a hundred thousand times better than you know, Abby," he cried. "Why, dearie, it was you converted me and made me give up preaching. What you trembling so for, lambie? Listen; it was this way: I read your sermons, and they worked on me. It was slow, for I'm slow. I don't know how to talk out things even to myself, and that makes me slow. But they worked on me. Abby, there was one sermon— you wrote it ayfter little Eli died——"

"Yes," said Abby, in a tense voice.

"I didn't seem to know where I was or what I was doing those days. I—I felt very bad, Abby."

Abby's hand stroked his brown curls, trembling; she could not speak.

"When I read that sermon, for the first time I could cry. And I was out in the willows by the river, and I kneeled right down and prayed to the Lord to have mercy and show me the way out and comfort us both! Abby, He will. But I couldn't preach that sermon."

"What did you do with it, Eli?"

"Wait a minute," said he. He put her out of his arms very tenderly, and went out of the room, while she waited for him, trembling.

She heard his footsteps moving about their chamber; they came back again. He was standing before her with the neat square sheets that she knew in his hands. And she read on the outside, in Eli's cramped hand, *"This sermon, which I thank God for, was written by my dear wife after the death of our dear son Eli."* There followed the date.

"Now you know," said Eli, "how you converted me. Ayfter that I felt I couldn't live a lie before you. But I wasn't strong enough, knowing the anxious notion you had of me being a minister, to stop right away, and I waited till I got things fixed so I can get a shop in this town; and you shall have the same money you had for the preaching, and more if you will take it, and we'll get a hired girl, so you'll have time to read your books; and, Abby, when it fell out this way this morning, I said to myself, 'Maybe the Lord ain't requiring a public confession of you, and maybe I could just say I didn't feel myself fitted, and quit.' What do you think, Abby?"

"I think," said Abby, "I'd go over to Brother Arnott and tell *him* all, and abide by his decision."

"I will," cried Eli, with a deep intake of breath. "I'll go now while you're getting dinner. Say, Abby, in your drawer on your bureau was standing this that you got for the rats; don't you think it's kinder dangerous having it there? Susy Nell——"

Abby caught it out of his hand and hurled the box into the open fire. "Yes, yes," said she; "it's a wicked thing. You go, Eli. And, Eli, you go tell your mother before you come home!" Then, as his footsteps echoed on the wooden walk, she sank lower and lower, and kneeled before the chair where he had sat.

THE WOMAN'S EXCHANGE
OF SIMPKINSVILLE

Ruth McEnery Stuart

"I'VE BEEN KISSED ONCE-T—with a reg'lar beau kiss—by Teddy Brooks." The puffs of smoke from old lady Sarey Mirandy Simpkins's pipe came faster after she had spoken.

"But I never kissed back. Hev you ever been kissed that a-way, 'th a reg'lar beau kiss, sis' Sophia Falena?" she continued, turning toward her sister, who sat, also smoking, beside her.

"Twice-t."

"Who by?"

"Once-t by Jim Halloway, time he spoken the word fo' me to marry 'im, an'—an' by another person for a far'well."

"An' you kep' two all these years an' never told 'em out, an' here I felt guilty a-hidin' one. Who was that various secon' smartie what done it to you, sis?"

"He weren't no smartie, Sarey Mirandy. He were Jim Dooley, an' it were time he 'listed in the army."

"Did you kiss back, Sophia Falena?"

"*Yas—I—did!* But what put kissin' into you' head to-night, sis? It's mighty funny, 'cause I was a-settin' here thinkin' 'bout kissin' too—an' I can't tell when I've studied about sech a thing befo'."

"I dunno. I was jest a-thinkin'. Sometimes it do me good to set an' think 'way back."

"Well, I tell you how I reckon kissin' come into *my* head. I was jest a-thinkin' *s'posin'*."

"S'posin' what, sis?"

"Well, s'posin' all 'round. S'posin' Jim Dooley had of came back from the wah, fo' one thing."

A faint blush suffused the thin face of the speaker at the very audacity of that which her supposition implied.

"An' s'posin' Sonny hadn't of taken to birds—an' died. An' s'posin' the bank hadn't o' failed. Why, sis, I could set here an' s'pose things in five minutes thet'd make everything different. S'posin' time Teddy Brooks give you thet special an' pertic'lar kiss, *you* had jest—ef not to say kissed back, not *drawed away* neither. S'posin' that?"

"Well, sis, since we got on the subjec', I've supposened it more'n once-t—pertic'lar sence I see how ol' an' run-down the pore feller is. Sally Ann Jones ain't been even to say a half-way wife to 'im. Seem like ev'ry time she lays a new baby in the cradle fo' him to rock she gets fatter an' purtier an' mo' no 'count; an' pore Teddy he sets an' rocks the flesh clean off'n his bones. Yas, sis, I've thought o' *that* s'posin' many a time, but it's a vain an' foolish thought—ef not a ongodly one. But the one I've s'posened about most is Sonny."

Both women sighed. "Somehow I can't get used to thinkin' 'bout Sonny dyin', noways. No two girls ever had a better brother'n Sonny. Sonny was a born genius, ef th'ever was one. Perfesser Sloane down to Spring Hill say hisself they warn't a young man in the county thet helt a candle to Sonny fo' head-learnin'—not to speak o' Sonny's manners. An' when I set an' look at this houseful o' stuffed birds in glass cases an' think o' what Sonny might 'a' been—Well, maybe it was God's will for Sonny to take to birds, 'stid o' drink or card-shufflin' like some brothers."

"It's mighty funny, sis, for you an' me to be sett'n' up here s'posin' an' lookin' back at this pertic'lar time, when it so p'intedly behooves us to be lookin' ahead. Lemme see that paper ag'in. Yas, here it is in plain 'Merican: 'Failure of the Cotton King's Bank of Little Rock'—a whole colume. Nobody to read that would think of its sett'n' two ol' women to studyin' 'bout kissin', now, would they? What you reckon we better do, sis?"

"God on'y knows—an' He ain't tol' me—yet. Twouldn't be no use to try takin' boa'ders, would it?"

"Twouldn't be right, sis. They ain't noboby in town *to* boa'd out but them as are boa'din' a'ready, an' twould be jest the same as askin' 'em to leave an' come to us—'special as we got the fines' house."

"Twould look that a-way, wouldn't it? I thought about takin' in quiltin', but there ag'in, you know, th'ain't mo' quiltin' give out to be did than Mis' Gibbs can do—an' she half crippled, too. No, no. 'Fore I'd give out thet you an' me'd take in quiltin', I'd starve—*that* I would."

"I taken notice to a pertic'lar word you spoke jest now, sis, 'bout 'God knows.' You recollec' what the hymn say?

'Hev we trial or temptation,
Take it to the Lord in prayer.'

Seem to me like our trial's been followed by two temptations a'ready. It's mos' nine o'clock, an' I'm goin' to read my chapter an' then lay this case o' you an' me out clear, on my knees, befo' the Lord; an' do you do the same, sis, an' I b'lieve we'll be d'rected."

Lighting her candle, old lady Sophia passed noiselessly into her own room. Her sister sat for some time longer in thought, then she too, after shovelling some ashes over the coals upon the hearth, took her candle and went to bed.

The Misses Simpkins were twins, and at the time of the civil war they had been fair blooming country maidens, both, and they were now, since the death, a year ago, of "Sonny," their bachelor brother, the sole representatives of a family that had stood with the best in the Arkansas community in which they lived; a family whose standards and traditions had been religiously observed in all things by the twin daughters upon whose frail maiden shoulders had developed responsibilities hitherto unknown to the women of the name of Simpkins. Their mother and grandmother had had slaves at their call, and by frugal care had accumulated what here in those days was counted as wealth.

They had worn their inherited frugality itself threadbare in the determination to "live like pa an' ma would like to have us live," and thus far they had succeeded.

Sonny, whose life, viewed retrospectively, seemed even to their loving eyes a failure, had been, when living, their pride and joy. Sonny was, in truth, a gentleman. His one year at college, which he left for the army in '61, had sufficed to introduce him into new realms of thought, and, it may be, had diverted activity from his hands to his brain. Certain it is that he never practically grasped the changed situation after the war, and the sisters and he had finally sold all the farm lands, reserving only the few acres surrounding the homestead. The proceeds, deposited in the failing bank, had yielded an income quite adequate to their modest needs.

Sonny had called himself a naturalist; and so he was—in a sweeter, broader sense than he knew. He was, as nature had made him, a true-hearted, unsophisticated gentleman. For more than twenty years he had been satisfied to pursue his chosen study, and take no note of time.

But Sonny was found one day, with a live bird still grasped in his hand, lying dead beneath a tree. Presumably he had climbed and fallen.

And now to the lonely sisters had come a second trial. Into their shadowed door had stalked unbidden and unexpected the informal guest called Poverty, with her startling command of "Work!"

It was dinner-time on the day following the conversation recorded before they reverted to the theme again.

"Well," said Miss Sarey Mirandy, "hev anythin' come to you, sis, thet we can do?"

"Hev anything come to you, sis Sarey dear?"

"Yas, it has. An' I'm 'fraid it's small comfort. Th'ain't but two things I can do, an' them's sewin' an' cookin'. Th'ain't any more sewin' needin' to be did in Simpkinsville'n them as are a'ready doin' it can do, an' as fo' cookin', you know how much chance they is in that—less'n a person'd hire out, which I *can't* do—not while ma and pa's ile-painted po'trait looks down from that chimbly at you an' me. Tell the truth, sis, what *to* do I *don't* know. Hev you thought 'bout it con- sider'ble?"

"Yas, I have, sis. You can cook an' sew, an' I can ca'culate figgurs, an' we got a-plenty o' houseroom, an' we're right on the public road, an'—"

"In the name o' goodness, sis hun, 're you wanderin', or what're you drivin' at?"

"Well, they's jest this much to it, sis Sarey Mirandy: I've got a idee; an' *my* idee is thet it's *the* idee—an' that's all they is *to* it."

Miss Sarey Mirandy readjusted her spectacles and scrutinized her sister's face. "Well, go on, honey. You've done got me wrought up!"

"Why, it's this—and I'd never o' thought o' sech a thing if

it hadn't o' been for my trip to the city, along with me subscribin' to that magazine, both of which, you know, hun, you pretty solemn discountenanced. I seen it tried in the city, an' the magazine is continual tellin' how it works everywhere."

"But for gracious sakes alive, sis, what is the thing?"

"*It's a Woman's Exchange*—that's what it is!"

"But, sis hun, we ain't got nothin' to start it with."

"That's jest the beauty of it. They get started on nothin'. We jest give out thet the Exchange *is started,* an' everybody who does any sort o' work to sell sends it, an' we sell it for her an' *deduc'* ten precent. You see?"

"Well, I dunno as I do."

"Well, here: S'posin' ol' Mis' Gibbs, 'stid o' totin' her heavy comforters all 'round the county, an' losin' maybe two whole days' time a-sellin' one for two dollars, jest sends 'em in here, an' we sell 'em for her. She gets—ten from one dollar leaves ninety cents, an' nine an' nine's eighteen, eight an' carry one—She gets—"

"You don't mean she gets eight dollar? Twouldn't never do in the world. People wouldn't pay it. An', besides, I thought you said she wouldn't have to carry none?"

"Don't put me out, sis; I'm all frustrated—'f I jest had a slate! Now I got it! You don't carry at all. Ought's a ought, an' nine an' nine's eighteen. She'd get a dollar 'n' eighty cents, an' we'd get the two dimes. Then you could put any kind o' cooked things in an' sell 'em. Them lemon pies o' yours'd sell like hot cakes."

"An' who'd get the precent on them, sis?"

"Well, reely, hun, I—I hardly know. We got to deal fair. We might give it to charity. How'd it do to give it to Mis' Gibbs to make up the *deduc'* on the comforts?"

"That might do—if it's got to be give; but look's if it would nachelly *b'long* somewhere, don't it?"

"It do seem so. Maybe we might keep that fo' rent o' the room."

"Well, I dunno. Ef we do, we had ought to give it out, so every person'd understand."

"Why not hev it called out in church? It's a good helpful work."

And so it was done.

When, on Sunday following, the minister stepped aside to read the notice, Miss Sophia Falena grew so flurried that she untied her bonnet strings and fanned vigorously. Her sister, however, though sniffling vociferously herself, nudged her, and she tied them again, and only cleared her throat at short intervals. The notice simply called a meeting of all interested in the project, which was duly set forth, on the next day at the Simpkins residence.

The response was most encouraging; all the chairs in the house and one from the kitchen being called into requisition to seat the attendants. Miss Sophia's voice trembled distinctly, as did the hand that held the paper from which she read, standing in the midst of the assembly, her "idees on the subjec'," which she had thought best to commit to paper.

The meeting was in all respects a success. Besides the assorted bits of advice which all gave freely on the spot, each promised to "enter" something. While Miss Sophia Falena, an atlas balanced upon her knee, made a note of articles promised, Miss Sarey Mirandy passed around raspberry-vinegar and crullers on an old silver-plated tray.

The two were similarly attired in gowns of shiny black silk, whose swishing sound at every movement seemed, with the clink of the high goblets against the silver waiter, reminiscent of a by-gone and more prosperous period.

The change wrought in the Simpkins household by the new enterprise was marvellous.

It was as if time had turned backward and they were young again, so quickly did they move about, so animatedly discuss the numerous details of preparation.

After considerable parley, they decided to use the mahogany centre table for cakes and articles of special showiness, while fancy-work could be advantageously displayed on the piano. If the time should come again when they cared to hear music in the house, they could move the things. Miss Sophia, who had been from home more than her sister, hated to open the old piano anyway. Indeed, she was once heard to say: "When that *piano* is shut an' kivered up, a person can look at it an' think music, 'cause the shape seems to favor it; but jest open it, an' I declare Methusalem ain't nowheres. It makes a person ponder on death an' eternity."

The Exchange opened briskly. The centre table fairly groaned beneath its burden of cakes: "White Mountain," "Lady Washington," "Confederate Layer," "Marble," "Dolly Varden," "General Lee," and score of others, iced, and decorated with reckless elaboration; while in the centre, completing the effect of a spread feast, stood—under glass, it is true—a glowing pyramid of wax fruits.

The piano was a bazar of many-hued zephyrs, from the miniature sacques and stockings of shrimp pink and kindred raw tints relegated by provincial taste to the adorning of babes, to the chinchilla and purple capes suggestive of grandmothers' rheumatic shoulders.

On a side table, wrapped in snowy linen, were heaped loaves of homemade bread, buns, rolls, lemon pies—the home contribution.

A stream of people were coming all day, examining things, pricing, but rarely buying. Indeed, nearly all had something in stock *to sell.*

The two old ladies flitted briskly about, ever and anon putting their heads together, only to dart off in other directions, as busy and buzzy as two happy house flies on a sunny day, only the bright red spots on their cheeks testifying to the unusual agitation of their minds. That they had need of tact, discretion, and judgment, not to mention patience, a bit of conversation caught up at random will perhaps best illustrate:

"An' who in the Kingdom sent in this curious cake, Miss Simpkins?" The querist was a patroness of influence.

"Kate Clark sent in that 'n', Mis' Blanks. It's a 'Will-o'-the-wisp,' made out'n five times sifted flour, 'n' whites of eggs. She says she *made it up,* name an' all."

"Seem to me she'd have 'bout all she could do makin' up rhymin' po'try. What price does she put on it?"

"She wouldn't name no sum. She says she never prices the work of her mind in money, an' thet cake is jest the same to her as a po'try verse. She'll be grateful for whatever it'll fetch."

"Well, I vow! Time a person taken to writin' po'try, seem like they all but lose what little sense they got. How you goin' to sell it, 'thout no price?"

"Well, we 'lowed thet anybody thet'd wanted it'd deal *fair.* I s'pose, bein' as they's nothin' but eggs, an' only the half o' them, in it, they mus' be consider'ble flour. An' *siftin'* it five times, you know that's worrisome work. An' the eggs is well beat; you can see that. Don't you reck'n it's wuth two bits?"

"Maybe it is for them as are willin' to buy a quarter's wuth o' wind. When I want air, I'll go out dohs an' sniff it! That's all

I'm askin' fo' mine, an' it iced all over, an' eight whole eggs in it, an' them beat sep'rate, an' a cup o' butter, not mentionin' the other things, nur the *extrac'*. They's a spoonful o' v'nilla extrac' in my cake if they's a drop, for I dashed it in by my eye—an' I've got what you call big eyes, come to measurin' food stuffs."

The speaker's little blue eyes snapped sharply, and she sniffed twice in hesitation, ere she proceeded, with some embarrassment:

"If you goin' to charge twenty-five cents fo' Kate Clark's pile o' baked bubbles—you can lift it an' see it's nothin' else—you better rub that twenty-five off o' my iced cake, an' put a forty on it. That's it, a four an' a ought, an' whoever buys *mine* gets four dimes' wuth o' good nour'shment, if I do say it." She moved on apace. "I see Kitty Baker's sent in a lot o' things. Well, them as want to eat after Kitty *can*—that's all *I* got to say.

"Kitty's a well-meanin' girl, Mis' Blanks, an' needy, too. S'posin' you don't say nothin' like that to nobody. I see the flour *is* caked some 'roun' the edges of her cakes, but that ain't sayin' they's anything wrong with her cookin'."

"Why, Miss Sarey *Mi*-randy Simpkins! I'm a perfessin' Christian, as you know—an' tryin' to live up to my lights. I wouldn't say nothin' to injure Kitty *fo' nothin'*. These remarks I make to you is jest 'twix' you an' me an' the bedpos'. One o' my motters is 'live an' let live,' an' another one," she added, with a laugh," 'what don't pizen fattens.' What you askin' fo' yo' lemon pies, Miss Simpkins?"

"Twenty-five cents, Mis' Blanks."

"Mh-hm! I s'pose they're made by yo' ma's ol' receipt—three eggs to the pie, savin' out the whites to whip up fo' the top?"

"'Deed, Mis' Blanks, Sis made 'em, an' I couldn't tell you jest how she po'tioned 'em, but I know she ca'culated thet they come to eighteen cents apiece, not countin' firewood, which, since pore Sonny's gone, we hev to hire to have cut."

"Cert'n'y; an' yet I'd think a little thing like a pie you could slip in whils' other things are bakin'."

"That's so; we do; an' yet—Do you think two bits is too much for 'em, Mis' Blanks?"

"Law, child, the idee! I was jest a-thinkin' *this*. You know business is business, Miss Simpkins, an' I was jest a-thinkin'—they *can't noways* be more'n *five* eggs in a pie, even if they was guinea eggs—an' they's eight in my cake, *an' it iced an'* flavored. Jest rub that *four*, please'm, an' put a *five* on my cake, will you? 'Cordin' to the gen'ral valliation it's wuth a half a dollar if it's wuth a cent. Well, I mus' be goin'. What you chargin' fo' yo' bread, Miss Simpkins?"

The old lady addressed scarcely found voice to answer. "Ten cents a loaf, Mis' Blanks."

"Well, you better gimme a loaf, please'm. You see, makin' cake an' bringin' it to the Exchange, I didn't bake to-day. I s'pose you make with salt risin', don't you?"

"No, Mis' Blanks, we raise with 'eas'-cakes."

"Jest so it don't tas'e hoppy, I ain't pertic'lar; but from hoppy bread *de*liver me! Well, good-by, Miss Sarey Mirandy, honey—*good*-by, an' I'm going to pray for you to succeed. Lemme know who buys my cake. I do wish I could be there to see it cut. Well, good-by again. Law! here comes Mis' Brooks with a bundle big as a Chris'mas tree. I *must* stop an' see what she's fetchin'. I do declare this here Woman's Exchange does tickle me all but *to* death. Simpkinsville ain't been so stirred up sence the fire. Howdy, Mis' Brooks? I see you keepin' the ball a-movin'!"

"You better b'lieve I wasn't goin' to be outdid by all you smart seamsters an' fancy cooks."

And Teddy Brooks's wife, drawing off their loose wrappings of paper, set upon the table a gorgeous pair of old crystal candelabra.

"How's them for antics?" she exclaimed, resting her hands upon her fat hips, and stepping backward.

These candelabra had been the proudest possession of Teddy's mother to the day of her death. To sell them seemed sacrilege to the loyal mind of Miss Sarey Mirandy.

"Are they—for sale?" she asked, with an effort at composure.

"Why, yes, indeedy; of course they're for sale, Miss Simpkins. Ain't nobody else brought in no antics? They're the special *speci*alities they sell *in* Exchanges, antics are. I wanted to fetch over Teddy's ma's gran'ma's belluses. The wind's all out of 'em, an' they're no good 'cept'n' *as* antics, which I nachelly *de*spise. But Teddy taken it so hard I had to leave 'em, to keep the peace. You asked if these're fo' sale— ain't everything here fo' sale, Miss Simpkins?"

"Ev'rything thet *is* is, of co'se, but they's some things thet *ain't.* Sonny's birds ain't, nor pa's and ma's ile-painted po'traits, nor none o' them things which them thet are gone seem to stan' guard over."

"Well, the way I look at this is, if the spirits thet stan' guard over things, as you say, would jest keep 'em dusted an' cobwebbed off, so's we could be sure they *was* keepin' up with 'em, they'd be some sense in it. Teddy took on some over sellin' the ol' things, but I tol' him he hisself was the only Brooks antic I cared to keep. How much you reck'n I ought to get for 'em, Miss Simpkins?"

"I'm 'feered I was too ol' a frien' to ol' Mis' Brooks, Sally Ann, to put a price on them candelabras, but you're at liberty to put whatever tag you like on 'em; an' sis an' me'll do our part, fair and square. I see they's one dangle missin' on this one."

"Yes; I give it to the baby to cut 'is eye-teeth on, an' he dropped it, an' it snapped. The things're no manner of account. They cost a hundred dollars, an' I doubt if I'll get ten for 'em, but I'm goin' to start 'em at that, anyway. I'm dyin' for a swingin' silver-plated ice-pitcher, an' have it I will. I've got the price all to seven dollars. Teddy laid it by to have the children's pictures took, but I told him the young ones could see their pictures in the side o' the ice-pitcher." And Mrs. Brooks laughed heartily at her own humor. "When I can swing back in my red plush rockin'chair an' tilt ice-water out of a silver-plated pitcher, I'll feel like some. I see you've got lots o' goodies for sale. I'm bound to have *somethin'* from th'Exchange for supper. What kinds have you got?" She slipped a piece of licorice-root from her pocket to her mouth as she began a circuit of the room, chewing vigorously the while. "Better do up that choc'late layer for me, Miss Simpkins," she said, finally. "Teddy don' eat choc'late, but I don' know but he's better off 'thout cake anyway. Jes' charge it, please, to Teddy—Mr. Theodore Brooks; that's it. Might's well open a 'count here first as last 'f you're goin' to have choc'late fixin's—that's the one thing I c'd get up in my sleep to eat. An' I don't know's I'll bother bakin', if you're goin' to have bread. Jest lay by a couple o' loaves every day, please."

When Mrs. Brooks passed out, the sisters, from their opposite corners of the room, managed to exchange glances, and both sighed.

When the first day was over, all the bread and rolls were sold; indeed, nearly all the housewives who had taken this first step in bread-winning went home with bought loaves under their arms. It was only after some days, when the gorgeous array of sweets was growing stale, that the sisters and their patrons began to realize that there were no buyers of luxuries in their frugal little village.

Besides several purchases of Mrs. Brooks there had been but one cake sold. The "Will-o'-the-wisp" had passed on the second day into the possession of a certain pale young telegraph operator—the same who was "keeping company" with its poetic fabricator.

Perhaps the materialistic circle of housewives, whose substantial contributions were further solidifying before their eyes, should be pardoned for the numerous pleasantries expended on this purchase. That the objects of their mirth, two ethereal young persons dealing professionally in commodities so unsubstantial as poetry and electricity, should choose "wind-cake" for nourishment, was a combination too prolific of humor to be passed by. The portly contributor of the still unsold eight-egg cake waxed especially facetious over it; and on the occasion of a unanimous vote of the "stockholders" to send the entire stale lot as a donation to the inmates of the poorhouse, she even went so far as to withdraw hers from them, and to bear it in her own hands as a gift to her friend the poetess, who, she declared, should have "one good bite o' solid substance, if she never had another."

The exclusion of confections, excepting those supplied to order, practically converted the Exchange into a bakery; for the fancy department, after passing through a fading process, had shrunken through many withdrawals, until a single glass case—an unused one among Sonny's possessions—held the entire stock.

Screened from the odium of professional bread-making by the prestige of the "Exchange," the Misses Simpkins were thus enabled to earn in this simple manner a modest living. True, the vocation had its trials, but there were compensations.

If their delicate wrists and arms were decorated with a succession of bracelets in the shape of burns from the oven doors, if they agonized many nights over the intricacies of numerous receipts sent in by kind advisers, and were oft disquieted in spirit by the vicissitudes of salt rising, compressed yeast, and potato leaven, it was yet a new youth-restoring life to be always professedly and really busy with work that left no time for repinings.

It was a sweet secret pleasure to Miss Sarey Mirandy to make the loaves Teddy Brooks paid for as large as she dared without attracting notice. And sometimes, on anniversaries—which perhaps she alone cherished—of their young days, it pleased her tender maiden heart to slip a few raisins into his loaf, with a suspicion of cinnamon, in loving memory of his boyish fancies.

For some time she was tortured with a dread that some one should offer to buy the candelabra. Should such a time come, she would calmly reply that they were already sold, when from an old stocking she would produce one of the ten-dollar coins that represented her own funeral expenses. It should buy Teddy's wife a swinging pitcher, and the chandeliers would descend by will at her death to Teddy's daughter—his mother's namesake.

For a long time she scarcely left the house, fearing her sister should sell them during her absence. Indeed, at times she was in such a state of suppressed panic over the matter that she would gladly have bought them outright were it not for gossip. People would talk. In her calm moments she knew that no one in Simpkinsville would pay half the amount for the useless old-fashioned bric-à-brac that they had seen all their lives. In fact, she had often heard the women jokingly wonder who would buy "Mis' Brooks's antics," and "if because she'd visited in Washington"—a distant town in the State, noted for its social distinction—"she was the only person in Simpkinsville who knowed about swingin' ice-pitchers." When they "had change to fling away, they'd buy ice-pitchers for themselves, an' not swap it off for glass Noah's-ark dingle-dangles."

So in time Miss Sarey grew to feel pretty secure about the chandeliers, and at night, when her sister knitted or nodded beside her, she would often half close her eyes, and looking thus at the crystal pendants, seem to see, as the fire sparkled from the prisms, bright memory pictures of her youthful days. Herself, a rosy-faced girl with curls, often smiled at the retrospective old woman from the familiar scenes; and Teddy was there, and Sonny, and another—a boy who had not come home from the war—and every one was young, and the trees were green, producing nuts, berries, persimmons, or sustaining grape-vine swings, as reminiscence required.

Only the missing dangle, on which Sally Ann's baby had cut his teeth, made a painful gap in the panorama. In this vacant place Teddy, grown palefaced and weary, seemed, somehow, always to stand, and while she looked at it, all the other pictures went out. So she would turn the defective side to the wall.

When the winter had passed, the Exchange had gone through some changes, shaping itself to the needs of the community by contraction or extension, according to indication. A few who seemed especially fitted to become at once its patrons and beneficiaries had resented its overtures as an insult, as did Mrs. Gibbs, the respected quilter of comfortables. From every point of view the Exchange was an offence unto her sensitive nostrils. To its bid for her patronage she had protested with a sniffle that "she hed never ast no mo'n they was wuth fo' her quilts, an' the day she took off two dimes on one, she'd own that she owed jest that much to every person as ever bought one. As fo' totin' the quilts around the country, she didn't know as 'twas anybody's business in special. The roads was free, and she reckoned her rheumatism was her own—not but what she'd be glad to give it to anybody that was honin' to take care of it. As to her time, she hadn't bound herself out to nobody but the good Lord, an' she 'lowed to claim the time He give her till He changed it for eternity, when she guessed she'd take that too, if the Simpkinsville folks didn't have no objections. The only visitin' she ever done was takin' orders in the spring o' the year and deliverin' her money's wuth *to a cent* in the fall. Them that thought she gadded too much was welcome to do 'thout comforts an' freeze, jest to give her the hint."

The truth was that the social side of Mrs. Gibbs's profession was her very life. A habit of spending a day with her patrons at both ends of each transaction kept her in touch with the home lives of the people. If she had conducted her business through an agent, she would long ago have shrivelled out of existence. There was much in her work to develop an interest in what to outsiders might seem trifles, such, for instance, as which among her patrons' families kicked in their sleep; and in her social rounds it became her pleasure to discover whether the solution lay in the eating of hot suppers or in guilty consciences.

If the Exchange failed to fulfil all its possibilities in some directions, it did unforeseen duty in others, especially supplying an oft-felt want in the open door which it soon offered to the passing stranger.

Simpkinsville had never boasted a hotel, and so it naturally came about that, in the common parlance of the village, travellers understood that "at the Exchange they could get comfortably et an' slep'" for a reasonable consideration. This was robbing no one, as previously it had been an unwritten law of hospitality of the town that strangers be entertained gratis. It seemed odd that its leading family, that which not only lent the dignity of its solitary gabled front to its highest eminence, but had bequeathed to Simpkinsville its name and traditions, should have been first to put a price on the bread broken with a stranger, but such is the irony of fate; for, with a sensitiveness revealed to the close observer by the slight pursing of their lips, which perhaps the wayfarer interpreted as having a mercenary meaning, these two old ladies did actually charge him twenty-five cents who consumed a hearty meal, reducing the bill with minute scrupulousness to fifteen, and even to ten cents, to such as failed in appetite. Further their most rigorous consciences did not lead them, as they agreed it was "wuth a dime to cook things an' then not see 'em et."

That they were sensitive to their changed social relations through the ever-present atmosphere of trade was evinced by a conversation one night, when Miss Sophia Falena broke a long silence by saying: "Sis hun, I been figurin' to see how we can contrive to move the Exchange out'n the parlor. When we *do* have outside comp'ny, I declare I hate to se 'em 'round that centre table piled up with sech as we been raised to offer our comp'ny free—an' it fo' sale. Time the Jenkses come in last week, an' we sat round so solemcholy, every now 'n' ag'in glancin' at the table which was covered up with mosquito-nettin', I vow if the thing didn't seem to me like some sort o' corpse, an's if we were some way holdin' a wake over it, an' oughtn't to laugh out loud."

Her sister chuckled nervously: "It's funny, sis, but, d'you know, I thought about that too—an' maybe I oughtn't to say it, but it 'minded me o' pore Sonny's buryin'—an' ma's an' pa's. But I don't see how we can help it. We might clear off the table entire, an' put the bread and rolls on shelves. I never knew of no dead person bein' laid on a shelf—not literal, though the way they're forgot they might's well be."

"Let's do it, sis, an' get shet o' that ghostly covered table.

89

Maybe you didn't take notice to it, but last Sadday when ol' Mis' Perkins sidled up to the table so stately an' raised up the nettin', she said the identical pertic'lar word that she said time she taken a last look at Sonny. 'Jes' as nachel as life,' says she, jest so. Of co'se she was referrin' to Inez Bowman's case o' wax fruits but it gimme the cold shivers to see her standin' there ag'in a-sayin' them same words. An' they's another thing strikes me, sis. When a day or a night boa'der *do* drop in, it seems to me the house mus' seem sort o' gloomy with nobody in it but a lot o' dead glass-eyed stuffed birds an' two old ladies—which you know to outsiders we are, sis—an' them dressed in black solid as Egyp'. Seem to me it's enough to sort o' take away a travellin' man's appetite. How'd it do fo' you an' me to baste a little white ruchin' in the neck an' sleeves o' our black comp'ny dresses—not meanin' no disrespec's to the dead, but in compliment to the livin'?"

"Well, ef you say so, sis hun. Seem like our first duty *is* to the livin'. Maybe ef we *do* lighten our mo'nin' a little these worldly drummers an' sech won't feel called to talk religion to us like they do. I can see it comes purty hard on 'em."

"An' I declare, maybe it's foolish, but I *do* wish Tom wasn't a black cat. He looks might doleful layin' asleep on the hearth of evenin's. A pink ribbon 'roun' his neck wouldn't look too worldly, would it—not for the pore soulless beast, hun, of course, but for us?"

"Why, no, I reck'n not—or a blue one. The blue bow on my valedict'ry is purty faded, but ef you think it'd do, why, th'ain't no use in keepin' it no longer. Ef Sonny had o' lived, an' married—which for a man, as long as they's life they's hope—they might in time o' been sech as would care for they ol' auntie's valedict'ry. That ribbon cost five dollars a yard, in Confed'rit money, an' tain't all silk, neither—but for a cat—"

"Tain't any too good fo' Tom, sis. He's been a faithful ol' cat. But they's another p'int on my mind. Don't you think maybe we better open up Sonny's room, an' sun it good, an' reg'late it, so's ef we're pushed fo' room we could let comp'ny go up there to sleep? As tis, we can't sleep mo'n three strangers *no* way, an' if a crowd *was* to come—not thet they're likely—but I b'lieve ef we'd do it, we'd be relieved ourselves. As long as we keep it shet tight, jest the way Sonny left it, we'll feel like death is locked in—an' I don't know as it's Christian. What you say, sis?"

"Well, maybe you're right, dearie. S'pose we go up in the mornin' together. I've done started up there three times a'ready, an' my knees trembled so they give way under me— but if you was with me, maybe—You don't s'pose strangers would mind sleepin' with so many birds, do you?"

"Cert'n'y not. Why should they, less'n maybe they was high-strung, an' their minds got excited? Ef so, they *might* imagine they was all singin' at once-t, quick as the light was out. If *sech* a person was to try to sleep there—well, I dunno. They's thirty-one hundred an' sixty-three stuffed birds in that garret room, an' all in sight o' the bed."

"Shucks, sis! you're talkin' *redic'lous*—I vow ef you ain't! D'you s'pose any right-minded man would think o' sech as that? Of course we ain't goin' to put no skittish person to sleep in Sonny's room noway—jest reel gen'lemen, an' only them ef we're pushed."

"It cert'n'y do behoove us to take in all we can, hones', sis, for seem like the Exchange money don't mo' 'n, to say, hardly pay our boa'd somehow."

The truth was, the profits of breadmaking were steadily shrinking. Not only did Teddy Brooks's loaves grow larger and larger as he waxed paler and more careworn, but among the "customers" of the Exchange there was scarce one whose circumstances did not seem to the old ladies an appeal for generosity—hardly one who was not, as they said, "mo' in need'n we are."

It would have been a hopelessly weary business but for its rich perquisites in opportunities of sympathy and helpfulness.

The spacious garret chamber was thrown open none too soon, as only a week later it was called into unexpected requisition through the arrival, late one evening, of a party of five dust-begrimed travellers, whom the ladies would have feared to receive had they not been accompanied by a neighbor, who had taken charge of their horses, and who, in a whispered aside, announced them as "Uncle Sam's men, with a-plenty o' greenbacks," adding, *sotto-voce*, with a wink: "Kill the fatted calf for 'em, an' then charge 'em with a cow."

While the strangers sat at supper that night night it was pathetic to see the solicitous scrutiny with which their hostesses scanned their faces in turn, eager for some sign by which to decide who of them all should be counted worthy to sleep in Sonny's bed. A chance remark settled the question.

"Well," said one, "I believe we are in the land of the myrtle and orange."

"Hardly," rejoined another; "but, better yet, we are in the country of the night-singing mocking-bird. Do you ladies ever hear them at night?" he added.

"From the upstairs bedroom," replied both sisters at once, while Miss Sophia continued:

"The winders open ri-ight out into the maginolia-trees, where they set and sing all night long some ni-ights."

The stranger's eyes beamed. "How delightful! If one might be so fortunate!" he replied, with a rising inflection, smiling.

"It's yore room, sir, for the night," said Miss Sophia, exchanging glances with her sister; "with whichever one o' the other gentlemen you choose. They's a wide easy-sleepin' bed in it, a-plenty broad fo' two."

"An' if you want to hear the birds sing," added Sarey Mirandy, "jest open any winder you like. They's four, not countin' the dormers, and they all open into trees, an' every tree's full of birds' nests."

"Isn't that rather remarkable? Are all the trees here full of nests?" the stranger asked.

"No, sir. Sonny—Mr. Stephen Decatur Simpkins, our brother thet's passed away—he had a gift. He got 'em to nestin' there."

"He was a lover of birds—do I understand?"

The sisters exchanged glances again, and Miss Sarey answered simply, "Yas, Sir. He was a nachelist."

"Ah, indeed!"

Around the speaker's mouth played that ghost of a smile which, being interpreted, means amused incredulity, while the conversation, becoming general, passed to other things.

With such an introduction, an hour later, Mr. John Saunders, of the Smithsonian Institution, of Washington City, accompanied by his associate Ezra Cox, proceeded, candle in hand, to the modest roof chamber that held the lifework of Stephen Decatur Simpkins, naturalist.

The next morning, though the twins appeared at breakfast in their spick white-ruched dresses, and Tom sauntered around the table resplendent in a blue neck ribbon, the ends of which hung to his knees, a distinct depression marked the spirit of the household. Despite their best efforts in the direction of cheerfulness, the twins were haggard and wan. The eyes of their guests, on the contrary, beamed with pleasure.

In the first interval of silence, after serving the dishes, Miss Sarey Mirandy, turning to the occupants of the room above, asked timidly:

"May I ask, sir, what perfession you gen'lemen perfess?"

"Certainly, madam," replied Saunders, his eye twinkling. "The three at your left, Messrs. Green, Brown, and Black— men of color, you perceive—are members of the National Geological Survey, whom Congress has sent out here to hunt up some mineral specimens. My friend here, Mr. Cox, and I—my name is Saunders—are from the Smithsonian Institution at Washington City, at present loafers, as we are off on a vacation. We are called scientists, I believe. Naturalists is a name we like better, but really"—he hesitated for a moment as if to gain entire seriousness— "here, in the presence of your brother's beautiful work, we should appropriate the name timidly, with heads uncovered. Is this collection of birds known in the State, may I ask?"

"Well, yes, sir. I reck'n tis. Tain't never been to say *hid*. It's been right here. Th'ain't nobody, black nur white, in the county, but *knows* they're here."

"It is not registered. I know of all the important recorded collections in America. I wonder if you ladies realize what a treasure you possess? My friend and I studied it until our candle burned out. Then we crept down and begged those of our friends, and burned them up—besides one we found in the dining-room. I hope we didn't disturb you ladies?"

The sisters exchanged glances and colored.

"Th'wasn't to say 'xactly noise enough to disturb nobody, sir, if we'd knew what it was, but th'ain't nobody slep' up in Sonny's room sence he passed away tell now, an' the sound of every footfall seemed like him back ag'in. So we nachelly kep' listenin' for 'em to stop, an' to tell the whole truth, sir, when we heard 'em so late, not knowin' nothin' 'bout you gentlemen, we got nervous an' scared like, 'n' we got up an' dressed, an' set up the live night long, 'th our vallibles all in reach—not thet you gentlemen look like peddlers, which even if you was, you might be hones'."

The professional gentlemen present thought it unsafe to

look at one another, while they expressed the sincere sorrow they felt at so unfortunate a misunderstanding. The occasion of their late hours, however, soon became the absorbing theme, resulting in a full restoration of confidence. Saunders's enthusiasm was genuine.

"I actually counted sixty-one beautiful specimens not existing in any registered collection," he said, addressing his companions.

"An' they wasn't all easy got, neither," replied Miss Sophia. "Why, Sonny slep' in a crape-myrtle tree ev'ry night for a week once't, jest to find out how a little he bird conduct hisself—ef he changed places with his settin' wife, or jest entertained 'er sett'n' on a limb beside her."

Her interlocutor smiled. "And how was it—do you remember?"

"Well, reely—how was it, sis?"

"'Deed, sir, I disremember. Either he did 'r he didn't—one. I clean forget, but—but it's put down in the book."

"So there is a book?"

"They's five leather-backed books, sir, with nothin' but sech as that *in* 'em. Sis an' me've read in 'em some, an' for anybody that *cared* for sech, I s'pose it's good readin'. They's *one* thing, it's *true*, an' thet's more'n you can say fo' the triflin' novels thet folks pizens their minds *an'* principles with."

"You have indeed a valuable possession here, ladies. Have you ever thought of selling it?"

"Sellin' Sonny's birds? No, sir. No mo'n we'd sell pa an' ma's ile-painted po'traits, or Sonny's Confed'rit clo'es, *ragged* as they be."

"No, sir. They's some things thet money don't tech. We wouldn't sell them birds, not if we got ten cents a head for 'em an' that's mo'n most of 'em'd be wuth even it they was baked in a pie—'n' the crust an' gravy throwed in."

"But, my dear ladies," said Mr. Cox, "they are worth far more than that. As a collection they are worth considerably more than a dollar apiece—"

"Sis," said Miss Sarey Mirandy, "the gentleman don't understand. Them birds, sir, ain't nothin' but feathers an' skin, an' it full o' rank pizen arsenic. Th'ain't a blessed thing in 'em but raw cotton, an' it physicked, an' nine out'n every ten of 'em never was no 'count for either cookin' nur singin'. We wouldn't deceive you 'bout em. But if they was birds o'

Paridise, caught before the fall o' Adam, jest swooned away, an' li'ble to come back to life any minute, 'n' you offered us the United States Mint for 'em, even so, th'ain't for sale—*noways.*"

This was somewhat of a rebuff to the first overture of the Washington scientist, who indeed seriously meant that the Institution should become possessed of the new-found treasure, if possible. He had inserted the edge of a wedge, however, and was satisfied to wait before pressing it.

Breakfast over, it was but natural that Miss Sophia should follow the visitors into the parlor, while she, with evident and pathetic pride, exhibited the additional specimens there. When, a half-hour later, she rejoined her sister in the kitchen, she was so full to overflowing of this tender theme that some time elapsed before she remarked, in a tone betraying a secondary interest:

"Well, I reck'n Sally Ann'll have her swingin' pitcher, after all, 'cause I've done sol' the candelabras."

Miss Sarey stood kneading dough, with her back to her sister. She came near falling for a moment.

"Wh—what you say, honey? H—who bought—*what?*

She kept on kneading, and did not turn.

"That slim, light-complected one, I say, has done bought ol' Mis' Brooks's candelabras, 'n' I mus' say I never sol' a thing with a worse grace. I'm a-puttin' the ten dollars which he give for 'em here in this pink vase on the dinin'-room mantel, an' do you give it to Sally Ann, honey. I don't want nothin' to do *with* it, nor with her neither. She gets me riled enough to all but backslide 'th her 'extravagance 'n' super*flu*ousniss!"

Miss Sarey had not realized until now how attached she had herself become to the old candlesticks. Their shimmering prisms were crystallized memories. Themselves, their long-familiar fantastic shapes, were friends antedating in association any surviving friendship.

When she had completed her task, great beads of perspiration stood upon her pale brow. Passing out, she nervously seized the ten dollars and hastened to the parlor. The purchaser stood admiring his new possession. Laying the money before him, she said, with a masterful effort at composure:

"They's been a mistake made, sir. Them candelabras is already sold."

"Indeed? I'm sorry," he said, bowing; and as she moved

away, he added, "I should be glad to give five times the price—if they could be secured."

Miss Sarey Mirandy hesitated. "Sir?"

There was something almost tragic in the apprehension expressed in this one word.

The offer was repeated.

Fifty dollars! Half her secret hoard! In a twinkling the sum resolved itself into a difference in the quality of a shroud and coffin. Without apparent hesitation she replied, firmly: "The lady thet's bought 'em don't ca'culate to sell 'em. Thank you, sir." And, her old heart thumping absurdly, she went out.

Declining the fifty dollars had seemed a simple matter of decision and principle at the moment, and the offer a bribe to her loyalty; but all day, as she moved about the house, her secret kept growing, first naturally from the germ, as the extravagance seemed to grow in enormity, and then by accretion, as one by one, the sundry deceptions it would involve gathered about it.

Of course, she would deal fair. Sally Ann should have the fifty dollars. But this soon became the slightest consideration. She must not be known as the purchaser, not even to her sister. If she hadn't told her of that long-ago kiss, it would be different. Sally Ann would naturally tell every one the price she got, and she would ask questions.

For the first time in her life she was shamefaced and afraid, responding even to her sister's enthusiastic remarks about Sonny in an incoherent manner. In the midst of her greatest apprehension the front gate was heard to slam, and Sally Ann Brooks did actually appear coming up the path. Seeing her enter, however, Miss Sophia said:

"Sis, you set Sally Ann down in the parlor and talk to her, honey. I'm 'feared if I'd see her tickled over that ten dollars I might not be perlite. Maybe, if a more Christian spirit comes to me, I'll come in after whiles; but it's mos' supper-time, anyhow."

As she passed through the parlor to receive Mrs. Brooks, Miss Sarey was astounded to perceive the "red-complected" coveter of the candelabra still standing before them. If the devious ways of deceit had been an old-travelled road to her, her dilemma would have been less trying. Not to introduce those who chanced to meet in her parlor would be a social dereliction of which she was incapable. To do so in the present instance would invite disaster.

She did not hesitate. Come what would, she would be a lady worthy the name of Simpkins. What she said at the door was, "Walk right in the parlor, Sally Ann, an' I'll make you 'quainted with a gen'leman that's here from the North."

"Law, Miss Simpkins!" exclaimed Teddy's wife, shrinking back. "I ain't got on no corset nor nothin'. I jest run over in my Mother Hubbard as I was. I wouldn't go before a strange gentleman the way I am, nohow, for nothin'."

Miss Sarey Mirandy was saved. Trembling within, and with two solferino spots upon her thin cheeks, she invited her guest into her own room.

"We hear you've got a house full o' Yankees," said the guest, taking a rocking-chair; "but Mr. Jakes says they're real ni-ice, an' he says the way they're a-praisin' up Mr. Sonny Simpkins roun' town you'd think he might o' been George Washin'ton, or maybe Jeff Davis hisself."

"Yas, Sally Ann. It's been mighty gratifyin' to sis an' me to hear them a-praisin' of Sonny. One of 'em's been a-studyin' over Sonny's books the livelong day."

"Is that so? If they read them books, they mus' shorely be educated. Kitty Clark's beau says they been a-telegraphin' all day to Washin'ton City—an' he says the name o' Simpkins has gone over the wire more'n once-t, though neither he nor she nor I got any right to tell it. Three of 'em, you know, 's been out to Mr. Jakes's farm all day a-spyin' dug-up things with a spy-glass. Mr. Jakes is diggin' a new cow-pond, an' they do say he's dug up enough to undo the whole Bible. That's the way the talk's a-goin', but I'm thankful to say I was raised a good 'Piscopal Church woman—not sayin' nothin' 'g'inst the Baptists, Miss Simpkins—an' the Prayer-book don't, in no place I ever opened it, make no mention o' Mr. Jakes's cow-pond, not the ins an' outs of it. An' talkin' 'bout the Church, Miss Simpkins, fetches me to what brought me here—not that I needed any excuse; but this is Lent, you know, in our Church, an' we're 'xpected to make some sort o' sacrerfice—if not fastin', some other—an' I thought, 'stid o' denyin' myself spring onions or maybe choc'let, since Teddy's mind seems to run on 'em consider'ble, I'd come over an' get them candelabras o' his ma's an' set 'em back on the mantel where she left 'em. Don't you think the Lord might take that the way it's meant, for a Lenten off'rin?"

"I do indeed, Sally Ann, an' a good one." And she added, in

97

a moment, "'Cause you know, honey they *might* o' sold for what'd fetch considerable worldly vanities."

"Yes'm, so they might, tho' I doubt if th'ever would."

A moment's silence followed, broken finally by Miss Sarey.

"But I'd advise you, Sally Ann, child, to examine yore deed purty close-t before you offer it to the dear Lord, 'cause you know, honey, He sees the inside *inness* o' all our purposes. Suppose somebody, now, was to offer to buy them candelabras 'n' pay a big price, cash down. How 'bout Lent, honey?"

The old lady's heart was thumping furiously.

"Well, Miss Simpkins, tell the truth, *they couldn't get 'em*—not if they offered me the first price of 'em." Teddy Brooks's wife's eyes filled with tears as she continued: "Teddy seems right porely these days, Miss Simpkins. An' another thing I come to ask you was if you had any more o' that blackberry wine o' yores left. It helped him a heap las' spring. Some days I get so worreted the way he seems a-failin'. Seem like if he'd get good 'n' strong, I wouldn't care fo' nothin' else."

When Miss Sarey went for the wine, she moved with the alacrity of a happier and younger woman than she who had entered the room ten minutes before.

For the first time in years she kissed Teddy's wife at parting, and bade her "keep good heart, an' not forgit the good Lord loved her an' hers." And as she turned to go in, she drew a long free breath as she said to herself, "An' yet some folks'll set up an' say th'ain't no sech a thing as a special providence."

The entertaining of five strange college-bred men, who talked familiarly of things beyond their ken, albeit the bird theme was a bond of sympathy between them, was a somewhat formidable undertaking to these old timid women of narrow and hitherto protected lives, though they had congratulated themselves many times to-day that "the household was perpared for 'em, even down to Tom."

When supper was over to-night, and Mr. Saunders, with a formality that was significant, begged an interview with the ladies in the parlor, they were seized anew with a vague distrust.

These Yankee men who wore the United States initials "promiscuous" about their persons, and made so free with the telegraph, might be—what? Spies? Detectives?

Neither confided to the other what, in truth, was but a suspicion of a suspicion, as they repaired together to their chambers to secure their turkey-tail fans and fresh hemstitched handkerchiefs, and slip bits of orris root into their mouths.

The gentlemen were already assembled, and the meeting lost nothing, but rather gained, in formality on the entrance of the twins, who, bowing slightly, proceeded to seat themselves side by side upon the sofa.

"Ladies," said Mr. Saunders, rising, "yesterday a party of tired men came to your door asking for supper and a night's lodging. They had come from a distant brilliant city, with its art galleries, its institutions of learning, its glare, its music. Coming into this little inland Arkansas town, they expected to find rich, deep forests, and fertile fields, tilled by true-hearted children of the soil. Within your hospitable door they hoped for what Solomon meant when he said, 'A dry morsel, and quietness therewith,' as they were both hungry and tired. Instead of a dry morsel, you have given us sumptuous fare, ladies; and for the quietness we sought, we have found—what shall I say?—the stillness of a temple, where, instead of sleeping, we have since sat in reverence. Two of us have spent a day and half a night in studying the beautiful lifework of Mr. Stephen Decatur Simpkins. Here we have found science, art, literature, romance, poetry— music, for the birds at our windows have filled the night with melody. There are in the world but two larger personal collections of birds than that we find here. There is none so exquisitely perfect in every detail. I have not found a gunshot in a single specimen, gentlemen, not a ruffled feather—"

"Th'ain't but thirteen shot birds there," interrrupted Miss Sarey Mirandy," and them was give to Sonny. He spent five years livin' 'mongst 'em, so's they'd know 'im, before he ever ketched one."

"All the valuable known collections," resumed John Saunders, "are on exhibition in public institutions. As its representative, ladies, I am authorized to say to you that the United States government wishes to place the work of Mr. Simpkins in the Smithsonian Institution at Washington—"

Simultaneously, as if electrified, the twins rose to their feet. Miss Sophia first found voice. What she said, in a quavering tremor, was this:

"If I may please speak, sir, Sonny lived a peaceful an' law-abidin' citizen clean sence the wah—an' he hedn't no more hard feelin's to them he fit ag'in 'n we've got—not a bit. If, after all these years, the North see fit to converscate his pore voiceless birds thet show *theyselves* how harmless Sonny spent his time—not havin' even to say a shot *in* 'em—why, all we got to ask is jest wait a few more years, till two ol' women pass away, an' then, why, if the North cares for 'em, they'll be nobody lef' to claim 'em."

As she sat down, her sister spoke:

"Them words we let fall to you Northerners 'bout Sonny's Confed'rit uniform wasn't intended fo' no insult to you gen'lemen. We jest prize it, bein' his sisters, 'cause seem like it's got all his young shape in it yet—that's all. Th'ain't a livin' bit o' strife mixed in our feelin's 'bout it—not a bit. That's all we got to say, I reck'n—ain't it, sis?

John Saunders was not the only man present who found it necessary to use his handkerchief before he could trust his voice again. There was a very tender note in it when he said:

"I have blundered shamefully, my dear ladies, and I beg you to forgive me. Your brother's property is yours. No power on earth can take from you. The war and confiscation are no more. Were Mr. Simpkins living, he could desire no greater honor than national recognition as one of America's first naturalists. This is what we would accord him now. His work lies buried in this little town. In the national museum thousands will visit it daily. His portrait will hang beside it, and his poetic and exhaustive treatises adorn the public libraries. These books alone, describing numerous hitherto unclassified specimens, and giving original methods of capture and preservation, are worth several thousand dollars. I am not yet authorized to name a specified sum. We cannot always pay as we should like to, but I can guarantee that to the estate of Mr. Stephen Decatur Simpkins the United States will pay certainly not less than ten thousand dollars for the collection entire; it ought to be double that. We feel quite sure that when you ladies fully understand, you will not let any feeling stand in the way of his getting his full honor."

For answer the sisters turned to each other, opened their arms, and fell sobbing each upon the other's shoulder. Thus they sat for some moments, and when they raised their heads they were alone.

"I hope," said Miss Sophia, wiping her eyes, "I hope pa an' ma's been a-lookin' on an' a-list'nin', sis. Twould make 'em happier even in Heaven."

"Yas; an' Sonny too, dearie; I hope he's been present, though I doubt if he'd care so much. I b'lieve he'd 'a' cared more to be upstairs las' night a-studyin' the birds with them gentlemen."

"I reck'n you're right, sis, an' maybe he was. I don't b'lieve the good Lord'd hinder 'im if he wanted to come."

If some supposed the fortune coming to the Misses Simpkins would prove a death-blow to the Exchange, they were mistaken. A comfortable income gave its machinery just the lubrication it needed for smooth and happy working according to the pleasure of its proprietors.

Three years have passed since Sonny's collection of birds went to Washington, and every spring the sisters plan to go East to visit it at the Institution; but each season finds Teddy Brooks "lookin' so porely" that Miss Sarey Mirandy finds an excuse to put it off. When pressed, she did even say once to her sister:

"Though Sally Ann is growin' in grace every day, an'll make a fine woman in time if she lives, you can't put a ol' head on young shoulders; an', like as not, before we'd be halfway to Washin'ton she'd run out o' light bread an' feed Teddy on hoecake, which always was same as pizen to 'im even in his young days."

WILLIAM WILSON

George B. Rose

I LIVE IN THE CITY of Little Rock. My best friend was a young man of about my own age, named William Wilson. He was a lawyer of brilliant talents and great promise, handsome of person, of engaging manners, and a universal favorite in society.

Last winter I left the city on a pleasure trip and was absent from about the first of January until the middle of April. Wilson accompanied me to the train, and I noticed that his face was strangely haggard, betraying evidence of great suffering or disquietude. I pressed him with questions, but he merely replied that he had had a slight attack of sickness the night before. Presently the conductor called out, "all aboard," and I stepped upon the train, which pulled slowly out. When on the platform, I turned to look at my friend. He was gazing after me, and his face was so wan, so drawn, so disturbed that I shuddered as I looked upon him.

As I have said, I remained absent until April, visiting the City of Mexico and Isthmus of Panama. I wrote to him several times, but got no reply. Owing to my frequent removals from place to place I received few letters, and these contained no reference to Wilson. At length I turned my face northward, and pursued my long and dreary journey across the plains of Mexico and Texas, and thence to Little Rock. I heard finally the long whistle that announced our approach to the city, and with keen pleasure looked forward to meeting the friends whom I had left more than three months before, particularly Wilson. I had written, informing him of the hour of my arrival, and confidently expected that he would meet me at the depot. We passed between the long lines of stationary freight cars, and at length came in sight of the platform. The usual crowd was there, hackmen, loungers, travelers with valises in their hands, women expecting the return of husbands or children, friends coming to see their friends off on the train. I leaned out of the window and peered among the crowd. I saw some chance acquaintances, but no friends. Rather disappointed, I descended, took a hack, and had myself driven to my boarding house.

There I was met by my landlady, an elegant and cultivated woman who had once been rich, but had been reduced to poverty by the war. She welcomed me warmly, and overwhelmed me with questions about my health, my journey and the places that I had visited. When her curiosity was in some degree appeased, it became my turn to ask questions, and I asked her how all were.

"Every one has been well," she replied, "except that Judge Savage is dead and poor Will Wilson has become insane."

"Wilson insane!" I exclaimed, "how did that happen? Where is he?"

"I do not know much about it," she replied. "It seems that at a ball given at Concordia Hall he suddenly became a raving maniac, and shortly afterwards was carried to the Lunatic Asylum."

It was a great blow to me. I had known Wilson from boyhood. We had been through school and college together, always in the same classes. At the University of Virginia we had roomed together for four years, and in this long and close intimacy I had come to regard him as a brother rather than as a friend. In our pleasures and in our studies we had been inseparable. And now to learn that he had lost his reason, he whose brilliant abilities and powerful, logical mind seemed to place him beyond the possibility of such a danger!

That afternoon I shut myself up in my room. I did not care to see any one. The blow was so sudden that it had unnerved me. Finally the sun went down, and one by one the stars peered out from between the vague forms of the tree-tops, waving spectrally in the breeze. The lights were lit in the opposite windows, and I sat watching them, my heart oppressed with gloomy forebodings. At length I sought my couch, wearied with my two thousand miles of incessant travel, and slept, but heavily and sadly, for sorrow can find the human heart even in the hours of sleep.

I awoke long before the dawn, and waited impatiently for the light. At length a faint streak in the east announced the approach of day. I arose and dressed myself, and sat down by the window. The red line grew broader and broader, became lighter of hue, till it changed to gold bordered with green, and then the majestic orb of day slowly arose. I had been tired, very tired, but when I saw the sun it infused into my veins its own power, and I arose, and stretched myself, rejoicing in my strength, and resolved to go that morning to see my afflicted friend.

After breakfast I told the landlady that I should probably not return for dinner, and went out. The roses were beginning to bloom, and the air was melodious with the twittering of birds. As I walked along new hope arose in my bosom, and I felt sure that the malady of my friend must be merely transitory. It seemed impossible that so powerful a mind could be utterly overthrown in so short a time.

I walked to the livery stable, and ordered a buggy. When it was harnessed I got in, and drove out westward. Arrived at the top of Capital Hill, the asylum stood before me, about a mile away, crowning the low range of pine-clad hills that arose beyond the intervening valley. The sun was shining brightly upon it, and as it stretched its long facade of simple but pleasing architecture across the western horizon, its appearance was truly imposing, reminding me somewhat of the pictures of the Spanish Escurial, and having something of the same sinister aspect.

Descending the long slope and then climbing the opposite hill, I found myself before the asylum. From the grated windows insane men and women were peering forth, with strange cries and questions. I got out and rang the bell. An attendant came to the door, and I asked for Dr. H., the superintendent of the institution. He showed me into a waiting room, where I sat down. Soon the superintendent appeared. He was a portly man, with strongly marked, handsome features and clear, piercing black eyes, who had been a practicing physician, especially valuable in times of emergency. A natural administrator, he was born to be the head of a large institution; and the cleanliness and order of the asylum bore conclusive proof of his rare capacities.

As we were old friends he greeted me warmly. After a few moments of pleasant conversation, I said,

"Doctor, I have come to inquire about my friend William Wilson."

At this his face grew darker, and he said,

"That is the strangest case that I have ever known. I have studied it a great deal, and can make nothing out of it. I have gone all through the books on mental alienation, but can find nothing to throw any light upon it. Every night he thinks that a hob-goblin, or something else, is after him, and he goes mad with fear. There is nothing marvelous in that. We have a great many patients suffering from similar hallucinations. It is the strange periodicity of the thing that troubles me. It comes on every night at exactly midnight. There would be nothing strange in that either if the patient knew the hour, and at first I supposed that the attack came on at that hour because he knew that it was midnight, but it is not so. I have locked him in his cell with no means in the world to tell the time, and have watched him. Exactly at the midnight hour the attack has come on with unerring accuracy. Then I put into his cell a clock that was too fast. He showed great uneasiness as he saw the hands of the clock approach midnight, but there was no symptom of his malady until the true hour, and then he suddenly became convulsed with fear. Then I put in a clock that was too slow. He was looking at it with the apparent feeling that the hour of his agony was some distance off, when suddenly his face became contorted with the most abject terror. I looked at my watch, and it was precisely midnight. I do not know what to think of this case. I have studied about it a great deal, and have written to several of the most distinguished experts in the matter of alienation, but their answers show that they think that I need treatment rather than my patient. And yet I have repeated the experiment so often that I know that I cannot be mistaken, and I wish that you would remain tonight to verify my observations."

I gladly consented, and inquired whether I would be allowed to see Wilson in the meantime.

"Oh, yes," he replied, "he seems entirely sane except during the time from midnight to dawn, and is allowed freely to walk about the grounds."

He led me out on the piazza in front of the asylum, and beneath the shade of a small oak tree I saw Wilson seated on a rustic bench. He was changed so terribly that I scarcely knew him. He was deadly pale, and his hair which when I saw him last was of jetty blackness, was almost white. He was terribly emaciated. His eyes were sunken, his cheeks were hollow, and his hands seemed almost transparent. His gaze was fixed on the ground, and his whole attitude was one of profound dejection.

I walked up to him, and laid my hand upon his shoulder. He looked up in a startled, frightened way, but when he saw me his face brightened, and he seized my hand in both of his, exclaiming,

"I am so glad that you have come back."

I sat down on the bench beside him, and we chatted pleasantly about my journey and about matters in general. He exhibited no signs of mental derangement, and so far as I could see his mind was as bright and as clear as ever.

Shortly after noon dinner was announced, and we went in, and partook of the plain but abundant and wholesome food provided for the inmates of the asylum. Wilson, apparently recalled to life by my companionship, ate heartily, and seemed to enjoy the repast.

After dinner we took a stroll around the grounds. It was a perfect day. The air was soft and balmy, and filled with the invigorating odor of the pines. Innumerable birds, orioles, red-birds, mocking-birds, wood-peckers, jays, filled the air with their songs or cries. The oaks, the hickories, the maples, were clothed with that light green foliage which makes the forest so beautiful in the early spring.

We wandered on in pleasant converse, and before we knew it the sun was sinking in the west. We returned to the asylum, and seated ourselves upon a bench in front. The setting sun was concealed from view by the great building behind us, but in the east there were banks of clouds, looking like mountains clothed in eternal snow, gleaming with a resplendent pink in the rays of light.

We sat looking at them, and the peacefulness of the scene appeared to soothe Wilson's troubled spirit. His eyes lost their restlessness, his features relaxed, and for the first time he looked like himself, though as he would look after a long attack of illness.

Presently supper was announced, and we went in. After supper the warden came to us, and indicated to Wilson that he must retire to his cell. I went with him, and entered behind him, and the iron door was shut and locked after us.

The cell was small, but beautifully fitted up, for Wilson was rich and a man of taste. On the wall were some handsome pictures, and in a corner was a revolving desk full of books.

We sat down, and resumed our conversation. I tried to make it as cheerful as possible. We talked of many things, and he seemed to enter heartily into the conversation. At length we became involved in an earnest discussion of the accuracy of Mommsen's views of the constitution of Early Rome, a subject to which he had devoted considerable attention. He went to the book-case to take down a book, and as he did so, I slipped my watch out of my pocket, and placed it open slightly behind me where I could see it, without attracting his attention. I knew that it was exactly right, for it was a good time-piece, and I had regulated it that morning by Stifft's chronometer. It was half past eleven. Seeing the fatal hour approach, I exerted myself to the utmost to interest him in the conversation, hoping that thereby it might pass without a crisis, and so the fearful habit be broken.

I kept my eye on the watch. The hand marked a quarter to twelve, then ten minutes, then five. How slowly it seemed to move! At last it lacked but half a minute. I looked up. Wilson had a volume of Mommsen in his hands, and was speaking with great animation in favor of his theories.

Suddenly the book dropped from his hands. His face was frightfully distorted, and grew of a livid, ashy paleness. His gray hair stood erect upon his head. His lower jaw dropped, his mouth fell open, and through it his breath came hard, with a hissing, moaning sound like that of a person with nightmare. But the most fearful thing were his eyes. They protruded from their sockets, staring frightfully at a foot-stool in one corner of the room. I had had no conception before of the horrors of fear. I was startled, I was frightened by the awful change, the more appalling from its suddenness. Involuntarily I followed the direction of his gaze, and my eye rested upon the foot-stool. It remained as before. There was no alteration, but in my soul I felt that It was there, It, the Unseen, the Unknown, the Supernatural. I felt my hair rising on end. I could hear my teeth chatter. Oh, the agony of that fear! I could have faced death without flinching, I believe. I know that no braver man ever lived than Wilson.

But before the supernatural, before this indescribable, unutterable, unknown thing, this emanation from the world of shadows which I felt to be there, there in the room with me, which I could not see, but which seemed to sear my eye-balls, I was utterly unmanned. My limbs quaked, my hands were convulsively clasped, and it seemed that my eyes would start from their sockets. I turned to Wilson. His expression had not altered. No Gorgon's face could ever have expressed a tithe of the horror depicted upon his. He was immovable, stiff, frozen with abject terror, his wide open, protruding eyes still fixed upon the foot-stool.

Oh, the horror of that night. As the moments passed the terror did not diminish, it seemed rather to increase. Time, habit, nothing could reconcile us to the presence of that awful Thing. I have suffered in my life, but all its suffering combined would be but an infinitesimal part of the agony of that night. We could not move, we could not cry for help. We were benumbed with fear. As a dream is but a faint reflection of the reality, so the most frightful nightmare that ever fastened itself upon the breast of man could give no conception of our agony.

And there we sat. The anguish of the damned, writhing in the infernal pit, could not surpass our own. The night seemed endless. The minutes seemed years, the hours centuries of pain. At length the day began to break, and as the light increased, we grew calmer, until, when the sun rose above the city, we were restored. I went to the window and looked out. There was not a cloud in the sky, and the birds were singing upon every tree. I opened the window, and a cool breeze fanned my fevered cheeks. I went to the glass. My face was strangely altered, ghastly pale, wan, haggard. My hair, which had been jet black the evening before, was tinged with grey. I looked at Wilson. He lay upon the bed utterly exhausted, and apparently asleep. I sat down beside him. True, he slept, but his face was twitching, and every few moments he would start painfully and mutter something that I could not understand. I watched his troubled slumber until nearly noon, when he awoke with a start. Seeing me he clasped my hand convulsively, looked at me a long time, and said,

"Such horrors are too much for you; they will kill you."

I did not contradict him, for I felt that I could not live through many similar nights.

He arose, washed himself, made a few changes in his toilet, not many, for he had not been undressed, and we went out and seated ourselves upon a bench in front of the asylum. After awhile dinner was announced. We went in, but ate nothing of consequence. The food stuck in my throat.

After dinner, we again went out and sat upon the bench. We said nothing for a long time. At length, he said,

"I feel now that all is lost. I hoped that your presence might scare it away, or that at least you might strengthen me in the hour of trial; but you are no stronger than I am."

I besought him to tell me what it was that besieged him thus, and he told me the following story:

"One evening I was walking along the street. It was about dusk, and a storm was gathering. Just in front of me was a young girl. She was walking rapidly in the same direction, apparently hastening to escape the storm. I was struck with the symmetry of her figure and the grace of her walk. After we had moved on a block or two, the storm burst and the rain fell in torrents. She was without protection, and I hastened forward and offered to shield her with my umbrella. She accepted pleasantly, and we walked along together. I learned that she was a young girl from near Lonoke, that she was an orphan, and was clerking in one of the large dry goods stores. Her name, she said, was Mollie Sparks. She was not regularly beautiful, but she was plump, fresh and pretty, and her manner was winning and attractive. At last we reached her boarding house, and she thanked me with a pleasant smile.

"I saw no more of her for several days, but when I met her casually on the street, she spoke to me so agreeably that I made it convenient to walk a few blocks with her. I do not know how, but I found myself very much attracted by the sweetness and amiability of this simple girl from the country, and the next day I passed by the store at just the hour when I knew she would be discharged for the evening, and walked home with her again.

"It would be a tedious story to tell. Suffice it to say, that before very long, she came to love me with blind devotion. I rented for her a pretty little cottage in the southwestern portion of the city, and fitted it up handsomely. There she was as happy as a queen, demanding nothing but my love. I always managed to spend two or three evenings out of the week with her, and then she was radiant with joy.

"After a while a son was born to us, a handsome little fellow. I felt that it was my duty to marry the mother, but I was ashamed. She was goodness itself, but she was almost wholly uneducated, had never seen anything of society, and I was unable to introduce her into the fashionable circle in which I moved, and unwilling to quit that circle myself. So time passed on and the child grew and thrived, and the mother seemed the happiest of mortals.

"All went well until one night at a private entertainment given in her honor, I met Miss Arabella Addington, whom you know so well. She had just returned from Paris, where she had gone to complete her education. She was radiantly beautiful, tall, of voluptuous but light and graceful figure, and hair that seemed spun from purest gold. She sang and played exquisitely, and in the dance she seemed to float through the air upborne on angel wings. Almost at first sight I fell desperately in love. My attentions were assiduous and devoted, and at last I became her accepted lover, her betrothed.

"It is needless to say that in the meantime I paid slight attention to poor Mollie. At last I received from her a piteous letter, badly spelled, but full of the sincerest pathos, begging me to return.

"I was deeply touched, but I felt that I could not be untrue to Arabella; so I sat down and wrote Mollie a long letter, informing her of my engagement, and stating that our former relations would have to be discontinued. I assured her that she should never want; that I had bought the cottage in her name; that on the first of each month she would find $150 deposited to her credit in the First National Bank, and that I would see to the education of our child.

"When I had sent this letter by special delivery I felt that a great weight was removed from my bosom, and I went out for a walk. That evening I called on my betrothed and enjoyed the charms of her society as never before. She sang and played my favorite pieces with exquisite skill and true sympathy.

"I went home, my heart overflowing with happiness, and slept well, dreaming of Arabella.

"Next morning I got up and called for the *Gazette* as usual. The first item that met my glance was this:

" *'DROWNED!*
'About 8 o'clock last night an unknown woman was seen to step on the government snag-boat

Wichita, lying back of the State House, and imme-
diately plunge into the river on the outer side. She
disappeared at once from sight, and nothing has been
seen of the body!'

"I was troubled when I read this, and at once sent my man-servant out to see if Mollie was at home. He returned in about an hour saying that he found the house wide open and no one about, and that the neighbors had seen nothing of her since the evening before, when she seemed to be in great affliction.

"At this news I was thoroughly perturbed, and went down and offered to the skiffmen a large reward for the recovery of the body of the woman who had drowned herself the evening before.

"I returned to my room, where I passed the day in great agitation. Toward evening a skiffman came and reported that the body was found. I accompanied him to the foot of Main street. There, stretched upon the muddy bank of the river lay the corpse of Mollie Sparks, horribly swollen and disfigured by her long submersion and foul with the mud and slime of the river. Clasped to her breast was our little boy just two years old. Even in death she held him pressed tightly against her bosom.

"At the awful sight my senses reeled, and I grew faint and sick. I turned away and staggered up the bank. Arrived in front of Hornibrook & Townsend's saloon, I fell heavily to the earth and lost consciousness.

"I awoke in my own room, feeling terribly weak. You were beside me, and you told me to lie perfectly still. I lay there for many days, and afterwards learned that I had had a terrible attack of brain fever, and that for two weeks my life had been despaired of. With returning consciousness came the agony of remorse, but still I gained in strength, and after some weeks of convalescence, I was pronounced well. I felt it to be my duty to conceal all from Arabella, for I knew that the revelation of my sin would render her unhappy and could do no good. And so, though there were moments when I felt an almost irresistible impulse to rush out into the street and proclaim to the world that I was a murderer, I kept silent.

"On the night before your departure for Mexico I was feeling particularly well. I seemed to have recovered my health entirely, and the fangs of remorse gnawed my heart less than at any time since the death of Mollie. I went to visit

Arabella. She was delighted to see me so much improved. We spent a charming evening together, and it was almost midnight before I bade her adieu.

"As I walked down the street I was again happy. It was a cold, clear, moonlit winter night. I heard the distant bell of the Blind Asylum striking the hour of midnight.

"Suddenly, sitting upon the curbstone close at hand there appeared a little child, entirely naked.

"Oh, you have never seen the supernatural, and you can form no conception of its effect upon a man. I believe I could die with a smile on my face, but before that little child sitting there naked on that bleak winter night I was utterly unmanned. An indefinable instinct told me that it was not of this world, but an emanation from the spirit land. My hair rose up, my teeth chattered, and for a long time I stood petrified with fear looking upon the child; and as I looked I perceived that it was my own dead babe. At last with a tremendous effort I shook off the lethargy, and began to run. As you know, I was a very swift runner, and that night I ran as I had never run before. But it was all in vain. Just behind me I could hear the patter of the little feet and a baby voice calling, 'Papa, papa.' Oh, the agony of that mad race! At last I reached home, unlocked the door with mad rapidity, and rushed in. But before I could close it the little figure had also glided in. I bounded up stairs to my room, taking four steps at a time, burst open the door and slammed it behind me. But quick as was my movement, the little one slipped in and took its seat upon a lounge, and there through the livelong night it sat motionless, looking at me. My blood was congealed with fear. I sat upon the side of the bed and glared at the phantasm all night. I could not take my eyes away. I was fascinated, I was overcome. I could not move, I could not speak, I could not cry out. Of all suffering, this abject fear, this indescribable, inconceivable terror, which only those few who have been brought face to face with the supernatural can comprehend, is the most horrible. I suffered a thousand deaths. Eternity does not appear longer to the damned in hell than that night appeared to me. Finally, when countless ages seemed to have rolled above my head, the day began to dawn; and with the increasing light the phantasm gradually faded away like a morning mist before the rays of the sun.

"That day I was naturally much agitated, as you observed. When night approached I was afraid to remain alone. I felt that the phantom could not pursue me out into the world. That evening there was a ball at Concordia Hall. I besought Arabella to accompany me, and we went. The assemblage was large and gay, the music good, and the ball room presented a scene of great animation and beauty. I entered into the dance with all my force, determined to distract my mind from its gloomy forebodings.

"About midnight I was waltzing with Arabella, when suddenly I heard behind me the pattering of little feet and a baby voice calling, 'Papa, papa.' I was petrified with horror, and there in the middle of the ball room I stood, my hair on end, my eyes dilated, trembling in every limb, and gazing wildly upon this strange phantom which no one else could see. The dancers crowded around me, the music stopped, but there close beside me stood the little form, looking at me with its wide open eyes in which I seemed to see the light of the tomb.

"How long I stood there I know not, but at length there came over me an insane impulse to seize this torment and crush it in my hands. I started after it. Before my distracted look the crowd parted. It ran before me, calling out, 'Papa, papa.' I ran after it. Round and round the room I chased it, begging the guests to help me catch it. But it was useless. However fast I ran, there it was just before me, and I could still hear the patter of the little naked feet upon the waxed floor.

"Finally my friends seized and overpowered me, put me into my carriage, and drove me home. All the way I could hear behind the carriage the patter of the little feet following on. We reached my room. The little one came in and sat down, and that night passed like the preceding, in unutterable agony.

"The next day my friends called in a physician, who gave me a strong dose of opium. I went to sleep about dark, thoroughly under the influence of the drug, but about midnight I woke up in awful agony, and sitting there with his eyes fixed upon me I saw my son. That night passed like the two preceding, but instead of becoming accustomed to the spectre, I felt that I was growing every day more utterly unnerved.

"For several nights my friends sat up with me, but after about a week the physicians agreed that I was insane, and I was removed to the asylum. I knew that I was not, but I made no resistance, for I did not care what became of me.

"Of my life since arriving here, you can judge by what you have seen. Every night the spectre appears, first in one part of the room, then in another, and we sit gazing at one another until morning."

He was silent. The sun was declining toward the west, and the great building cast its broad shadow far across the valley. I felt that I could not spend another such night, that I must have an opportunity to collect myself, and alleging reasons of business, I prepared to depart. He made no resistance. My buggy was brought round, and I drove slowly to town.

That night I slept little, but toward daybreak I fell into a heavy slumber. I was awakened by a knocking at my door, and sitting up in bed, I heard the landlady call out: "They have telephoned from the Insane Asylum for you to come out at once. I told them that you were asleep, but they told me to wake you."

I hurried into my clothes, and ran rather than walked to the livery stable. I told them to bring out their fastest horse. Immediately a powerful bay was brought out and the saddle and bridle thrown upon him. I leaped upon his back, and giving him a severe blow with the whip, he started forward with a prodigious bound. At the risk of killing every one I met, I drove him at full speed across the city; arrived at the top of Capital Hill, I again beheld the long facade of the asylum, crowning the western hills. It was but a glimpse, and we dashed into the valley between, and up the opposite slope. Arrived at the asylum, I leaped from my foaming and panting steed, whose bridle an attendant seized, and ran to the door. There I was met by Dr. H., who, without a word, led me to Wilson's cell, where a sight that froze the blood in my veins, met my eyes.

Bolt-upright upon the side of the bed, his hair standing erect, his lower jaw drooped, his mouth open, and his eyes almost bursting from their sockets, and fixed upon a corner of the room, sat Wilson—stone dead!

The shock was too much for me. I staggered back and sat down on a bench in the hall. An attendant brought me some brandy. I drank it, and felt better, and suggested to the Doctor that we had better lay him out. We went in and laid him down on the bed, but he maintained his sitting position.

He seemed frozen. After several efforts we perceived that we could not straighten the poor emaciated limbs without breaking them, and desisted from the attempt. We tried to unclasp his hands, but they were clinched like iron. Again and again we endeavored to close those fearful, wide open, staring eyes, but in vain. They protruded so far from their sockets that the lids could not be made to meet, and when our hands were withdrawn they flew open again, staring more horribly than before. Contorted as he was it was out of the question to put him in a coffin, and so we had a large square box made, and in this we placed the wretched remains of him who had once been so handsome, so brilliant, so full of life.

He was buried in Mount Holly Cemetery, where as his executor, I have had a handsome monument erected to his memory. The inscription speaks only of his happy days, and those who read it have no suspicion of the frightful, contorted body and staring eyes that lie beneath.

ERIC

Charles J. Finger

ONE DAY LAST SUMMER, the derailment of train No. 16 came as
a welcome interlude in a tiresome journey. Because of it I
found, and lost, an opportunity, though it was nothing much
in the way of excitement. We were rolling along one minute,
dully enough, gaping unseeing at the flying landscape, then
there was a swift change in the manner of our progression, a
queer bumping noise and a sudden stop. A child at the water
cooler stumbled and fell. The conductor woke up and
waddled down the aisle and the brakeman went running.
The rest of us stuck to our seats and asked one another the
cause of it all. Then, the eye of authority being withdrawn in
a time of incipient calamity, we, the passengers, clambered
out, made our way painfully over the ballast and walked the
length of the train looking for something startling—the
fascinating sight of a dead or wounded man, for instance. But
there was nothing. The locomotive leaned out of the
perpendicular and it soon became clear that the drivers had
left the rail. A few ties were broken, seeing which, some of us
made sarcastic and revolutionary remarks about railroad
managers and their habits of playing with danger. A couple
of tattered negro children, who had evidently been gathering
blackberries, stood wide-eyed. These the brakeman
promptly and boldly ordered off the earth. Some one burst
out with a question regarding the schedule, but no one
answered. Presently, the fat conductor assumed control of
operations, and the engineer, smoking his pipe, looked on

calmly from the height of his cab window. No one was alarmed or excited. There were some futile attempts to do something, a gathering together of jacks and of rerailers, some necessary cursing and swearing, a little running and much shouting; then it being apparent that no one had confidence in the conductor, and equally apparent that he had no confidence in himself, one of the train crew started to walk back to telephone to headquarters, interest waned, and we passengers disposed of ourselves as best we could.

Now from the track, a little way off, I chanced to see a tiny rivulet shining opaline in the sun, and also the arching green of a tree clump, so there I went. The change, seated in the hollow of deep, cool shadow, was grateful, for the day had been hot, oppressively hot, and the Pullman car was stuffy, so it was good to be there and to remember that so short a while ago I had found the touch of the red plush seats unpleasant, as giving a little thrill of misery. It was good, too, to be alone and to remember the three passengers in addition to myself who were aristocratic enough to endure the discomfort of the parlor car. One of them, I remembered, had been asleep the whole morning and another had turned a cold eye on me when I approached with friendly intent. The third I had deliberately avoided, he was of the dramatic southern-colonel type, one who might be set down as a dignified man or a pompous ass according to the way one chose to view him. Certainly he had the fixed and glittering eye, the skinny hand of Coleridge's Ancient Mariner and I knew instinctively that, once given the opportunity, he would engage me in a monologue on civil war days or on the merits of the towns of Tucumcari and Alamogordo. As for the smoking car, that had been quite impossible, for not only was it dirty to an intolerable degree, but, while the electric fan buzzed brightly and hopefully, it was fixed at such an angle that the breeze it stirred passed directly into the open ventilator in the roof. Accordingly, I had left the more polite end of the train and gone into the common car, the partitioned place marked FOR WHITES, where the old time train butcher still plied his nefarious trade. His book corner held me, for there were volumes unknown to the northerner except as curiosities. There was Mrs. Southworth, for example, and a Life of Jesse James, and "Did She Love Him," and Ingersoll's "Mistakes of Moses," and a very wonderful production purporting to be the scripture in verse. That I took to my seat and opened, reading this:

> "Sometime, somewhere, out in space,
> God felt it was the time and place,
> To make a world, as He did claim,
> Would bring some honor to His Name"

when the crash came. As I have said, it was a welcome interlude.

When the noise made by the men working at the derailment had become a kind of *pianissimo obligato* to nature's music, I caught a glimpse of blue overalls through the leafy screen, and Eric came into my life.

He was the kind of young fellow one likes to look at, the kind of lad who might pick up a hundred and fifty pound sack and make no ado about it. Brown-skinned he was, and onyx-eyed. To me he was the tan-faced boy of whom Whitman sang, a being so rare in the country as to be noticeable. He stood with the characteristic stoop of the overworked son of the soil and had about him an appearance of clumsiness. He was slow of speech and incurious, and his was that raucity of a lad whose voice had but recently broken. Noting all of which, it came to me that the American peasant is doubtless no less lumpish than his foreign brother, and that he is neither bright-eyed, nor quick-witted, square-shouldered, upright and beautiful, though the pinchbeck and patriotic orator had led me to believe otherwise. Nor, as I saw, in spite of war and military training, has he been changed, as the recent sight of groups of country boys showed. The slouch still persists, the square-shouldered, deep-chested illusion has fled. Indeed, I remembered then that looking through the kodak albums of my friends, there had been revealed the fact that there is all about us an incredible amount of healthy and vulgar ugliness. However, to the lad I spoke presently of my body's needs, of my desire for milk, eggs and country-made bread; so in time we set off walking to his house.

On the way he spoke of his father, who had farmed there, as he said, for nigh on thirty years; but there was no joy in his voice. Now I was not without some preconceived notions as to the manner of man I should meet, for, having read widely, my mind's eye readily conjured up visions of Mr. Wardle, the friend of Samuel Pickwick, the more stately Roger de Coverley, the "prompt decisive man" of Whittier, and, while of quite another type to these, the florid and beer-drinking, good-natured, gusty Allworthy: not to mention the yeoman of the politician, so sturdy, upright, virtuous, just and god-fearing, hope of the race and backbone of the nation, supporter of church and state, the builder of a myriad separate, isolated little paradises. Neither did I forget the simple tiller of the soil of Harold Bell Wright, nor the countryman of the popular stage, a fellow jovial and hearty, free with words of counsel and wisdom, serene in the belief that rags are royal raiment when worn for virtue's sake; a man ever ready to make the welkin ring with mirth and song.

My man, I soon perceived on arriving, was none of these. Rather was he of the kind I had seen sometimes at country fairs and lounging about small town depots, or, more frequently, squirting his tobacco juice into inaccessible corners in rural post offices. So often had I seen him, indeed, that I had ceased to notice him and did not see him at all. Looking again, I found him strangely familiar and it came to me with a shock that I recognized him as a brother of the sullen, hopeless peasant of Gorky, the man who seemed to live always on the verge of penury and whose means of subsistence suffice, at the best of times, to procure him only the bare necessities of life, who rarely had enough sleep, who seldom enjoyed the satisfaction of having quite enough to eat, whose clothing was inadequate protection, whose dwelling was destitute of comfort. His was the dull, ox-like resignation seen in the convict under life sentence. He was dressed in patched and faded overalls and his bare feet were thrust in loose, ill-fitting shoes. On his chin was the gray stubble of a couple of weeks, and the sun had baked his skin, and wrinkled it, and furrowed it, and, looking closely, it was seen that there was dirt in the wrinkles. His teeth were yellow and stained, and his hands gnarled and knotted, and his nails broken. About him there was an air of general, vague unhappiness, and in repose, his features seemed to show the stamp of misery and despair. Later, sitting beside him at meal time, I became acutely aware of the rank smell of stale perspiration. He had, too, an unpleasant habit of spitting on the floor and was, moreover, loudly flatulent.

Nor was the meal all that my fancy had painted it. The food I found unsatisfying and tasteless, the surroundings incredibly filthy, and I was driven to the verge of distraction by the buzzing flies. Sweet potatoes formed the staple, butter was handled as hoarded gold, and milk was a scarce commodity. It had not occurred to me that modern methods and cream separators presignified so much, and, in a flash, I saw the meaning of our latter day fatless, stringy beef and its connection with the pot-bellied, skim-milk fed calves. I congratulated myself privately on the fact that I was a city dweller who paid absurdly little for the best of things.

The day being Sunday, there was time for talk and we had a rambling conversation. Our subjects were, generally, far from things of material nature, and I gathered much of his beliefs and opinions. Listening, a great despair fell upon me. The despair was not so much because of what he said, as that those who sat about him, his dull, hard-faced, moody, slatternly wife who cringed rather obviously, his two sons and two daughters, heard, yet spoke no word of disagreement, but rather seemed to drink in what he said as truth beyond question, to doubt which was blasphemy. So it was that I sat for the most part silent and a little angered. Almost, I felt hate for him.

Of odd things I will not write, of beliefs and things told me by him with all the seriousness of a professional theorist, such as that the lay of the Milky Way indicated the direction of the prevailing winds; the position of the horned moon, or rather her phases, told of the coming of wet or of dry weather during the month, according to the manner in which the hollow of it held, or failed to hold water; of the best time to lay shingles according to the light or the dark of the moon; of the foretelling of weather by observing how a cat sharpened her claws. These things, and many more, he told me in heavy seriousness, the youngest there gathering it all in open-mouthed, her father, to her evident thinking, a very Sir Oracle. Meanwhile, he gave me the Law, seated outside, with his chair tilted against the house wall, his feet on the uppermost rung, and his head stooped, so that his chin almost touched his knees.

Lightly, he sketched in his religious beliefs, and incidentally, those of his neighbors, for the community attended a little wooden church close at hand, at which preached a coarse-featured fellow who kept a grocery store. Him I saw before leaving. The man of God acted also as community barber, traded in hogs, and kept an open Bible on the cash register. He breathed noisily, looked stupendously grave, and whenever I spoke, regarded me dubiously.

From the lips of my host, with promptings from the preacher, I gathered that we were soon to witness the most terrible catastrophe of the world's history, and a century of sorrow and of gloom was to follow. The end of things human was at hand and the blowing of the great trumpet was to be momentarily expected, at the sound of which my host, some of the children of his loins with a few of the elect, would leap into the light and enjoy the spectacle of the destruction of the human race, pyrotechnically arranged with dramatic effect, by a vicious, evil-minded, sadistic god for the entertainment of a select few. In contemplation of this speculative bliss, a ray of optimism showed itself and my host became fluent.

Touching lightly on matters sociological, he discovered to' me a belief that all who dwelt in cities were panderers and prostitutes, parasites and wastrels, lascivious-minded sinners and outraged innocents. Government was organized brigandry. The farmer, and the farmer alone, was the producer. Strangely enough, he quoted Dr. Frank Crane in support of his contention regarding this last, doubtless at fifth or sixth hand, for he spoke of that moralist as being one high in the counsels of the government.

Regarding the matter of education, and learning, and culture, he was bitter as gall. His voice grew lower and more cunning. "Me," he said, "I ain't had no book learnin' an' look at me." He threw out his hands as he spoke, and his family regarded him, the wife with a cynical side glance. "Books is nothin'," he added, repeating that again and again, but looking frowningly at Eric the while, and that lad shifted uneasily. There was a far echo of Ruskin too, when he advanced the opinion that education did but result in the turning of literature to lust and of arithmetic to roguery. "By God, I'd burn every book, and put every writer of 'em to honest labor, I would, if I was the gov'ment," he said, and there was a fierceness in his tone.

He became comminatory, too, bundling together theatres, music, pictures, drink, automobiles, stenographers, picture shows, magazines, tobacco, Catholics, Jews, jewelry, silk stockings, universities, professors, railroad officals, and all elected persons. He was in an ecstacy of anathema. The rose leaves of love grieved him sorely.

Life itself, he held, was as an imprisonment. There were

days when something that had an appearance of happiness and joy chanced to appear, but such were temptation periods, and, did man or woman but unbend the slightest, condign punishment would ensue. No radiant optimist was he. In life there were no honest cakes and ale. Happiest was he who was tortured with awful spiritual anguish. So firmly was he, and his family through him, impressed with this point of view, that, did a hog fall sick of colic, did a chicken chance to die, immediately there was a searching for the cause in past happiness. To bear ills, then, was the portion of humanity. To suffer was to gain. Life itself was but a wringing of blood from the heart.

As we listened, we had fought flies, mosquitoes and gnats, and I was sometimes inattentive, being suspicious of chigas.

II

The thin ghost of a new moon was melting into the violet, when, wearied of all this, I rose to return. Eric walked with me to my train, and, I was glad to find, grew more communicative. I remember that walk very distinctly. Almost I could vouch for the words spoken. Referring to his father's mention of the folly of education, I told him of my interest in literature and books, and thus happily touched a chord that pleased my companion. He had plucked a blue flower and looked at it admiringly as he walked.

"The trouble is," he said presently, "things I've read don't tell of things as they are. I bought some of them there books off the train once. You know 'em. They sell 'em on the train."

It was difficult to understand his meaning sometimes, and I groped. It came out then that the only books permitted in the house were "The Sins of Society," Tupper's "Proverbial Philosophy," the speeches of William Jennings Bryan, a Bible, and a mail order house catalogue. He listed them rapidly.

"Paw, he won't allow no books," he said. "You heard him. . . . They spoil for work, he says. . . . I'd like to tell you what I'm tryin' to say, but I can't."

"Yes," said I. "I understand. I think I know what you mean. Go on," I urged him. Then, after a short silence, "I'm interested. I'll send you some books as soon as I get home."

Eric picked up the thread of his musing presently, for it was more musing than talk. He reminded me of a foreigner unacquainted with the language, trying to make himself understood.

"I was thinkin'," he said slowly, "thinkin' that somehow I'm just plum crazy to tell about the things what I see and like I see 'em. . . . In different words somehow to them what we talk. . . . Just a few words, you know, and them the right ones. . . . Tell exactly, and sometimes what seems the right words comes to me."

He compressed his lips. Carefully I had to lead him into explanation. He seemed to make an effort by way of example, but it was abortive.

"Look at the country," he said, stopping and pointing to the low confusion of hills in the distance. I attempted some commonplace. Again there was silence for a space.

"I don't know how it is," he went on presently. "Once at the meeting house there was a new preacher, and he said this here word—'decorum.' I didn't know it. . . . 'Twas new to me. But somehow what it meant came to me sudden like. When I sat there and looked at them old trustees and elders, this came to me, this here what I'm tellin' you. . . . Maybe it's silly, but it seemed to fit. This was it. 'Blank decorous faces and bald heads.' Just that. Them trustees and elders, you know. . . . I'm telling you it fitted 'em. Well, at odd times I think of things like that and then the words stick. Of course, they don't come in a rush and all ready, like that there one did. You kinder got to work it up in a way. Just a word and the notion comes. It's like weedin' a garden. The way you talk every day is like weeds. Then maybe you find a flower, and you got to hoe it and tend it and favor it. It worries you till you get it right. I just got to stop what I'm doin' and think about it and if I do, I get it fixed good and proper. Paw, he yells at me and then it all goes like a dream. You know them dreams when you think you'll remember, then wake up and find there ain't nothin' left? . . . Sometimes I'm alone when I get a notion, then it sticks.

"Now there's this here. . . . It fits the little road leading up to our place. You didn't see it, of course. It's on yonder side of the hill. There's bendin' lilacs, you know. Bending over the road. It goes this way. 'The lonely lane lost in the leaning lilacs.' I like that there. There was other lines come, but I forgot 'em. But what I told you fits the place like you made a

123

picture of it. To me it does."

Eric looked at me as he spoke and his expression was profoundly thoughtful. I thought that his clear eyes contemplated conflicts and triumphs and I had a silly impulse to shake his hand.

"Work keeps me busy though," he continued. "There ain't no end to it all. Up at five, then the cows. What's worse, I get 'em gentled, 'an paw, he comes blusterin' and it's all wrong again. Then there's hitchin' up after milkin' and the field all day an' milkin' at nights and fool odd jobs too. Even the kids don't never play. I never played in my life. Wouldn't know how to. Work all day an' every day. It ain't work. It's . . . it's weary strife. That's what it is. That's the right word. . . . Still, the body bein' tired don't stop the thinkin'. . . . Say, tell me this. You say you know all about books. Well, was there ever a fellow what worked on a farm and yet done things?"

There was a slight pause, then he put his case more compactly. "I mean this. Does workin' in the clods make a man a clod? Is there any hope? Will I be here always, my work unfinished, my self undone, do you think?" He was earnest and there was a change in his diction. He squared his shoulders as one preparing for a burden.

At that I remembered Burns and had to search my memory diligently, for Burns the lover, and Burns the excise man, blotted out the memory of that boy on the wretched Ayrshire farm. Luckily a passage in a letter written by him came to my mind, the heart-stirring letter in which was told the tale of that home where, for several years, meat was a rarity. Then came the memory of the thirteen-year-old boy threshing, and of that life worse than a galley slave's until he was sixteen. Eric listened attentively, rigid in his interest, for we had stopped in our walk for a moment.

"But what did this fellow Burns do?" He was eager. His eyes were ablaze. "What did he write?"

At that I was distressed privately. For a moment we looked at each other mute. It seemed to me that all I supposed I knew, all that I took for granted, all that I had learned and placed away for ready reference, had vanished completely. I tried to quote. Nothing came. In vain I searched my memory, cudgelled my brains. Nothing could I find but the banal "a man's a man for a' that," which clearly would not do. But Byron came to my rescue quite unexpectedly, so I lied roundly, using the only passage that I clearly recalled in the whole universe of literature. Nor was I perfectly sure that it was from Byron. I thought so, but could not place the passage. Yet it was all that I could do just then. So I quoted:

> " *'I had a dream which was not all a dream.*
> *The bright sun was extinguished, and the stars*
> *Did wander darkly in the eternal space,*
> *Rayless and pathless, and the icy earth*
> *Swung blind and blackening in the moonless*
> *air.'* "

Secretly I cursed myself for a humbug.

" 'Blind and blackening in the moonless air' " repeated Eric very softly. " 'Blind and blackening in the moonless air' . . .and a farm-hand like me made up that, you say?"

I nodded, then, after a pause, attempted some explanation with a notion to square myself with my conscience, but gave up when I saw that he was not listening.

He repeated the line once more, almost whispering this time, gazing intently the while to the west where crimson and gold streaks shot upward, to die in the violet. Then this extraordinary young man put his hands to his face as though he feared to lose the line. "I wish I'd thought of that," he said, simply and sincerely. It seemed as though there was a moment of acute bitterness, a jealousy almost. I opened my mouth to say something, for part of the "Cotter's Saturday Night" had suddenly occurred to me, but he made an arresting gesture and asked me to repeat the five lines again. Seeing his appreciation, sensing it dimly rather, I felt little and contemptible. I had a swift thought of Bunyan with his intense, pictorial sort of imagination. There came on the heels of that an idea that my own love of literature was but a thin veneer lightly laid over a common surface.

"Now I got that forever," he said with a little air of triumph. "Paw, he can't touch that now. . . . Paw's chock full of pizen hate. . . . He's bitter. . . . Once he called me a hell-hound for nothin' at all almost, so I have to hide everything."

He broke off at a tangent then. "When I think of something, getting words right for things as they are, it's a good day for me then. There was one dull day last fall, just about the time the air had the first nip in it. I was out after the cows and seen that the woods was all brown, while the day afore they'd been green. This came to me then, came like talkin' in a dream, you know, 'marvel of godlike change.' It seemed that, and just that. You see, a gray mist hung there in the valley, but it was still green, but higher up the slope where the wind had beat and the night had been chill, there was streaks of yellow and patches of brown, and here and there scarlet. I seen it all otherwise the evening before, so to me it was just what I said, 'marvel of godlike change.' There was more of it, of course, but the chance slipped. I wanted to think and tell of the earth, all brown and bare, like it was tired and in pain, and glad to rest under the snow, because that's how I felt real often. But paw was plum awful that day. They'd been trouble at home. Trouble about a girl.... No. I don't mean there was that you might think of. 'Twas different. It's kinder hard to tell."

Eric meditated for a space. I feared that there was to be some preposterous self-revelation, some stupid confession.

"It's kinder hard to tell," he repeated, and hesitated. His brows were knitted and his air abstracted. "I suppose it might look like something, but it wasn't really, but it looked so darned suspicious against me I can't explain. Paw, him and the preacher, is the Anti-Vice Society.... They started that after the Chatahqua. Well, once the school teacher she loaned me this here Geographical Magazine out of the school li'bry, with a story about savages in it, with pictures. The savages, of course, had nothin' on. Paw, he got aholt of it. He said it was vice and talked about bringin' it to the Grand Jury. Him and the preacher got the teacher fired. Then another day, him and the preacher they had a raft of pictures they'd taken from the feller who keeps the drug store an' they was all of women. Well, I seen 'em where they'd hid 'em under paw's bed. They was one with a woman takin' off her robe, most beautiful. Standin' sideways she was. You know.... Anyway, it set me wantin' to see a woman like she was. I never seen one. Well, the women folk they take a dip down at the creek, for there ain't no bath tubs hereabouts. I wanted to see a woman an' how she looked without clothes and against the green, you know. So when Sara and her sister, they're my cousins, went down to the creek, I hid in the thicket. An' paw he found me. He jumped out from in under the bush an' they was trouble. I never seen him so mad. That's when he called me a hell-hound like I told you.... Bein' country girls, I expect, they wasn't at all beautiful like them pictures, so they wasn't nothin' to it at all but trouble,

126

with paw madder every day, sayin' he wouldn't have maw know my hound's heart for anythin.' But the jawin' kept on an' on an' him ahoundin' me all the time till I wished I was through with it all. One night I got this here:

' *'Twill soon be o'er,*
A fateful calm succeeds
The storm of passion that has
    wrecked my life.'

"I liked it pretty well, but not so well as this here, because you see there was more of it, and I got to thinkin' and makin' the tale up to where presently I found a feller who'd understand, an' who'd be with me 'warming the winter of my loneliness.' That's the line I liked best, that 'warming the winter of my loneliness.' It's fine, I think, an' I was real glad to get it."

III

Climbing the right of way fence—it was barbed wire and a mean thing to have doings with—I saw that a large gang of men were at work and that the locomotive had again reached the perpendicular. Through the window of the dining car I saw the waiters going to and fro with their loaded trays, and the white-covered tables looked pleasantly enticing. After a little persuasion, I prevailed upon Eric to take a meal with me.

Across the table, half in shadow, his face looked to me like the face of Sandburg. There was the same light of enthusiasm, the same earnestness, the same eager, seeing, questioning eye. Yet the lad was not the same type as the Chicago man. There was that lack of crystallization, for one thing. And, looking at him, I decided that with all his intellect, his health, his passionate appreciation of things about him, he was but born to waste. The idea was monstrous, intolerable perhaps, but still I know that there are thousands and tens of thousands of seeds dropped to die scorched.

For a while we talked of farm life, and, while it was my intention to get some data for an article, I fell to boasting of what I had read and what I had seen, then, a little ashamed, checked myself sharply. That memory is very clear and full, the memory of my immense self-consciousness. Then he fell to talking of the flowers and the trees and the birds, especially the birds, and telling me of the glory of them. He spoke of a little spot on the farm where was what he called his Pool of Dreams. Back he came sharply to birds, describing them and naming their names. To be sure, the names were familiar, but I sat, a little oppressed, knowing that for the life of me I could not conjure up a mental picture of more than one or two.

"Did you ever watch a mockingbird, now?" he asked, looking at me fixedly. Somewhat grudgingly, I admitted that I would not with certainty recognize one, and at that an expression of perplexity came into his face. It was almost a swift mood of depression, but it soon passed and he went on with frightened eye.

"I seen 'em many's the time, and watched," he said. "In Siss's school book it says 'The song of the mockingbird is beautiful' an' that's all. That don't tell nothin'. What they ought to do is to set it down as it is for men like you who don't get no chance to see one. I've set and watched, an' watched. Day after day I seen it. I've thought it all out, thought it out word for word. You see I always sleep outside in summer and from my cot before the sunrise, I——"

"Wait," I interrupted, as a notion struck me, and I reached for the menu card. "I want to take a note or two of what you tell me."

"Write it down?" he asked incredulously. "Write down what I say?" Then he protested. "But it's nothin', you see. I seen it so often that I can see it now just as it is an'——"

"I know," said I. "Don't mind. Just tell me. Go on from the first time you see it."

Thus it came that I took down his words in shorthand. But I noticed this: In his deep interest his very voice was changed. Gone entirely was the rustic huskiness, and he was low and kindly in intonation. So saturated was he with his theme, so thoroughly had he assimilated it all, that he spoke as one who had learned a lesson by rote, or as one reading aloud. He had chosen and re-chosen his words, refining and rejecting and memorizing with patient care. I transcribe my notes then:

"From my cot, and before sunrise, I see my mockingbird on the ridge-pole of the house. It seems to have dropped there to bathe in the first sun shaft

and it is the fifth morning that I have watched.

"My bird commences to sing as he gains his perch and pours forth at least half a dozen songs in quick succession. There is one note like gold, a peculiar note almost bell-like. Perhaps it is part of a new song to be well considered before he adds it to his——what?"

he questioned, at a loss for the right word. "I ain't got nothin' there."

I suggested the word 'repertoire' and Eric repeated it. "It seems hard, hard, that word," he said. "Hard in the sound of it. Why not say 'stock' or 'list' or 'collection'? He considered a moment, then went on:

"At times, still singing, the bird runs a few feet, flutters in the air and dives, dives as into a pool, lighting again like magic on his perch. It is as though his joy overflowed and could not find outlet in the song alone. The little leap is almost a somersault and I catch him at one moment in the air, and, as he makes his turn, the black and white bars on his wings are plainly seen against the sky. Two tiny fluttering fans."

Here he paused in thought. I noticed that, reciting, he had fallen into a sort of monotonous half chant, analogous to our recitative, and the effect was soothing. Some of what he said seemed to fall into shape, into lines like much that passes as free verse, and has offered a subject for serious reflection to the student of literary phenomena. Certainly, he had some sense of the musical qualities of words, though it was badly overlaid. His rusticity had disappeared. He went on, unstirred by his surroundings:

"No pause, no stay in his music. One song follows another as if he challenged the birds of the world. There is the song of the blue jay, for he always starts with that, and he seems to hurry through with the warble of the Carolina wren to get to the song of the tufted titmouse. The cry of the cat bird too he makes and the call of the cuckoo, then just as a musician sounds a harsh chord, there comes the call of the guinea fowl like wooden machinery clumsily stirring.

"Sometimes, though not often, he will drop one song to begin another, an outburst, it seems, as if he tried to drown that other song I hear from some cousin of his on the hill side. At such times there is a bold little run with wings outstretched, and my bird drops to the ground—flashes like an arrow rather— his song never ceasing.

"Over and over again there is the running along the ridge pole, a leaping into the air, a darting to the ground to return swiftly, then, of a sudden, and in the midst of a burst of melody, I hear his voice through the whirr of wings as he darts to the distant wood, his song growing fainter until he is lost in the silver green that hides the hill, gone to meet the challenge of his cousin, the unseen songster."

Eric ceased, and I looked to see some sign of expectancy on his face, but there was none. He had talked as the bird sang, without looking for praise or blame.

I pocketed the card and began to recall passages that I had a mind to quote as being likely to interest him. Shelley's "Skylark," for example, or a line or two from "Hyperion." I mulled things over in my mind. It seemed to me that perhaps in him was what we were looking for, what Whitman had expected, and Emerson foretold, the untutored singer of the soil. Indeed I said something of the sort, though not so definitely as I should have, and I noticed that Eric puffed out his cheeks to blow a sigh.

At that moment the conductor came through the car very breezily, smiling as one that had done a worthy deed, and as he reached for the signal cord, he quoted loudly and in high good humor.

" 'Off agin, on agin, gone agin, Finnegan.' "

Hastily we rose, and Eric had barely time to seize his hat and to give me a handshake before the train began to move. He made for the rear platform, I following, and as I waved a good-bye, I caught a glimpse of his face happily radiant by the light of the brakeman's lantern. Then I saw him silhouetted against the sky as he climbed the right-of-way fence, shrinking in size fantastically as we gathered speed.

THE BEST MAN IN TOWN

Thyra Samter Winslow

WHENEVER HUGO DAHLMER passed down the street someone always said: "There goes the best man in town."

Hugo Dahlmer was a German Jew. He had come to my home town when he was thirteen, at the close of the Civil War. He had started out, around twelve, a brave immigrant boy with a pack, determined to become a great merchant. He separated from his cousin who had brought him to America and found himself alone—and lonely—in the South and a war going on.

Without knowing a thing about the war—he couldn't speak English well enough to find out who was fighting and just what the fighting was for—he happened to come across a Confederate army, saw other boys doing the tasks that in a later war were to be assigned to kitchen police, and he joined on.

He spent nearly a year peeling potatoes, driving mules. When the war was over one of the prominent men of the town, who had become interested in him, brought him back to his home. Dahlmer found himself not only with a new home but with an adopted nationality. Immediately, because of his activities in the war, he became an ex-Confederate soldier, a part of the old South. When he learned English, it was with a Southern accent. His family, in the years that followed, thought of themselves as an old Southern family.

Hugo Dahlmer's patron died, penniless because of the war.

Dahlmer took care of his patron's family until death claimed them. He worked hard. He got together a little money, bought a stock of goods, started a store in a small vacant building.

The store grew. Dahlmer learned merchandizing. The shrewdness that had made him come to America, that had made him dream of becoming a great merchant, developed. One building after another was outgrown until he had a huge—and dull-looking—store, a curious mixture of wholesale and retail. He sold at retail to the neighborhood ranches and farms and plantations and wholesale to the stores in the smaller towns. Several times a year he went to St. Louis and later to New York, and because he had a keen sense for bargains and for buying he bought remnants of stock, "job lots," the whole output or the left-overs of small wholesale houses and factories.

In town there was never anything too small or too big for him. On every charity Hugo Dahlmer's name came near the top of the list. He was always helping out poor families.

"Go to Hugo Dahlmer, he'll take care of you," the ministers of the various faiths would say, if a man's home burned down or if he were ill or needed clothes for himself and his family. Dahlmer would supply felt hats and overalls and Mother Hubbard wrappers, barrels of sugar, sacks of flour. It was all part of living. He was making money, had more than enough.

When Horace Hogge and Joe Barton wanted to start in business they didn't have a cent of capital. No one else would even give them serious attention so they went to Hugo Dahlmer. He knew well enough that they would be in direct opposition to him. He knew that no one else would help them. He felt that they were honest and deserving young men. What was one more business rival, anyhow?

Hugo Dahlmer took a small stock of goods from his own store. He loaned it, without a cent of charge or interest, to the two young men.

"Pay me back whenever you can," he said, and gave them a lot of fatherly advice in the bargain.

Hogge-Barton was successful immediately. The men were young and ambitious. They planned—and built—a far more citified establishment than Dahlmer had ever dreamed of. They paid him for his merchandise when they could spare the money easily.

Dahlmer helped out a dozen other firms with stock and with money. He took half-a-dozen young men, one at a time, to work for him, most of them leaving to go to bigger firms or to start in business for themselves. He was the man to whom folks turned when they needed to be helped out of difficulties.

When Hugo Dahlmer was middle-aged he married Freda Stillman, a young girl he met through some business acquaintances in St. Louis. They bought a huge old house, a bit given to gimcracks on the outside, set in a sort of miniature estate, with an iron fence around it and a row of outhouses, stables and barn, and chicken houses in the rear. They had one daughter, Taube, whom they called Taubschen—little dove, an odd girl with curly hair and brusque ways.

There were always the family surrey—or, later, automobile—and a couple of other buggies or cars in front of the Dahlmer place. They were always having company, guests for dinner or overnight, and the hired man and the cook and the second girl were always rushing around, frying platters of chicken, baking huge cakes, pulling chairs around, getting ready for company.

In spite of this constant activity, the elder Dahlmers didn't actually go with any social set, though Taube went with "the crowd" when she was young. They were always entertaining people from ranches or from plantations or from other towns. They went "in society" only when some charity entertainment demanded their attendance.

Mrs. Dahlmer's mother lived with them, a dignified little white-haired woman, as charitable as Dahlmer, who was always being called upon at odd hours to look after sick folks, and whom you'd see any day in the family surrey delivering a huge basket of food in the poorer section of town.

The Dahlmers were, in a way, in spite of their out-of-town guests, almost alone socially, and yet curiously an important part of the town. They were solid. Substantial. Folks liked to tell about all the good the Dahlmers did. You could count on the Dahlmers.

Hugo Dahlmer was always a gambler. Most of the important men in town gambled. For years Dahlmer kept his gambling activities harnessed to poker games. Poker was played for pretty big stakes, then, in my home town. As he grew older Dahlmer began to speculate in cotton.

He speculated once too often. The market didn't go the way he expected it would—and he had carried his expectancy too far. He lost everything. In two days he saw the fortune he had built through the years disappear. Five hundred thousand dollars, the town said. That was a lot of money to lose, everyone agreed.

Dahlmer gave up his immense and ugly store. His huge and mid-Victorian house. He sold his wife's ugly diamonds, "sunbursts" and the like. He sold Taube's pony. All but one of the servants went away.

Dahlmer paid every cent of his debts. The family moved into a small cottage on Oak Street, and Taube quit going to parties. She was sixteen, then, and being a Jewish girl would have stopped being popular automatically at eighteen anyhow.

Dahlmer started looking around for something to do. He was a fairly old man now, but he took it for granted that some of the many younger men he had helped would come to his aid. He had never asked aid for himself before.

He walked into the Hogge-Barton store and asked for Horace Hogge. Joe Barton was dead, and Horace and his son, Horace, junior, owned the store now. It was large and fashionable.

Dahlmer, embarrassed, hesitatingly asked if Horace had something for him. He felt he knew merchandising. Buying. He still had a good many useful years ahead of him, he said.

Horace Hogge looked at him. He saw an aging, round-shouldered man, not very well dressed, with a worried look in his rather faded eyes. Horace looked at his sleek and prosperous establishment. He forgot how Dahlmer started him in business. Men forget things like that.

"I'm sorry, old man," he said patronizingly, "there isn't a thing here for you."

Dahlmer didn't say anything. He just looked at Horace Hogge. He went out of the store. He never asked anyone else for any sort of a job. After all, he never had worked for anyone.

A man of another caliber would have broken completely. Dahlmer, looking older and more worried, started all over again. A small store in a town a few miles out in the country. Not a very good business town, but the only one that didn't have too many stores. He worked harder than he should have at his age. He managed to make a living—which was all he wanted to do, he said. He also managed to help a lot of people who were poorer than he was and who had no one else to turn to.

The only person who ever did anything for Dahlmer was a man named Ferd Buyton, one of the many young men Dahlmer had taken into the big store with him. Ferd Buyton offered Dahlmer any amount of cash he needed. Dahlmer found out that his credit was good enough so that he didn't have to take the loan. Instead of taking Ferd's kindness for granted—for he was a rich man, and Dahlmer had helped him get his start—he always talked of Ferd's generosity as if it were absolutely unparalleled.

The Hogges, Horace and Horace, junior, were dead when I last visited my home town. The sharp-faced Hogge daughter was still alive and was very busy with her club work. Her folks had left her well provided for, and she had been married a long time. Her husband doesn't amount to a great deal.

I asked about Hugo Dahlmer. He and his wife were dead, too. Taube had married a man in the East, someplace, and no one had seen her except when she came to town for her father's funeral.

The young folks didn't even remember the Dahlmers. One of the older folks said: "Hugo Dahlmer, he was the best man who ever lived in this town." And someone else added, "And a lot of good it ever did him."

A WOMAN LIKE DILSIE

David Thibault

ON A SATURDAY in June Easter, George and John were walking home from the commissary, each with his rations slung in a gunny sack upon his back. Now and then a wagon passed them, going toward town. In one of these sat Aunt Minnie Graves, with her husband and the girl whom Easter had seen at the revival the August before.

George pleasantly called the old man by name.

"So dat's Peter Graves," commented Easter. "I know Mis' Minnie since I wuz 'bout seventeen."

"Don't you know 'im?" George asked.

"I seed 'im at chu'ch wid Mis' Minnie. I figgered who 'twas. But I ain't to say *knowed* 'im."

John laughed his slow, provoking laugh. "Now you done ax 'bout all of 'em but de onliest one you thinkin' 'bout."

"Who dat?" demanded George, smiling. "Dilsie?"

"Who you think East been stud'in'? Not de team of mules."

"Shucks!" said Easter. "I ain't even knowed her name till now."

"She a fine gal, East." For once George was not ribald. "Her ol' folks is fine too. You heahed of de Peter Graves Lake? A big cyp'us brake ovah across de bottoms?"

"Co'se I is."

"Hit named fo' him. He homesteaded fawty acres ovah dare. Good lan' as a crow ever flew ocross. He got nigh twenty acres cleared."

136

"Dat's all he *kin* clear," said John, "lessen he hires catfishes an' mud turkles to roll de logs. De rest of it runs out in de lake."

But George pointed out that this was no tragedy, because the pond acres bore a good stand of big cypresses. These Peter Graves felled and rived into boards and pickets. Everyone knew that Peter Graves kept a stock of clear, air-dried boards on hand, and that his count and his price were fair.

"He done well 'fore he got agable," George concluded. "Now he got to hire de timberin' done."

Easter said no more. Here, after nearly a year, he was tapping information he had longed for since his first sight of Dilsie. It was a part of her peculiar effect on Easter that he had asked no one about her, not even her name or where she lived. He had been afraid of this girl, and then there was Annie C., the kind of woman to occupy any hard-working man's spare time completely. Annie had comfortable ways, she was cheerful and not at all terrifying. Once or twice a year she might fly off the handle and mark you with a bed slat or a poker, but she never hit as hard as she could, and ten minutes afterward she would be laughing and joking and comfortable. Easter could take a rest from her, and she could take a rest from him, and when they came back together it was as though all were new.

Easter left George and John at his own turnrow and tramped on alone to his cabin. He unlocked the door, stored his rations, and brought out a chair, which he tilted back against the walnut tree. Then he thought about marriage. It must be a good thing, after a man has run round over the bottoms like a stray boar shoat, to marry a woman like Dilsie Graves. A man should do this in time to have his children coming up ready to lend a hand in the field when he began to fail and lose his teeth and get old. He wondered if Annie C. could have children even if she wanted to; and he wondered why he thought of Dilsie, whom he had seen twice, in connection with marriage, and not of the comfortable Annie. "Annie, she jest ain't marryin' kind," Easter muttered half aloud.

Today's encounter with the Graveses had focused the dream of Dilsie which Easter had entertained since the revival. While he kept this dream vague, and played it against the immediate and usable flesh of Annie C., his emotional setup was ideal. He could not have explained it, but that was why he had not sought to know more of Dilsie. Knowing her better, he might have needed her, and the things she meant to him, intolerably. As it was, he had of her all that he needed. Dilsie was merely a tenuous memory made into a beautiful dream which Easter delighted to evoke when, as now, he sat with his eyes half shut, his thoughts turned to pasture. This dream could not displace the grappling realities of Annie's breasts and thighs. But neither could poor, everyday flesh, frankly real, obviously limited, destroy the dream.

That afternoon Easter took his gun and struck out through the bottoms toward Peter Graves Lake. "I needs to kill me a squirrel fo' some freshenin'," he told himself. "H'm," said Double-Actin'. "De squirrel you is atter wears a blue calico dress." Easter resentfully denied it, a course always dangerous, because his conscience was irascible in argument, personal, and sometimes vile. "I *is* gwinna hunt me some squirrels!" he insisted and put a cap on each nipple of his gun. "Sho'!" jeered Double-Actin'. "Sho'! But dis squirrel ain't got no bush tail." Stung and disgusted, Easter crossed half a dozen narrow straits between cypress ponds, skirted two fair-sized lakes, and came to the Graveses' clearing. The double log house was locked and still.

Knowing the family was in town, Easter boldly approached the house. There was a front gallery and a water shelf loaded with cans and buckets and broken crocks full of moss roses. The unfenced yard was clean swept, the sizable woodpile was neat, and a sound wooden tub stood under the spout of the pitcher pump. Between woodpile and pump, handy to chips and to water, two big washpots stood, each with its three legs resting upon half bricks. Look at the crops and you know the man. The front gallery, the yard, and the wash place tell you about his womenfolks. True as a mirror, everything here reflected Aunt Minnie Graves—brisk, clean, kindly. Easter turned back to the house. Against the house, under the gallery roof, hung festoons of red peppers, bunches of herbs, and loops of well-roped onions. On a tiny three-legged stand stood a handleless earthenware pitcher filled with old-fashioned cabbage roses. At this Easter looked long. He was sure Dilsie had placed those flowers there.

He crossed the lead between the lake and a smaller pond adjoining it and plunged into the thick woods beyond. For two hours he hunted squirrels as he never hunted them before. By late afternoon he had killed eight. He tied their necks together with a strip of elm bark and returned to the Graveses' clearing. The place was still deserted. Easter ambushed himself near the foot log across the lead and waited. It was nearing sunset, and the mosquitoes were about him in booming clouds when he heard the wagon approaching. When Peter Graves stopped his team in front of the house, Easter crossed the foot log and walked briskly forward, perfect picture of a belated hunter hurrying homeward.

Peter had helped his womenfolk out of the wagon and they were all three busy with their packages when Easer came up to them.

"Well, Lawd bless my heart!" cried Minnie Graves. "It's Easter, dat Malissa Thomas raised. How is you, honey?"

"I's all right, Mis' Minnie." Then to Peter. "Kin I he'p you wid de team, Mistuh Graves?"

"Glad to see you," said the old man. "Dems some fine squirrels you got. I kin unhitch. You go in an' take a cheer."

Easter insisted on helping with the team. It staved off by so long the beatific terror of looking at Dilsie. But for all that, the corners of his eyes saw her demurely attending to her own business, helping her ma the way a gal does who is used to it. Easter was miserably afraid. He presented Peter Graves with all the squirrels and prepared to bolt. The old man herded him with difficulty to the front gallery, calling cheerily to the women, "Dis boy done gimme *all* his squirrels. I's gwinna make 'im stay an' he'p eat 'em."

"Sho'!—course he is!" Minnie followed her voice through the door. "Come in an' have a cheer, Easter."

But the stiffening had gone from Easter's bones. He reeled off lie after lie to get out of doing what he had schemed and worked half a day to do, rejecting the fruits of the victory he had not even dared to hope for.

"Den effen you *got* to go," said Minnie, disappearing inside, "wait jes' a minute." She returned with a pie tin piled full of something over which a clean white cloth was tied. "Heah you some beef we bought in town. You kin bring back de pan sometime."

"Sho'," said Peter Graves. "Now you know de way, come an' visit. Don't many come across dese bottoms—'cepen a lot of boys dats a-settin' up to Dilsie."

What barbed information for Easter to pack home across the swamps!

Easter cooked his supper and ate it, washed the skillet, pans and cups, and then sat down on his door block under June stars to think of Dilsie; and he came to the image of her in his mind as a famished man faces manna. Not even old Peter's mention of many rivals hurt him now. When at last he went to bed he was convinced that just thinking about a woman like Dilsie was more exciting than possessing any other woman he had ever known, except Annie C. Here he was thinking of those two at the same time again. He wished to goodness he could keep his thoughts about them separated. But it wasn't his fault, he maintained to his vision of Dilsie. Thoughts of those two girls ought to be more alike than they were different, or more different than they were alike.

Sunday Easter attended meeting at Zion Wheel, hoping and fearing the Graveses would be there. They were not. He saw Loda Green, Annie and Elsie in the congregation. How had he ever come to marry Loda? Elsie's remembered fascination was nearly as incredible. He studied her face as the sermon thundered on: a tired, leaninsh woman of forty, with one eye. . . . When his meditative glance fell on Annie C. she flashed her wide smile, and his lips flashed an answer; but he was thinking of that broken pitcher full of pink cabbage roses on Peter Graves's gallery.

Monday morning Easter hoed in his own crop. Between quartering time and noon it showered; so little that he had trouble convincing himself that it would be too wet to work in the afternoon. However, he managed it and was just ready to set out across the swamps to return Aunt Minnie's pan and cloth when Mr. Henry rode up.

"Easter," said Mr. Henry, "I want you to help us out this afternoon. We're chopping the upper eighty." It had not occurred to Mr. Henry that it was too wet to work, and Easter didn't argue the point this time.

That was the heartbreaking pattern of events for three weeks of grinding work. On the first Saturday following his visit to Graveses' clearing he had to drive the wagon to town for rations, substituting for Pink Dawson, who was down with chills and fever. Sunday, dressed in his best, he crossed the bottoms to find the Graveses' house locked and silent. He learned later that they had attended meeting. The following week his own crop needed him. A blessed thunderstorm halted field work Friday, but Mr. Henry sent Easter to town again, and on Saturday had him help issue rations in the commissary. Sunday Easter was at meeting again—and the Graveses were not. But Annie C. was there.

"How come you ain't been down to see me?" she asked.

"Gal," said Easter, "dey is tryin' to work me down. W'en nighttime come, I jes' falls on de bed."

"I b'lieves you, East. Whut I wants to know is *who wid?*"

Easter had been thinking so often of Dilsie and so seldom of Annie that he looked half guilty, but Annie's laugh made him comfortable again. "East"—she was solicitous now— "you is lookin' kinda ganted, sho' nuff. Whatever you is doin', you better not do much of it as you is."

Wednesday of the next week he met Aunt Minnie Graves herself in the big road. "Easter, boy, why ain't you been to see us?"

"I's been layin' off to come, Mis' Minnie. I sho' is. I ain't forgot yo' pan and de cloth. I washed 'em *good.*"

"I done forgot 'em, myself. I don't need 'em honey. When you gwinna come and see us?"

"You-all be dare Sadday?"

"We'll be dare all day Sadday."

"Den effen I lives an' nothin' happens, I's sho' gwinna come."

Seedy though he had felt for days past, Easter did strike out for the Graveses' clearing Saturday morning. Every step he took increased his lassitude. He began to feel a shiveriness despite the June sunshine, and every fifty yards he yawned. With about half his journey done, Easter was seized with nausea. Afterward he lay on the ground on the sunny side of a log and shivered. He and malaria were old acquaintances. He lay in the sun until the dumb ague passed; afterward, when his fever mounted, he crawled into the shade and slept. It was noon when he awoke. No visiting that day. He knew he would feel comparatively well until next "chill time": the same hour tomorrow or the next day. But right now it would be well to get on up to the big house and ask Mr. Henry for quinine.

For a week Easter wrestled with malaria. Mr. Henry knew the malady thoroughly and fought it with broken doses of calomel and six ten-grain doses of quinine daily.

By the middle of the following week Easter reported for work. He was still a bit "ganted", but the hoe gang was busy again, and hoeing was child's play to him. Easter finished next the leader, Flint, and, resting on his hoe, turned toward the gang which was strung out for a hundred and fifty yards back along the rows. When you finish your own row it is your privilege to rest until the others "cut out"; but seemly conduct requires that you rest only a moment and then turn back and "he'p out" some slower hand. You pick a friend's row or that of some woman whose favor you seek. It is an orthodox means of sparking as well as a gesture of friendliness. Also it is a point of honor for the leader not to start ahead of the gang but give everyone the chance to displace him each round.

Easter turned to the row next his own, without noting who carried it. As he began chopping, three other men chopped out and hastened to that same row. But Easter was ahead of them, already several yards along the row. Astonished that so many should rush to a row far from the stragglers where most of the women worked, he looked for the first time at the hand he was helping out. It was a girl . . . Dilsie Graves. For the moment Easter lost his awe of her in amazement and admiration. A gal carrying third from lead in a gang of fifty hoes!

When he and Dilsie met, the girl gave him a tiny scared smile. "Thank you," she said, and they walked back to the end together.

"How you been?" Easter ventured.

"I's been well. Dey says you been sick. I hopes you is better."

"I is," Easter mumbled.

It was well that he was better, for that was the fastest day's hoeing Easter ever put in. There were three or four of the best hands who raced him for the privilege of helping out Dilsie. He held his own and thanked his stars that the lead row was carried by Flint Winfrey, the best hoe hand in the bottoms.

"Don't let 'em git de inturn on you East!" Flint would chuckle. " I sho' never saw so many lazy niggers hoein' dis fast befo' in my bawn days. Jes' look at 'em! Dey's kicking up dust like a cow a-runnin' in de road." Flint weighed close to three hundred. He moved his body as clumsily as an erect bear, but in his thick hands an eight-inch hoe became a rapierlike thing.

Easter had time for no more than a quick grin acknowledging Flint's banter. Nathan Grant, Dick Mickings, and others pushed him hard. Once or twice Nathan finished a stroke or two before Easter, and the latter was saved only because his place in the gang was next Dilsie's. By quartering time that afternoon Easter knew he was slipping, though his performance gave no sign of it.

"You is sweatin' too free, East," said Flint. "Hit ain't *dat* hot, boy."

"I kin hol' it."

Easter was in the grip of one of his fits of bullheaded stubbornness, and he would have hoed until he dropped. Dilsie saved him on the very next round. When they met in finishing her row, she said to Easter in a rush, frightened:"You mind he'pin out my mommer 'stead of me? It shames her so to be behin' all de time."

Thereafter Easter helped out Aunt Minnie Graves, and Nathan Grant, swiftest of the remaining rivals, got Dilsie's shy, stimulating thanks.

However much this stung Easter, there was balm in Aunt Minnie's good nature, her appreciation of his help, and her evident liking for him. He refused to consider another palliating circumstance: he would surely have "fallen out" had he kept to the racing clip.

That same afternoon he learned of another of Dilsie's accomplishments. The squad of women had begun to hum. Often an hour of this precedes actual articulate song. Finally, when even the men were leavened with harmony, one of the elder women called across to Dilsie, "Pitch it, gal!" Clear and true Dilsie's voice rose across the perfect accompaniment of their humming:

" 'Oh, Cav-a-reee! Hit's a mighty high mountain!' "

They all swung in with the mellow antiphony:

" 'Look how He died! Look how he died!' "

Then Dilsie's voice, alone as one star at nightfall:

" 'Oh, Cav-a-reee! Hit's a mighty high mountain!' "

And their response, deep from the men, wailing as Rachael's own from the women: " 'Oh, don't you hate dem cruel, cruel Jews!' "

That carried them half down the field.

That night Easter, loose limbed with fatigue and the weakness of his convalescence, sat on his chair under the walnut tree and thought of Dilsie. The day's scenes flickered through his head: Dilsie's hand on her hoe handle; Dilsie's figure with the wind molding her skirts about her. He thought, too, of the girl's popularity with all manner of folks. He had seen men race to "he'p out" gals before . . . but these wenches were of a pattern flamingly different from Dilsie's. For the first time Easter stood Dilsie and Annie C. side by side in his mind and examined them without flinching; he realized with joyous amazement that, after just one day's association with Dilsie, it was Annie C. who was now the tenuous dream. "An' Dilsie, she got good hips an' breastes her own self," said Double-Actin'. "I wasn't stud'in' 'bout dat!" cried Easter, perhaps aloud. "H'm," grunted Double-Actin'. "Dat how come you sees 'em in yo' haid so strong now?"

There was another glorious day with the hoe gang; then a thunderstorm split open the skies to soaking rain, and work ceased. That was on Thursday. Friday morning Easter shouldered his ax and tramped across the bottoms to the Graveses' clearing. Long before he reached it the sound of three busy axes rang in his ears. Aunt Minnie had told him that Peter would be at work in the timber and that he had no one hired to help him. Easter was puzzled, chagrined, at the sound of the axes. His own purposed offer of help would depreciate if two hirelings were already employed, and the hirelings would not be pleased by it.

But he found Peter Graves's helpers were two young men with motives as high perhaps as his own: Nathan Grant and Dick Mickings. Easter had liked these boys before they had raced him in the hoe gang for Dilsie's favor. Since then he had marveled at the faults with which they suddenly bristled. Nathan was plump and aggressive and biggity. Dick smiled to himself all the time, like a possum, making everybody round him uncomfortable.

Easter saw the three men at work in the timber before he himself was seen and he came within an ace of turning back. His feet, more than his volition, carried him toward them.

"Hello, East," called Dick Mickings.

"Good mawnin', Easter," said Peter Graves.

"Whut you doin' ovah dis way?" Nathan Grant asked, pleasantly enough, but with point that stung Easter to the quick.

"I come ovah to he'p Mistuh Peter—same as you."

"He got he'p enough," said Nathan, eyeing the slight-built Easter less pleasantly.

"Dat fo' him to say." Easter knew Nathan could lick him,

but he would hold his ground.

"We all done done 'nuff to earn a cold drink ob water," said Peter Graves. "You-all come up to de house."

The three young men shouldered their axes and followed their host to the pump.

"Dilsie!" called Peter. "Bring us out de drinkin' gourd, gal! Dis rain," he continued conversationally, "done made my turnip groun' just right to turn, but heah I is: Mistuh Keatts a-callin' fo' boards. Mistuh Mitchell a-callin' fo' two hundred posties, an'—"

Here Aunt Minnie came out with the dipper. "Mawnin' Easter. Boy, you got no business ovah heah wid no ax. You been sick."

"I's well now, Mis' Minnie."

"Dat's zackly whut I tole 'im," said Nathan Grant. "A man whut is too light fo' timber work when he is well ain't got to be tryin' it when he under de weather."

"You *is* been sick." Peter Graves turned his kind old eyes on Easter. "I ain't gwinna have you swingin' no ax." Easter protested, begged, became nearly eloquent. Peter and Minnie were too much for him. Finally Peter said, "Effen you is *bleedged* to he'p, you kin ketch up de team an' turn ovah my turnip lan'."

Easter preferred any field work to timbering, but under the circumstances this was defeat; bitterly he hitched Peter's team to the twelve-inch turnplow. Peter and his volunteer woodsmen prepared to return to their work. Minnie Graves stood on the gallery, the gourd dipper in her hand. "Easter, boy," she called. "I'll send Dilsie down wid some fresh water fo' noon."

The turnip patch was stumpy, half-subdued new ground, but Easter never knew the day when plowing was not fun to him. Now, besides this workday satisfaction in it, he could hope for Dilsie's coming. But hours went by and she didn't come. Finally he was sure she wouldn't, and he spoke sharply to the astonished mules.

Easter stopped his team, swung them left in a right-angle turn, and started the new furrow. This brought him facing toward the house, which was invisible behind an angle of a dense thicket of second-growth ash. The mules set their ears forward and slowed up; Easter followed their gaze, knowing a mule is harder to surprise than a watchdog. "Whoa!" said he, and he stopped without knowing why. A moment later

Dilsie came into view round the thicket. She wore a sunbonnet and dress of crisp blue, and she had a tin bucket in her hand.

"Don't you walk 'cross de plowed groun'," Easter called to her. "I'll come git it." He tied the lines to the plow handle, and stalked across his furrows toward Dilsie. "I ain't scairt of her no mo'," he thought. "Didn't I call out loud and tell her not to walk in de plow dirt?" "H'm," said Double-Actin'. "Dat wuz jes' part of yo' plowin' sense. Effen you ain't scairt, how came yo' heart pattin' juber?"

Easter took the tin bucket from Dilsie, and their eyes met in quick frightened acknowledgement.

"You jes' keep de bucket," said Dilsie, beginning to go away. "Effen you don't mind you kin bring it up at noon."

"Dis groun' turns good—after de rain," muttered Easter.

"It sho' do." Dilsie neither stopped nor continued her flight. She merely half turned, pausing like a swamp blackbird alighting on a swaying willow, wings still a-flutter. Easter's craven tongue found no further words. He watched the blue figure recede across the clearing. When it vanished behind the thicket Easter uttered an impatient oath and dashed the untasted water to the ground.

Through that summer and fall Peter Graves had no labor problem. Five or six stalwart young men placed their spare time at his command. Of these Nathan Grant, Dick Mickings, and Easter were most constant. And with the tactlessness of their kind, the old couple showed their strong partiality for Easter. The rivals must have felt it, since it was meant to be felt; Dilsie undoubtedly knew of it for the same reason. Easter sensed it, even through the wistful panics and jealousies of his condition. He could turn the advantage to no use. He worked harder with plow, hoe and cotton sack, winning golden opinions from the old folks, while bolder blades found the opportunities for laughing words with Dilsie which he was too fearful to engineer. And along another march circumstances built a wall against him: none of his serious rivals lived on Mr. Henry's plantation. If he had been thrown with them anywhere but at the Graveses' clearing, Nathan's biggitiness, Dick's possum grin, would have bred trouble, from which, since he had the lasting rage of a man of slow anger, Easter would have emerged perhaps badly beaten but with his emotions unshackled. Not even this doubtful solution was possible. The boys, for all they thought of one another, were average good field boys. They were not bloodthirsty enough to seek out one another for a quarrel, and they met only at Peter Graves's.

Through that winter Easter kept up his own work and managed to help Peter Graves lay in wood, pick cotton, and pull corn. There were beautiful days when no other suitor was there—when Dilsie, her parents, and Easter were snug round the table at noontime. Peter Graves even let Easter build up the fire; and any man who relinquishes that function in his own home expresses complete confidence in the one to whom he grants the privilege. Easter couldn't think of any person in the whole world whom he would want tampering with his own fire; not even Dilsie. God made men to build fires, and He made women to put them out. Those winter days were good days, and the clearing became home to Easter; but he got no mastery over the panic that sparkled through his soul when he and Dilsie were alone together; and in so far as he knew, he drew no step nearer to her.

April came, and there was no change, and Easter was gaunt and lean faced with protracted anxiety and ecstasy. May boomed in, with trees full leafed, the bottoms full of water and roaring with life. It seemed to Easter that folks meeting him on the road grinned a Dick Mickings grin at him. But he couldn't help it; he had lived so long with his cowardice now that he knew which was master. If Dilsie had once made him angry, slighted him, or showed marked favor for a rival, the proper mechanism within Easter might have clicked; but the girl minded her own business and dealt with her suitors with appalling equity.

One day in mid-May he met Annie C. in the big road. Neither of them smiled. Annie spoke first. "East, you gwinna wanna take me to de dance week atter next?"

"Whut dance?"

"You knows. Dey is givin' a frolic at de Tom Brown schoolhouse Thursday atter dis nex' one comin'."

"Gal, I's workin' so hard——"

"I knows whut you workin' at. Dat ain't none of my business. But I's been axed plenty fo' dis frolic——"

"Den go ahaid on! Who's a-stoppin' you?"

"Ain't nobody," said Annie musingly. "East, you ain't got much sense, but I sho' is liked you, boy, you long, rusty, no-

'count blacksnake!"

"Who is no 'count, gal?"

"I's done said." Annie had to smile. She could go just so long without it. "Now git on. You'll see me at de Tom Brown schoolhouse wid some low-down mink whut ain't no better dan you is. An' me, I'll see you a-buggin' yo' eyes at Nathan Grant a-dancin' wid Dilsie Graves."

"Dilsie don't dance! She in de chu'ch."

"Well, git on down de road." Annie smiled mysteriously and walked away. "You know how long it's been gone since you been to see me, East?"

"Two-three weeks. I's been——"

"Six months, East. Effen you wuz a ol' sow, you could a-done drapped two litters ob pigs in dat time!" Screaming with laughter, Annie C. swung away. Easter felt down in himself the full gallantry of her; but there was nothing he could do about it. In five minutes he was absorbed in her news of the party and had forgotten Annie. Would Dilsie go? Would her ma and pa let her go? Could he find courage to ask her to go with him? He side-stepped that last by a craven inspiration: he would not ask Dilsie to go with him; he would ask her parents, of whom he had no fear at all.

Whether he could have carried through even that anemic campaign was in doubt until he met Elsie Lewis in the big road. He would have grumbled a greeting and trudged on, but Elsie stopped him peremptorily.

"Whar you gwine—shovin' along de road wid yo' head down, like a sow in heat? Answer me, boy!"

"Nowhar. Jes' down to George's."

"Nowhar. You is right! East, I couldn't believe it till I seed you. Now I knows you is even a bigger fool dan dey says." Elsie's lean face was kind. She tilted back her head and looked steadily at Easter with her one eye.

"East," she said briskly, "I ain't whut I wuz onct, but I knows wimmins. Now listen at me: you standin' off, an' you standin' on. But a woman want to be stood on all de time. You is he'pin' her paw, an you's he'pin' her maw. But whut you doin' 'bout Dilsie *her own self*? Git busy, boy! Work like a red sow rustlin' overcup acorns in deep leaves! . . . How is crops up dis way?" They exchanged the universal shoptalk of earth. When they parted Elsie called, "Don't forgit whut I done tole you!"

Easter found George Mack sitting on his door block. The

two men walked to the rear to look at the frame of seed sweet potatoes George had bedded.

"I ain't bedded me out none," said Easter. "I'll have to buy me some slips, 'gin time to set 'em out."

"You knows you can git all de slips you need heah. You been busy crossin' de bottoms," laughed George.

"Ev'ybody I sees, dey got to talk 'bout dat same ol' subject."

"Well, don't git mad at *me*, East. Git mad at yo'self. East, is dese damn blacks like Nathan an' Dick makin' you stan' back? You scairt—or is dat gal done tamed you?"

It takes a man to lay a man's wounds wide to the beginnings of healing.

"She done tamed me, George. I can't lay a finger on her. I done lost my rabbit-foot on Dilsie. All I kin do is jes' *want* her like you needs vittles at noon when you ain't et since sunup. My belly's weak right across de middle—jes' de same way."

"East," said George, "you is ridin' fo' yourself a fall effen you don't make 'ase. Too many good mens is around atter dat gal. She sho' a fine 'un too. But, East, 'tain't but one way to git any of 'em. You got to go atter 'em like guttin' a dawg."

That night Easter recalled Elsie's and George's words with the wholesome resentment recipients of good advice should feel.

"One thing"—he was near bitterness as he crawled into bed—"dey is sho' plenty folks to tell you whut to do in dis yearth. An' plenty misery." He believed that summed up and dismissed these two encounters. But back in his rational years he had regarded Elsie and George as experts. Doubtless what they had said worked deep down in him, unknown to himself.

It didn't work hard enough to pump his courage up to the point of asking Dilsie to go to the frolic with him. He put that request to Minnie and Peter. Peter promptly side-stepped, leaving the decision with Minnie.

"Dilsie *wants* to go," said Minnie; "an' two-three done axed her. I didn't want any gal of mine traipsin' round wid jes' *anybody*. But I do want her to have her pleasure. You won't make her dance, will you, East?"

"No ma'am! I sho' won't." He meant it.

"Den you kin take her."

The horrible swiftness, the dazzling sweet torture, of the days and nights which followed! Finally the revolving earth turned up that particular Thursday morning, dealt out a day of May with soft clouds and slow wind, folded the clouds and put them away at sunset, and the—night.

When they set out together through the young night and entered the path which tunneled the purple tree-shadows, Easter turned and saw Minnie Graves silhouetted against the gleam from the open cabin door, and it turned him weak; he longed to run back there, to seek the peace of which that light and Minnie's blurred figure were symbols. But life had him by the hind leg. He walked silently beside the silent girl, too afraid of the inexorable events which lay coiled in the hours ahead. Then, in crossing a foot log, he took her by the hand—for the first time; and the stark business that had laid so heavy upon Easter broke up, leavened with light. But his warmed and glowing panic was still panic, and when he spoke to Dilsie his voice was oppressed.

"Dem stars is a-winkin' like mo' rain."

"Sho' is. An' we don't need none, does we?"

"Sho' don't. We needs choppin' weather."

"Mr. Henry hirin' any choppin'?"

"He ain't dis last past week." Easter was nearly at ease; agriculture was always his tutelary deity.

They came to the next foot log, and the recurrent thrill of touching Dilsie's hand swept Easter to new boldness.

"We been choppin' de lower field. It's so fur a man can't go home at noon to cook himse'f suthin' t'eat."

"Does you fix up a bucket at breakfus time?" Dilsie's own voice was stronger; here was her province.

"Naw. When my belly's full of breakfus seem like I can't bother my haid 'bout lunch—wid it so fur off."

"Umph! Dat jes' like a man!" murmured Dilsie, and then her lips seemed to freeze at her own boldness, her panic swept through herself to Easter, and they walked on in silence. Without words and with no contact Easter knew, with swelling heart, that Dilsie loved him; it made a white light of the gloom under the trees to know it; but the surging lift of this realization brought with it new fears. If he could take Dilsie in his arms he was sure the thin, strong barrier that held them apart would dissolve. But he could no more raise his two arms and put them about this girl than he could have plucked up one of the trees that made a leaky roof against the sprinkle of May stars. Each time their hands touched, whenever they were close together in the narrow path, Easter felt a warm, triumphant flood rise up inside him. And when it rose, and receded and came again, it came stronger and higher. When its heartening current flooded over, beyond his control, he could take this girl—this woman Dilsie—in his arms; but not before then. Shakily his mind compounded his vigorous strength, her slenderness, and the lonely dark into a compelling reason, a divine compulsion; but reason and experience were no helps for him with a woman like Dilsie. The rising of the tide inside him was his only hope, and it receded after each intoxicating surge.

They had traversed the woods; an open plantation road lay before them with the feel of wide fields about. Easter knew every step of the way as well as he knew the gear for his own mule, but tonight it was like walking out into a world remembered from a dream. He lifted his face to the night sky and got strength. Now he knew that the next wave of courage would sweep him out of his shackles. He wanted to sing his triumph as he walked, and he drew close to Dilsie in the path; and she seemed to shrink away, without actually moving off—while leaning closer.

They turned the angle of a dense thicket. Laughter floated through the warm air. A dim light glowed ahead. They had come to the Tom Brown schoolhouse.

It stood at the edge of the fields. It had only one room, with windows three to a side. There were two kerosene ceiling lamps, but only the one farthest from the door was lighted. The rough school benches were lined up along the walls; the tiny rostrum had been converted into a refreshment stand. From Ziek Bell the revelers could buy hard candies at ten cents a pound, a plate or sandwich of barbecued pork, coffee hot but tenuous, and lemonade mixed in a wooden tub.

Easter and Dilsie were early, and with others they sat uneasily on the benches, waiting until numbers gave them courage to be gay. In the field, at work, that faculty never failed them. Stalking fun purposefully, focusing gaiety in time and space, and going at it like laying rails require more practice than they could ever acquire. For that reason parties were oftener matters of excitement, hilarity and brawl than events of carefree pleasure. But sitting here in the dim schoolhouse, Easter could not imagine any event more exhilarating. His eyes shone; he felt his lips stiff with involuntary smiling. He felt as though he had taken three fingers of whiskey.

Later, when others had arrived and noise had warmed them, when they had begun to stamp and clap rhythmically, and the more sinful felt their feet tingling, Easter saw Dick Mickings come in with Annie C. Behind them, towering above the crowd, was Nathan Grant.

The clapping and stamping settled into an even, compelling roar. Now and then a woman's voice keened an excited "E-e-e-e Yah! E-e-e-e Yah!" in time to the jungle beat of it. It was not gay—it was as deadly solemn as lust itself.

"Lemme at dat flo'!" yelled Hezekiah.

They pressed back, walling an oval opening with their heated bodies, and in this space Hezekiah capered. John Mack followed, then George, Nathan and half a dozen others. Only sinners will dance, and this being a respectable party no women joined in; but the boldest of them clapped and stamped, and when the rhythm drummed irresistible compulsion, they shouted an excited accompaniment to the clapping.

The first mechanical austerities of the dance flowed off and into the grace of primitive abandon. They leaped and whirled, they shuffled and swayed, they wiggled out the full repertory of sound, earthy obscenities, interpreting that universal essence of rhythm as it has shaken the cypresses of Mylitta's groves and the spotted canvas of revival tents. Easter did not dance; he was too clumsy, and tonight he would have been too self-conscious. He clapped and stamped with glowing eyes. Sweat stood on his forehead. The women shrieked their high-pitched triple "E-e-e-e Yah!" and the schoolhouse quivered. Ziek Bell suddenly struck the bottom of a dishpan with his huge iron spoon.

"Time t'eat! Time t'eat!" he bawled.

The dancers stood, the clapping died a fluttering death like the stopping of a furious machine, the crowd broke, and the first gay shouts and genuine laughter of the evening swept through it.

Ziek Bell's hospitality was mercenary but hearty. Opulent couples crowded up to his table. Thoughtful men fingered through their jumper pockets under the intent, encouraging smiles of their womenfolk.

Easter led Dilsie to Ziek Bell's table as soon as he had located the errant six bits among his pockets. Dilsie would have taken only coffee, but Easter pressed a sandwich and lemonade upon her; he also bought a bag of hard candy for them to eat on the way home. The other women greeted Dilsie pleasantly—until their men began offering to buy things for her.

"I's buyin' for Dilsie," Easter stated boldly, and they desisted. The code was simple and plain. But this was a challenge Easter's rivals could not ignore completely.

"I b'lieves I'll take Dilsie home my ownself," said Nathan Grant genially. "I kin jes' tuck her under one arm an' East under de yuther."

"You can't make no crop wid one arm," retorted John Mack loyally; "an' you'd be sho' to git *one* of 'em gnawed off."

When the laughter eased up, Dick Mickings said, smiling his dead-possum smile, "Whut effen Brother Nathan an' me double-teams an' *bofe* takes her home? Would he gnaw us bofe, Brother Johnnie?"

"Naw! East is got good toofs, but dey couldn't stan' up to dat."

The crowd howled, Nathan and Dick with the rest. They were fairly routed; they knew, besides, that Easter was fully backed by his friends and by the approval of Dilsie's parents.

"Tell you whut us *kin* do!" cried George Mack. "All de mens heah kin make a congregation an' walk home wid Dilsie an' East—t'keep de snakes off."

"Sho'!" they shouted, and John added good-naturedly, "East, he kinda timid anyhow."

"It ain't only snakes he's scairt of—round wimmins," laughed Hezekiah Jones.

Easter's lips rolled out and his eyes blazed. The jest had been harmless in the hands of his two rivals. It was rapidly becoming fatal now that his friends had taken it up: there were so many of them.

"Hot dawg! Dats de thing!" said Hezekiah. "East can't do nuthin' wid *all* of us!" As the effects registered on Easter the others increased their efforts. George Mack silenced them to explain more fully the perfections of the scheme. "Effen jes' *some* of us tries it, East mout kill us dead. But effen *all* of us——"

They cut him short with shouts of acquiescence. The party had focus now, and a butt whom everyone liked and nobody feared. The ring formed again, the dance thundered into full fury. But now it was lightsome. The dancers would shout, "Who gwinna take her home, Lawd, who gwinna take her home?" And the triple response came spontaneously, shouted to the accompaniment of redoubled clapping and stamping:"*I* is! *I* is! *I* is!"

Easter looked at Dilsie. She was frightened and she tried to smile back at him. Suddenly a red wave inside Easter rose up behind his eyeballs, and he turned and plowed his way to the door.

The old Tom Brown house which had stood a hundred yards from the school, had been destroyed by fire years before. Easter knew he could find brickbats on the house site and he steered for the weedy ruins like a serpent for its hole. Where the old blacksmith had stood he saw the spread fingers of a ruined wagon wheel. The tire and felloe were gone. He laid hold of one of the spokes and wrenched it from its mortise in the hub. The spoke was sound oak, twenty inches long, tapered, and had the perfect balance of a war mace. It could crack a man's skull like a walnut, but it was as handy as a rapier.

Without haste, because the full flavor of his dish of martyrdom lay before him with no check and hindrance of sanity, Easter turned and stalked back toward the lighted door. "Whut you up to, East?" demanded a voice at his shoulder.

"Watch an' see."

"Wait, East!" Easter had not even recognized George Mack.

"I ain't waitin'!"

"Stop, you damn fool,—listen! I wants t'help you."

"Don't need none."

"You'll git kilt fo' nuthin! Some of dem boys is got guns on 'em."

"I'll gun 'em!"

George sprang from behind and pinned Easter's arms to his sides. "I wants to *he'p* you, you mule-headed fool! Listen...."

They wrestled, despite George's advantage of hold and greater strength, Easter's madness would have prevailed if George had not pleaded and cursed.

"I wants to he'p! Listen, East: I knows how we kin do it!"

"Talk in a hurry den."

Easter rested, panting. George did not relax his grip.

"East, effen you starts a rookus dey'll lay you out——"

"I don't care!"

"—an' effen dey don't, somebody 'll pull a knife or a gun——"

"I don't care!"

"You *will* care—wid a bullet in yo' guts! Lemme tell you whut us kin do——"

"I ain't gwinna leave. I's gwinna——"

"All right! All right, boy! But listen at me *furst.*"

"Talk fast, George."

"I's got my gun on me. You stan' by de do'. I'll shoot out de light through one of dem back windows. Dese damn blacks'll run. I knows 'em! Dey'll run. You stan' at de do'. 'Tain't but one do', and de windows is nailed shut. When dey comes out——"

"Come on!"

"Wait!" George released Easter now, sure of him. "Be sho' you lays yo' mark on all de men—not 'scusin' Nathan an' Dick."

"Come on!"

"Wait, fool! Now listen at me *good:* Effen you jes' scares a nigger or jes' lashes him, he mout bust you from behin' a bush someday. But effen you makes yo' mark on him wid suthin' like a wagon spoke, he know who de boss is. Now git to de do'. Don't show yourself till dey starts out. Dey'll run! I knows dese damn blacks."

George vanished and Easter moved to the door. He spat generously into his palm and sunk his fingers into the wagon spoke.

Almost at once George fired through the rear window nearest the lamp, and the party exploded with the noise and velocity of shrapnel. It took the third shot to fetch the lamp and bring it crashing down. By that time the door was vomiting a screaming tangle of bodies, and Easter's right arm rose and fell with mechanical regularity.

Now and again he recognized a friend or a woman in the struggling mass and tried to hold his hand with an effort that nearly stood him on his head. Mercy was impossible; too many got by unmarked. He abandoned discrimination and went to work with grim thoroughness. Even when the frame of the glutted door fell down among them he missed no lick, and the clear crack of oak on skull beat on. Five or six lay on

155

the ground, heaped up. Those inside dived over the rampart of bodies. While fresh victims still fell, some of the first revived enough to stagger up, and these followed the impulse to run which had been interrupted by Easter's wagon spoke. When the supply slackened, George's pistol roared again, and stragglers who had huddled inside plunged out, often cheating Easter by tripping on the wrecked doorframe and stunning themselves on the ground.

Finally after a quick eternity of bliss Easter found no fugitives under his club. The last of the fallen had made off. George's pistol shots could evict no more. Only the shrieks of the women responded. They had not run with the men. Easter could see them in his mind's eye: a pile of them, hugging one another, burrowing under one another's bodies, kicking and scratching to crawl under, to put bodies between their own bodies and the terror—like a clot of lively fishing worms in a tin can.

George came to the door. "Heah—dese is matches. Go in an' git her."

Easter snatched the matches. He was already going in.

He dropped the wagon spoke and cupped his hands round a lighted match. The women had crammed themselves under benches and in corners. A dozen were stuffed like tattered, shameless rag dolls under the teacher's table on the little rostrum. Their struggles had spilled Ziek Bell's edibles over the floor. Wild eyes caught the gleam of Easter's match.

"I wants Dilsie!" Easter called. His match flared and died, and while he lighted another he wondered how he could ever have been afraid of that girl. "Dilsie!" he called, and the next match blazed up.

"I's comin'," she quavered.

Easter blew out his match. He did not wish to see her untangle herself from the mass of frightened flesh. He walked to the door and stood just outside in the starlight. When the girl came out to him he curved his right arm round her shoulders and led her through the fields toward the level shadow that marked the edge of the woods.

"My first wife," said Easter, "lemme go hongry in de field. Whut do you think of a woman like dat?"

"She ain't hardly no woman—she jes' a mess!"

"Effen a man make de money an' bring home de rations of a Sadday, he got a right to find cooked grub in de house, come time t'eat."

156

"He sho' is."

"An'—Dilsie"—Easter made the name precious in the saying—"I wants me some chullens."

"Don't—don't *ev'body* want 'em, Easter?"

It was enough now to walk under the trees side by side. When they came to the edge of the Graveses' clearing, Easter drew Dilsie off the path toward a new, clean log. "Not *on* it!" he breathed when, half hesitating, she sat down upon it. "We kin sit on de groun' an' lean our backs again' de log." He drew her down beside him on the short grass, which was cool with dew.

The stars had steadied to the unshaken air of deep night, and quiet lay on the wide bottom lands. A cock crowed, and the sound came to them as strained silver through the miles of sweet air.

"Don't!—not t'night, Easter!" Dilsie murmured, but she clung the closer as his arms, suddenly harsh and hurried with his long hunger for her, bent her down.

LOCUST

Mary Elsie Robertson

IT WAS THURSDAY and so they had to walk together—to Edna Lynn's and Carl Roger's house this week—and it was May and already hot so that their book-satchels bent around their thighs like so many dead fish and left damp, hot places on their skirts, their jeans' legs. Murphie walked a half step behind, stepping on all the cracks; she had her head down and so when Edna Lynn suddenly stopped walking and started hopping around on one foot with one finger in the heel of her other shoe, Murphie butted her head into the small of Edna Lynn's back and sent her hopping ahead even faster, three dainty little hops like a dancer.

"My goodness," Edna Lynn said, "my goodness, don't you ever look where you're going?" But then she stood still on one leg with her other foot dangling down where her finger crooked inside the heel as though she had forgotten it. She looked out toward the feed mill with a faint, almost blissful smile on her face. There wasn't anything to see at the feed mill except a thin column of chaff blowing straight up in the air and then curling lazily off to the north. "I have such trouble with my shoes," Edna Lynn said, graciously letting them in on her train of thought. "My feet are so narrow I have a terrible time getting shoes that fit. I don't ever get any that really fit." She had long pale yellow curls that hung down to her shoulders like slender, rather sickly fingers, and a dimple like the dent a baby's finger might make right in the center of her chin.

"You have big feet," Carl Roger said, jealous. "My feet are ever so much littler." He put out one foot and arched it as though he were going to rise up on the tips of his toes.

"You're three years younger than I am," Edna Lynn said, walking on primly as though she thought someone was watching her. "You're a boy and your feet will get real big. They'll get so big you probably can't even get shoes to go on them and have to go barefooted half your life."

"They won't either done it," Carl Roger said, enraged. He looked down at his feet as he walked and he walked on his toes so that it was hard to tell if his heels even touched the ground at all.

"Your feet will get big too," Edna Lynn said to Murphie without looking around.

"I don't care if they do," Murphie said. "If they want to get big just let them."

Mary Catherine was already in the yard when they got there. She went to the parochial school and so had come through town. She had a honeydew ice-cream cone and yellow drops were falling out of the tip and the cone was all gummy there where she had sucked on it. They watched her take the first leisurely, crunching bite out of the cone. She chewed it up slowly and let it slide down her throat—a faraway look in her eyes. She took another bite before she held it out to them. "You can have a bite," she said. Murphie and Edna Lynn shook their heads, but Carl Roger stuck out his head and took a big bite on the opposite side from where Mary Catherine had been eating—such a hard bite that one whole side of the cone tore away leaving the little pat of ice cream on the inside exposed. "He tore it all up," Mary Catherine wailed, looking at the wreck of the cone.

"I'll tell Mother on you," Edna Lynn said. "You're just a bad old greedy boy."

Carl Roger, choking on the cone, with the tears coming in his eyes, didn't answer.

"She offered it," Murphie said unexpectedly. "He just took one bite."

Carl Roger ran up the steps into the house. "I'm not an old boy," he said, from just inside the screen.

"What are you then, a girl?" Edna Lynn said.

"I could be if I wanted to," he said mysteriously.

"How?"

But Carl Roger, running down the hallway, dim through

the screen like the ghost of a boy, didn't divulge that secret.

They all followed him into the house, Mary Catherine licking her sticky fingers with her tongue, arched and curled up at the tip like the petal of a lily. They could hear the soft rise and fall of their mothers' voices from the living room at the left of the hallway—telling, they wondered, what stories, what secrets? The faint click of china cups on china saucers—the rich smell of coffee and, like an undercurrent running through all of it, the smell of late lilac and spicecake. They hesitated a second before opening the door, feeling the somehow mysterious and exciting atmosphere of the room—an atmosphere rich and moist and sweet like the center of a just-opened flower.

They pushed open the door and the atmosphere in the room was suspended, with all the heads turned in their direction, and then it changed suddenly so that the other, secret, atmosphere might never have been. "The children," someone said. "Here are the children." And the older women who no longer had children of their own, or the old maids who never had any, clicked their tongues and waited for an opportunity to ask them how school was, for a chance to say, "Mary Catherine, dear, your sash is untied behind." Their own mothers looked up from their sewing and held out one arm proudly to their daughters, smiling at them in a way they never smiled at them unless there was someone else to watch. Mary Catherine's mother, carried away by the moment, put her arm around her daughter's plump middle and kissed her round red cheek—that had the same smoothness as a winesap apple—with a little smack that carried all over the room. The women smiled, remote smiles, behind their glasses, their crocheting needles.

"I got an A in spelling," Edna Lynn said, showing off. "And Mother, these old shoes are too big. They keep falling off. I want some straw ones with flowers on the toes like Annabelle has." Annabelle lived next door and was sixteen years old.

"Just listen to that," the women said. "You're going to have a grown-up daughter on your hands pretty soon, Janet. Ten years old and already a little lady." They beamed at Edna Lynn and her mother tried to look modest.

"Oh, they do grow up fast," she said. "She'll be grown up and with babies of her own before I know it." Edna Lynn stood looking down at the floor, smiling, as though she already saw those babies crawling over the carpet.

Murphie watched Carl Roger come into the room with his strange bouncing walk, his nose wrinkled up so she knew he was smelling the coffee and the cake and the furniture polish and lilacs—he was crazy about smells. She had taken off her book-satchel and she swung it against her mother's chair and it hit with soft little thumps. "What did you do today?" her mother asked her, in a lull in the conversation, and she tried to think of something. The day had already fallen back into a dim hole somewhere.

"I was the best in the class in reading," she finally said, bored. She was always first. "A hundred in arithmetic. And I wrestled with John Berry at recess," she said in a burst of inspiration. "I won. I held him down until they counted ten." The women laughed softly, a little embarrassed.

"Oh, she's only nine," they said, as though to comfort her mother. "In another year she'll be wanting fancy clothes too. Don't you worry about her a minute," they added, but their voices didn't sound very reassuring. Murphie's mother sat straight and looked back at them as though she didn't want any comforting. "She's the smartest one in her class," she said. But the other women only smiled back, indulgent. Murphie stood kicking at one of the roses in the carpet with the toe of her shoe.

"Oh, they must try on their dresses," Mrs. McGee said excitedly, from one corner of the room, looking out from the great mass of afghan that covered her lap and the back of her chair like the carefully draped body of a dead animal. She had been doing nothing but crocheting afghans for the last six months.

"Oh, yes," everyone else said. "Let's see what they will look like." And Murphie's and Edna Lynn's mothers bit off the thread where they were sewing and held up two gold-colored dresses, without hems and with the sleeves basted in, and shook them out. They were just alike except that Edna Lynn's had two flowers embroidered in the front—there was going to be a row all the way across but they weren't finished yet. Murphie had refused to have flowers.

Edna Lynn and Murphie took their skirts and blouses off and stood in their straight petticoats, their shoes looking much too big and heavy for their thin bodies. Edna Lynn lifted her arms straight out from her sides and whirled around on her toes, bobbing up and down in one place—right in the middle of a flat rose with purple leaves. Murphie stood straight, with her arms down stiffly at her sides, like someone waiting for a cold shower to touch him.

"How cute they look," the women said when the dresses had finally been eased over their heads. "How sweet. But Murphie, dear, you should let your mother put flowers on yours."

"No," Murphie said.

"They look ugly," Carl Roger said, jealous, curled up on the arm of his mother's chair.

"Of course you'd think so," Mrs. McGee said. "You're a little boy. Of course you don't see anything to a dress."

But Carl Roger only stuck out his bottom lip and didn't answer.

"I think Murphie looks funny," Mary Catherine said. "Her arms hang out."

"Why, she looks nice," the women said quickly. "She looks like a regular little lady."

"They both look awful," Carl Roger said. But no one answered him this time.

Finally they were allowed to leave and they remembered to let the door go to softly behind them—Edna Lynn's mother calling behind them that there was cake and milk in the kitchen for them.

"But let's don't eat it yet," Edna Lynn said. "Let's save it for a while and have a tea party. We can dress up for it."

"We always dress up," Murphie complained. "Every single time we dress up and play movie stars."

"But that's more fun than anything," Mary Catherine said.

"If you don't want to do that, you can go out and climb trees with Carl Roger or something," Edna Lynn said.

"I'm going to dress up," Carl Roger said. "I don't want to climb any old trees."

They went up the stairs Indian file, Murphie trailing along behind, poking her hands through the slats of the railing as she walked. They went to the storage room where there were winter clothes packed away and odd pieces of furniture and a clarinet belonging to Edna Lynn's big sister who was away at college and old clothes they had packed in a trunk waiting for somebody to burn out or for the Methodist church to have a rummage sale.

"I get the pink evening dress," Mary Catherine said. Edna Lynn opened her mouth to protest—Mary Catherine always got the pink evening dress—but she knew she couldn't say anything because Mary Catherine was visiting at her house.

"It doesn't become you," she finally said. "You're too fat for it." But Mary Catherine ignored her until she had pulled the dress over her head and stood holding up the front under her armpits with both hands. "You're too skinny," she said then. "You're just going to make a beanpole. I'm going to have a real good figure. My mother says so."

"Oh, your mother says, your mother says," Carl Roger sang in a high, whining voice. "You're always saying what your mother says."

"I don't care," Mary Catherine said. "My mother knows everything. Which is more than I could say for some people's mothers." She said the last with great satisfaction—it had the rhythm of something she'd heard before.

"Marecatherine's mother says, Marecatherine's mother says," Carl Roger went on singing, up and down, like a droning little wasp.

She slapped at him but he danced away—he wouldn't ever fight. He reached over in the trunk and pawed through the clothes—there was a particular thing he was looking for.

Edna Lynn had gotten the second-best dress—the filmy black one with silver sequins across the front. It had long sleeves so she had to hold her arms up when she wore it, and her arms looked strange, thin and white, coming out of the soft mass of material.

"You've got to put on something too," Edna Lynn said, looking over at Murphie. She felt vaguely insulted that Murphie hadn't put on anything yet—she just sat cross-legged on the floor fingering notes on the clarinet, a deep, intent stare on her face as though she were looking at something inside her head.

"You hadn't got anything I want to dress up in," she said. She'd gone all the way through the clothes several times before, hoping there might be a soldier suit or something, but the only men's clothes in the whole trunk were a pair of socks and a wine-colored tie with a tan horse's head painted on it.

She got up and put on the first dress her hand touched, which happened to be a faded blue one with a little round collar that turned up, and then she put on the tie and the socks—the socks reached almost to her knees, the empty bulges of the heels loose around her ankles.

Carl Roger had found what he was looking for—a blouse that pulled low over the shoulders with cutwork on the front, and a red skirt with a fringe around the bottom. Mary Catherine and Edna Lynn had gotten out the box of stub ends of lipsticks, powder boxes, mascara, and they put two crooked lines of red across their mouths and little daubs of green in the corners of their eyes, but Carl Roger was very careful and put just a little rose-colored lipstick on his mouth, squatting down over the cracked mirror, wrapping his skinny fingers tight around his wrist to hold it steady.

"Look at Carl Roger," Mary Catherine said. "He looks pretty."

He stood up and turned around so they could get a good look at him. He held the skirt up in both hands as though he were dancing some kind of old-fashioned dance. "My dear," he said, and waited for more words to come to him but they didn't. "My dear," he said again, sticking his nose up in the air and wrinkling it. "My dear, my dear."

"He's a better-looking girl than either one of you," Murphie said. She stood up and put the clarinet back in its faded green velvet case. She started slinging her arms around and around as though she were warming up to do something, and then, as though her whirling arms had reached the right speed, had lifted her to a certain peak, she ran out of the room and down the stairs, making a whirring noise in her throat. The others ran after her, walking all over the bottoms of their dresses, but she didn't stop until she was outside and up in the maple tree as far as she could go—the smooth branches like a warm body under her, the leaves half grown and a tender yellowish green. She sat high above the others, not even looking down at them, and when the wind made the branches sway she felt a happiness tight inside her—she took off her shoes and the men's socks and then her own socks and dropped them, one at a time, down into the grass where the shoes bounced, twice, the others looking up at her with still faces as though they were watching some animal that they didn't think very much of. And then they ignored her completely and began having a party, walking around on the grass holding their skirts up with one hand and an imaginary cigarette in the other. Murphie didn't even bother to look down at them—she looked out even beyond the town where there were blue mountains against the pale-blue sky, and no telling what beyond them.

But after a while she got tired of being up in the tree by herself and she looked down at the others right below her—squatted around an imaginary table drinking imaginary coffee and eating imaginary cake. "This is the most delicious cake," Mary Catherine said. "I do wonder if you could loan me the recipe."

Murphie felt a sudden urge to jump right down in the middle of them and squash them all down in the ground—they would go down just like nails in a board so there was just the shiny tops of their heads showing, and then she'd put dirt on top of them and that would be that. She laughed to herself, showing her white, wide-gapped teeth. And then she swung down from the tree, holding the limb she had been sitting on between her hands and swinging her body down so that her feet were almost in their faces. They jumped back out of the way, rolling on the grass, and she jumped down right in the middle, her feet stinging but she standing right up and pretending it hadn't hurt at all. Mary Catherine let out a surprised squeak and began bawling. "She jumped right on me," she said. "Right on top of me."

"I did not," Murphie said. "I didn't touch you." She was always wary of Mary Catherine because she got hurt over nothing at all and then she would cry and her mother would come hurrying out, giving them all poisonous looks.

Mary Catherine still lay in the grass with the long pink dress bundled and twisted around her like a pink mummy cloth—big tears rolling out of her wide-open eyes and becoming absorbed in the shiny glaze of tears that covered her cheeks.

Murphie backed up to the maple tree and then she called the others. "Come here," she said. "There's the funniest-looking bug thing." But they wouldn't come—they thought she was only trying to get Mary Catherine interested in something so she would be quiet. Mary Catherine thought so too and she let out another thin wail, proving that she really was hurt—that she wouldn't be diverted from her hurt by anything as unexciting as a funny bug.

"No, it really is funny," Murphie insisted. "It looks like a big eye." She was squatted down at the foot of the maple tree looking at something at nose level.

Carl Roger was the first to give in—he crawled over to her and looked and didn't say anything for a few seconds, though he knew the others were waiting for him to. "It's splitting out of its old shell," he said finally. "It's going to come out that place in its back." Edna Lynn and Mary Catherine came too then, Mary Catherine pulling her dress around on her body—the front had gotten pulled to the back. They all squatted around in a semicircle in front of the place where a locust had fastened its old shell and was now splitting out of it—the eyes of the old shell already dead, the eyes having been pulled back inside the shell. There was a wide split down the back where the new body bulged like a pink, blind eye—they could see it pulsating.

"What will he look like when he gets out?" Edna Lynn asked. But none of them knew. They sat and watched until their feet went to sleep and began stinging from sitting in one place too long.

Carl Roger jumped up suddenly. "I'm going to eat," he said, and ran in the back door—the others following more slowly. They let him cut the pieces of cake—he was more careful than any of the rest of them and he measured and poked at the cake with the long butcher knife, his turned-up, soft nose almost touching the cake. He passed around the plates with a wedge of cake precisely in the middle—they all looked furtively, jealously, at the pieces of cake on either side of them.

"My piece isn't as big as Edna Lynn's," Mary Catherine said, her fat chin making a round smooth roll underneath like a Vienna sausage every time she bobbed her head to compare the two pieces.

"You old stuffpot," Edna Lynn said, enraged, feeling that her whole family was being attacked. "You're so big now you can't get all your stomach under the table."

Carl Roger stood up and leaned over, propping himself on one elbow on the table, and put his finger against the side of Mary Catherine's piece of cake, the icing clinging to his finger when he took it away, up to the second knuckle. Then he put the finger against Edna Lynn's piece. He licked the icing from the finger in one long sweep of his tongue, contemplatively, making delicate measurements inside his head.

"See there?" Edna Lynn said. "Just the same, you old pig." But at that moment Carl Roger reached out two fingers like a crawdad's pincer and tore off a piece of Edna Lynn's cake and dropped it onto Mary Catherine's plate. Mary Catherine popped the piece in her mouth and swallowed it like a frog swallowing a gnat, before she even took time to laugh at Edna Lynn.

"I hope you choke," Edna Lynn said. "And you too," she added, looking at Carl Roger, "you sissy old outfit."

Carl Roger didn't pay any attention. He sat with his knees almost under his armpits making two little bulges in the full skirt that fell in a deep crease between his legs. The blouse had fallen off one of his shoulders down to the elbow and it gave him a half-naked, coy look.

They put bites of cake in their mouths with their fingers and washed them down with milk, looking at each other over the rims of their milk glasses furtively, like squirrels, without saying anything.

Mary Catherine finished first and suddenly, for no reason at all, she reached out and pushed Carl Roger half off his chair. He looked at her surprised, his mouth half open so they could see the last bite of cake in his mouth. And then Edna Lynn pushed him from the other side, and he sat slapping his hands at them like a well-dressed lady trying to keep a dog from jumping against her. But it was Murphie who picked up her fork and spoon and rapped them on Edna Lynn's and Mary Catherine's heads, hard, so that they yelled and jumped to their feet.

Carl Roger and Murphie were already ahead of the others, running into the hallway and slamming the door in Edna Lynn's face and turning the key in the lock. They ran up the stairs, feeling giggles so tight in their chests that it hurt. At the top they couldn't think where to go—there were no good hiding places in the bedrooms and they imagined Edna Lynn already at the front door. In desperation they ran into the upstairs hallway again and Carl Roger opened a door and they slipped inside without looking behind them.

The door closed but there was no lock and they stood in the dark-brown darkness that seemed almost to pulsate like the beating of their hearts. There was a musty, slightly soured smell around them, but it was only after they stepped backward from the door, their eyes black and blind like a rabbit's in its burrow, that they fell into the pile of dirty clothes. They wriggled down into the pile so that they could see out only down a little tunnel—like looking down the length of a sleeve—at the end of the tunnel they could see the white shape of the keyhole.

They squatted with their arms and thighs pressed together so that they were sticky and hot—so close that they could sense the trembling in the bottom of each other's stomach. The smell of their damp bodies and the dirty clothes around them mixed together so that it was the ripe, near-decaying smell of human flesh, the undertone of smell that lingers in a steamy bathroom.

"They won't find us here," Carl Roger whispered, and they giggled, a conspiratorial giggle, as though they were one child. They could hear Edna Lynn and Mary Catherine come pounding up the stairs, and they squeezed even tighter together, holding their breaths and then gulping to keep from giggling.

"They aren't here," Edna Lynn yelled from one of the bedrooms. "Not here."

Murphie could hear them on the landing then, walking around, not sure whether to leave or not. But at the last minute, when Mary Catherine had already started down the stairs, Edna Lynn walked down the hallway—moving even deeper in the clothes they could see the white of the keyhole go dark—and then she opened the closet door and the white light poured through their tunnel and they were caught. They struggled to stand up but Edna Lynn had already jumped on top of the clothes.

"What'll we do to them?" Edna Lynn asked.

"I don't know." Mary Catherine spoke from the doorway.

Murphie and Carl Roger stood, giggling, their feet still tangled in pillowcases.

"Make Carl Roger kiss Murphie," Mary Catherine said.

"I don't care," Carl Roger said, turning betrayer. "But you'll have to hold Murphie."

Murphie looked at him amazed. "Old two-face," she said. "You always have to get on the right side. You're not about to kiss me." And then she ran away from them and down the stairs and was at the end of the yard before the others came outside.

They didn't chase her. They were sick of the game and anyway she was too fast for them. They squatted around the base of the maple tree and Murphie could hear them talking. "He's almost out," Mary Cathrine said excitedly. "Look at him."

Murphie didn't have any intention of joining them and yet she was tired of standing there by herself. There wasn't anything to do except to pretend she was looking at something in the tree above her. A grasshopper was making a crunching noise as though he were biting into a metal plate; time passed very slowly.

Finally she walked across the yard, pretending she was looking at something on the next lawn. But the others weren't watching her anyway. She had to kneel behind Carl Roger and look over his shoulder.

The locust had just gotten his feet uncurled and he gripped the old shell with them and pulled the back part of his body out so that he was all free, and then he was curling and uncurling his legs. "Oh," they breathed. "Isn't he pretty!"

He was pink and gray and clear-looking, almost translucent, and as he still sat curling and uncurling his legs he began to open the wings that had been glued to his sides. They were transparent, and when he had opened them fully the sunlight caught in them like a rainbow. "He's so beautiful," Edna Lynn said. They were all almost holding their breath, feeling the pressure to say something, to do something, to show how they felt.

"He's gorgeous," Mary Catherine said. "He's all grown up," she added in a burst of inspiration.

The others let out their breath. "Yes," they said, "he's all grown up," feeling relieved as though this were the answer to the mystery.

The locust sat slowly waving his wings, letting them harden in the air. And then, effortlessly, with a sort of joy, he let the air pick him up and he flew slowly out into the sunlight and then, as though he knew just where he was going, he flew high up in the air and over the top of the house so they couldn't see him any longer.

Carl Roger and Edna Lynn and Mary Catherine followed him out in the sunlight, waving their arms up and down and jumping every once in a while as though they wished the air would pick them up too.

Murphie sat still beside the tree, picking the old locust shell off where it clung with its dead feet. She sat pulling apart the little shell with her fingers, pinching off bits with her sharp fingernails. "He won't live any time," she said suddenly, with satisfaction. "He'll be dead in a few days." But the others, running out in the light, flapping their arms up and down as if they wanted to fly, caught up in some feeling of ecstasy, didn't answer.

"He was so lovely," they said. "Did you see his wings?"

This story originally appeared in Jordan's Stormy Banks and Other Stories *(New York: Atheneum Publishers, 1971) and is reprinted with permission of the author.*

THE BAPTISM

Mary Elsie Robertson

THEY GOT THE CARD on Wednesday and on Thursday Authur drove the children down and left them, carrying a little cardboard suitcase that looked like doll clothes had come in it. He'd been too busy to pay any attention to them and that was what they'd packed in. He only stayed a few minutes, and after absent-mindedly kissing his sisters and his children he'd gotten back in the car, mumbling something about he'd come and get them, in a day or two or so, as soon as Norma was better. And then he drove away again, leaving the children in a wilted little row in the driveway. They had never been left at their aunts' house alone before. Sara Bernice felt sorry for them; they looked like orphans. Patrick's pants were buttoned up all wrong, one leg hung down further than the other, and Lorena's hair looked prickly where bits of it had started slipping out of the braids. Even John Robert needed a haircut; his hair was nearly in his eyes and he blew up on it every once in a while, making it stand in a peak on his forehead.

Sara Bernice and Minnie stood behind them, not knowing what to say, and nobody moved at all until Authur's green car turned a corner two blocks away and they couldn't see it any longer. Then they went in the house, the children sitting in a stiff row on the divan, running their fingers around the flower designs behind them and between their legs.

Minnie didn't seem bothered at all. She sat very straight and waved a palm fan in front of her face and looked at the children. "You're going to get very hot sitting on that divan," she said finally. "It's got wool in it."

But they didn't look up at all. They sat perfectly still except for their fingers moving slowly in crooked little paths over the divan, tracing the design of a pale-green or blue flower.

Sara Bernice sat turning her rings around and around on her fingers. She remembered, like a dank breath of air blowing suddenly from somewhere, how the house had looked to her when she was a child—big and dim with marble-topped tables with claw legs that were particularly horrible somehow, especially at dusk when they were in the shadows. And the smell of flowers from her mother's room. The smell, when she thought about it, still seemed to linger in the corners of the house, a stale, rotten smell, like unwashed vases. She knew that she and Minnie must look frightening—old and thin and gray, sitting on the edges of their chairs like two old half-asleep vultures.

They didn't cry though, not even Patrick who was only four. And Sara Bernice was proud of that; but Authur hadn't cried either that time Minnie pushed him in a wet cowpile when they were visiting Uncle Leo. It had been against all the rules to cry.

She got up quite abruptly without even looking over at Minnie. "We've got some fresh cookies in the kitchen," she said, standing stiffly by her chair as though she were issuing a formal invitation. They dutifully slid off the divan and followed her in a little string, still not looking up.

"You'll spoil their suppers," Minnie said, still waving the fan.

But Sara Bernice went right ahead. She could be stubborn when she wanted to. And in the kitchen it was nicer. The sun came in the big west windows, and the jar of green-and-red pickled peppers on the table caught the light, really very bright. She set the plate of cookies down with quite a defiant thump. They reached out and politely took only one apiece, nibbling carefully around the edges, around and around, like mice.

The cat came to the door then, the gray-striped one that Sara Bernice let in the house furtively at night sometimes when she went in the kitchen in her gown to take her vitamin pills. She would open the door ever so quietly and it would come in, putting its gray paws down cockily on the floor. Then it would sit on its haunches, moving its front paws up and down as though it were beating up a feather pillow, and look up at her through its slits of eyes, bulging just a little with greed. And after she fed it, it would raise its tail straight behind it and walk to the door, waiting to be let out. She felt hurt sometimes that it was so anxious to get out again. But it had a strange, mysterious life of its own, paths among the shrubbery to walk and hollow places in the grass to take naps in, and other cats to meet on full-moonlit nights. Shadowy silver and white and yellow cats. Moving slowly around each other in a sort of ritual, their eyes very big and very green in the moonlight.

Of course the children had to let the cat in and pet it and put it over their shoulders. "We have two cats at home," Lorena said suddenly. "They're John Robert's and mine."

"Doesn't Patrick have one?" Sara Bernice asked.

"No," Lorena said shortly. "He's too little. Just John Robert and me."

Patrick was sitting on the floor with his legs straight out in front of him, softly knocking his shoes together; he didn't look up.

That night the children only played with their food. "I told you you'd spoil their suppers," Minnie said, pleased.

Sara Bernice was caught unprepared and so she used the weapon she generally used only as a last resort. "Just because you were married one time," she said, "you think you know everything."

"I do not," Minnie said, very dignified, "think any such thing."

"For six months," Sara Bernice said. "Not much to brag about."

"That's more than you can say."

But Sara Bernice didn't answer.

The children's shyness seemed to have simply evaporated by the next day. They were running and shouting all over the place and Sara Bernice couldn't do a thing with them. Minnie didn't try. She sat and crocheted and called out every once in a while, "What are those children doing now? You'd better watch them better."

And Sara Bernice hurried from one window to another, pushing the curtains aside and sticking her nose against the glass, squinting up her eyes in the light. "I can't seem to see them," she said apologetically.

"Well, for heaven's sake," Minnie said. "Go outside and call. What do you expect to see, poking your nose through the curtains that way?"

"I thought maybe I could see," she said vaguely, giving Minnie a quick, guilty look. Finally she did go outside and walked around in the yard, looking in the bushes and up in the maple tree and even pushing aside the big canna lilies and looking behind them, as though she were looking for a cat. When she did finally see them she hurried back in the house without calling them at all.

"They're playing with those little Foot children," she said desperately.

Minnie put down her crocheting and looked at her, really irritated. "Sara Bernice," she said carefully, "you go get those children away from those trashy little things this minute. I have never seen a bigger ninny than you are. Sometimes," she added in way of concession.

Sara Bernice hurried back through the back door, sticking her hands down so deep in her smock pockets that she was on the point of ripping them. "John Robert!" she called, but it even seemed to her that she might as well as be a mouse squeaking for all anyone would pay any attention.

The children were just on the other side of the forsythia bushes, just in the Foots' yard. They were doing something out under a scrubby elm tree, and when Sara Bernice saw what it was she began jumping up and down and waving her arms like a scarecrow the wind has just hit. Patrick was tied up to the tree with an old, broken bridle, and one of the Foot children, a fat little boy with red hair and a sunburn, was waving a rusty old hunting knife around his face. Lorena and John Robert were sitting cross-legged on the ground, complacently watching the redheaded boy. They all looked around when they saw Sara Bernice and they all frowned and stood still, staring at her.

"You leave that poor little child alone," she said, her false teeth positively clicking together. "And you, Lorena and John Robert," she said while she was untying Patrick, "letting your own little brother get all tied up and scared half to death."

"We were the Indians," Lorena said, bored, chewing on the end of one braid. "We let him be the white settler. We

174

generally don't let him be anything."

"They were going to scalp me," Patrick said.

Sara Bernice clumsily pulled him against her sharp hipbone. "They're not going to scalp poor little Patrick."

But he pulled angrily away from her. "They let me be the white man," he said accusingly. "They were going to scalp me too." He stood looking defiantly at her through his soft lashes.

She still misunderstood. "I came as fast as I could," she said. "I wouldn't let them hurt you for anything."

But his face got quite red with anger. "I wanted to get scalped!" he shouted. "I was going to get to." He looked as though he might start crying and she looked around the yard as though she'd forgotten which way to go. There was a little group of wide-eyed children standing at the Foots' back doorstep, staring, and Sara Bernice saw their mother's fat, round face at one of the windows, laughing fit to kill and showing the gap space where she'd gotten a tooth knocked out.

She grabbed Lorena and Partick by their arms and pulled them along, pushing John Robert from behind. The rest of the morning the Foot children lined up along the bushes and threw squashy tomatoes at John Robert and Lorena and Patrick every time they went in the yard. A truck had lost a crate of tomatoes right in front of the Foots' house and so they seemed to have an endless supply. The redheaded boy sent the little children through the bushes to pick them up between throwings so they could use them until they were nothing but a bit of mush and seeds.

But in the afternoon the Foots had company, some of their kinfolks from Reunion, and Mr. Foot came home early from the strip-pits, as dirty as a hog, but he never bothered to wash as far as Sara Bernice could tell, and they all sat out in the yard eating watermelons. The children had sticky pink watermelon juice all over them, and it made Sara Bernice hot just to look at them. They lined up again along the hedge and saw who could spit seeds the furtherest.

"They sure do have a lot of relatives," John Robert said, looking out the window at the row of children.

"You ought to see them sometimes," Sara Bernice said. "House and yard full. They're kin to everybody in the countryside."

"Your grandfather ought to be alive," Minnie said, leaning

forward in her seat. "He wouldn't have let poor white trash like that move in the city limits, much less right next door. He was a judge, you know." She shook her head wisely up and down. "District judge."

"Was he?" John Robert said.

"Why, surely you knew that," Minnie was shocked. "Whatever does your father mean not telling you that? Of course he was a judge. Everybody knew him."

"I think that would be fun," Sara Bernice said, unexpectedly, still looking out the window.

"Well, I suppose," Minnie said. "But how many women judges have you ever heard of?"

"Not a judge," Sara Bernice said dreamily. "Those Foots. With all those kin folks and it's like a celebration every time they have company. It would be nice."

Minnie was almost speechless. "Those horrid people," she said finally. " Whyever would you want to be like those horrid people? Four United States senators have sat right in this room," she said, looking at the children. "Four."

"The truth is," Sara Bernice said, quite loudly, "we don't really know anybody in this town."

Minnie simply stared at her. "Insanity has never run in this family to my knowledge," she said. "But there's a first time for everything. You've lived here all your life. How can you stand there and say you don't know anybody?"

"Nobody," Sara Bernice said. "Nobody at all."

Minnie closed her mouth and didn't say another word. She knew the symptoms. Sara Bernice had acted just the same way that time she'd gotten all up in the air about tick fever in cows and had gone traipsing all over the countryside poking around in dirty barns and stepping in old manure and walking through pastures that were full of chiggers and ticks. Talking about vats and dips and all sorts of things, but their father had been alive then to do something with her.

They thought surely they would hear from Authur by Saturday but they didn't hear a word. They didn't know if his wife was better or worse, and they didn't know when he was coming after the children. It was getting to be a problem.

Saturday night, when they were in bed, the windows up all the way but still the breeze just barely ruffling the curtains, Sara Bernice asked, "What about church tomorrow?" And the question just hung there in the air. They both knew they'd been thinking about it.

"Well, I just can't face it," Minnie said finally.

Sara Bernice didn't bother to answer. She knew she couldn't do it—get them dressed up and herded to church and then keep them quiet for an hour. "What will we do with them then?" she asked, and turned over and went immediately to sleep without even thinking about an answer.

It was late when she woke up. Minnie was still asleep, the sheet pulled up to her chin, snoring lightly. She dressed quickly, listening to the house sounds. It was too quiet. There was just the heat, fairly shimmering outside, and a rain crow calling from somewhere, on the outskirts of town probably. But she didn't hear a thing in the house until she heard just the faintest little rustling sound outside the door.

She stepped out in the hall and saw Patrick, all alone, sliding carefully on the floor, barefoot, moving his legs as though he were skating. He didn't look up.

"Where're John Robert and Lorena?"

"Outside," he said. "Somewhere." He went on skating, slowly, looking down at his feet.

She let the screen go to very quietly and she walked around the yard, the dry grass making a little crinkling noise. She saw them at one corner of the garage then, half hidden by it—Lorena and John Robert completely surrounded by Foot children. She thought they would probably have them beaten to death before she got there, but when she got closer she saw it wasn't that sort of thing at all. The little group was quiet and very still, and while she watched, the little redheaded Foot boy leaned over with his hands behind his back and kissed Lorena with a loud, sucking noise. "He did it!" all the Foot children shouted. "He'll always take a dare."

"I don't care," John Robert shouted. "I'll climb to the very top of that tree." He pointed to the big maple. "The very tiptop."

But Sara Bernice caught him before he even started and took them both into the house. She didn't say anything to them, or to Minnie either when she got up. At breakfast John Robert said, all of a sudden, "R. P. Foot's getting baptized this afternoon."

"Who's he?" Sara Bernice asked, quickly, before Minnie

had time to say anything. "The little redheaded boy?"

"Naw," John Robert said, disgusted. "It's his cousin."

"Out in a creek," Lorena said. "We've never got to see anybody baptized in a creek."

"The Foots over here can't go though," John Robert went on, ignoring his sister, "because some kin of theirs is coming down from Springfield. And they're having dinner on the ground," he added sadly. "The people at the baptizing are."

"At Six Mile Bridge," Lorena added.

Minnie suddenly looked up. "Isn't that one of the places you went when you were running around about tick fever?"

"I guess," Sara Bernice said shortly.

"What's a baptizing?" Partick asked. But no one answered him.

There wasn't a breath of air stirring all morning. The children lay on the cool, bare dining-room floor, their arms out straight from their sides as though they were being crucified. There was a curl to John Robert's mouth that made Sara Bernice realize that not only was he being crucified but it was his aunts who were doing it to him.

Sara Bernice had all the dinner to fix herself. Minnie just sat in the biggest rocking chair, rocking back and forth with her eyes half closed, sighing every once in a while with the heat. Sara Bernice stood it as long as she could and then she stuck her head in the dining-room door. "It's a wonder to me," she said, "that it's the oldest in this family who's spoilt. Who can't ever do a thing. It's a small wonder to me that some people's husbands walk out on them after just six months without a with-your-leave or a by-your-leave."

Minnie simply opened her eyes wide and looked at her for a moment, and then she went right on rocking. Sara Bernice felt afraid after she'd gone so far and she jerked her head back in the kitchen. "He was carried off," Minnie called, finally. "Some mean people just carried him off. Dead more than likely not two hours after he was last seen in this town. Poor man."

"Strange thing to me then they never found hair nor hide of his body. *If* anybody was silly enough to kill him."

They ate dinner early, all the windows in the dining room open as far as they would go, and a fat little vase of wilted-down nasturtiums on the table. But the children hardly ate at all. Patrick held his fork in his hand as though it were an ice pick, trying to spear the plate.

"We could go out driving somewhere this afternoon," Sara Bernice said timidly, out of the clear air.

The children instantly perked up. "There's nothing to see anywhere around here," Minnie said. But no one looked discouraged.

Right after dinner then, without even washing the dishes, Sara Bernice went to get the car out of the garage. This wasn't a simple operation as far as she was concerned. Her backing up was quite perilous. Minnie had been too peeved, though, to learn to drive and she'd had it to do. However, in a way, she'd never considered the car her fault. It wasn't her fault she'd been alone the day the man came around. He was a young man and she noticed the first thing that even though his clothes were a little bit greasy, from being around cars, she supposed, he had still washed his face and arms until they were quite pink. He said he was one of Claude Jones's boys, and Claude had been a good friend of her father's so of course she had to let him in. He'd just sat on the edge of a chair and said that really it wasn't his fault; that he'd never have thought about bothering her, but somebody had *told* him they'd wanted a car. And he had some good secondhand ones; he wouldn't think of cheating her or anything. He'd laughed nervously.

In the end she'd felt sorry for him—getting all cleaned up to come around and see her, taking an interest in whether they had a car or not. He said that, really, it wasn't even safe not to have a car these days. You never knew when you'd need a car. And two ladies living alone. . . .

She saw what he meant. She imagined some horrible men, thieves or murderers, silently slipping a flat knife around the door crack and getting it open. And then running into a table or something with just the slightest thump so she'd hear them. Shaking Minnie awake and creeping out the back door, or through a window, and then in the yard in just their gowns. So of course it would be a great comfort to have a car sitting there. All ready to go and they would jump in and drive madly away to safety.

She'd bought a car, sight unseen, on the spot, and Minnie, when she got home, had had a perfect fit. Not because of the money, they had enough to last them until they were two hundred if need be, but because no one had asked her anything about it. So Sara Bernice had pretended to be very fond of the car, and had even, with great difficulty, learned to drive it.

Sara Bernice turned on the ignition but the car only made a strange buzzing noise. She tried and tried until she was quite flustered.

"What are you doing out there?" Minnie called from the back door.

Sara Bernice tried once more but the car only buzzed. "I can't seem to get it started," she said finally.

"You'll have to call a mechanic," Minnie said cheerfully. She was always happy when something went wrong about the car.

Sara Bernice went in the house, frowning and licking her lips too often as she did when she was nervous.

"You do it," she said suddenly to Minnie. "You call."

"Now you just go ahead," Minnie said, looking at her with her eyes as hard and smooth as marbles. "It's your deal from first to last. Be practical for once."

Sara Bernice sat down, guiltily, at the telephone and called. She always felt guilty that she wasn't practical. Minnie gave the air of being able to do anything, though when Sara Bernice thought about it it was precious few things she could remember that Minnie had ever done.

The mechanic drove with a flourish into the yard, expertly turning his truck around with one hand. Sara Bernice gave Minnie another guilty look and went out to the garage to watch him. She moved from one side of the garage to the other, trying to keep out of his way. It seemed to her that they were going through some rather weird but very polite dance, she stepping aside for him and he stepping aside for her. He kept moving his tongue around on his teeth.

"Did I get you away from dinner?" Sara Bernice asked.

He wiped his hands on his back pockets as though he had to do that before he could answer her. "I was about through anyway. It doesn't make any difference. My wife burned the biscuits again." He winked. "She can't cook much."

Sara Bernice felt suddenly warmed toward him. He seemed such a nice young man. "Oh, I'll bet she's a very good cook," she said teasingly.

"What do you know about it?" he said gloomily. "She's the worst damn cook I ever saw. Spark plugs are wet," he added.

"That's all it is."

He went out to his truck after something and Sara Bernice stood as far back in one corner as she could. He came back into the garage but neither of them said anything and Sara Bernice felt the silence weigh down on her, first just on the top of her head and then sink slowly down until her eyes felt half shut with it. He whistled nervously through his teeth for a few minutes and then, as though it scared him to put that little bit of noise into the silence, he stopped, the last note trailing off to a dismal little hiss. "You going to take this car out somewhere this afternoon?" he asked finally.

"Just out driving. We've got my brother's children here this week," she said, feeling she should say as much as she could.

"Oh," he said. "That's nice."

"Oh, yes," she said. But without much conviction.

"You've lived here quite a while, haven't you?" he asked.

"All my life." She sounded almost apologetic.

"Thought somebody'd told me that."

Finally, when he was finished and the car was running, he picked up his tools and hurried out. "Ball game this afternoon," he explained. "I've got to get there and pitch. I'm the best pitcher they've got." His shoulders, under his shirt, seemed to have a separate life of their own. They moved as though a fly were perpetually landing right between them, just in the center of his backbone. She watched him, envious without quite knowing why.

At last, when they were all in the car, the children in the back seat, Sara Bernice couldn't decide which direction she should go. She drove through town and simply took the first dirt road leading off on her side of the highway. The dust boiled up behind them, catching up with them every time she slowed down for a chug-hole, and made an absolute mist of fine dust in the car, gritty in their throats. John Robert had an arm out one back window and Lorena one out of the other. They looked, almost hypnotized, at the strange little movements they were making with their fingers, twisting them into all sorts of patterns. Patrick was squeezed up between them, holding his bottom lip down with his teeth, quite red in the face from anger. He'd wanted a window.

Minnie pointed out various things along the side of the road, as though she were an announcer for a tour bus. "There's a nice-looking corn patch," she said. "John Robert, there's a white horse over in that pasture."

John Robert only made a sound that sounded like a growl deep in his throat. He carefully avoided looking at the pasture where the white horse was supposed to be.

Patrick, to show his anger, refused to look anywhere except directly in front of him at his bare knees and his hands placed exactly on top of them.

Minnie was unaware of the hostility in the car. "Look at the darling cow," she said, to no one in particular.

John Robert looked, his eyes narrowing down to slits as though he were looking at something far away over on the ridge of the mountains. The cow was just in front of him, on the side of the road. No one knew if he saw it or not.

Sara Bernice simply drove without having the least idea where she was going. She always got immediately lost on country roads, so that she didn't even know which direction she was going; they all looked alike to her. She fussed when she came to a place where there were cars and pickups parked on both sides of the road, leaning over halfway in the ditch, the blackberry bushes and sunflower stalks touching them as though they were balancing them. She crept between the rows of cars and over a wooden bridge with no side rails. "It's the baptizing," Lorena called when they were right in the middle of the bridge. "You brought us right to the baptizing." Sara Bernice didn't say anything.

"You don't need to take the credit to yourself," Minnie said. "I know you always get lost."

Sara Bernice turned the car in behind the last pickup and stopped. "You aren't going to stop here, surely?" Minnie asked. But the children were already halfway out of the car. "You'll get chiggers," she called. "And mosquitoes and gnats and flies'll cover you." But they slammed the car doors behind them and were gone.

By the time Minnie and Sara Bernice walked back to the bridge the children were already there, sitting and dangling their feet off the edge. Sara Bernice put her foot down on Patrick's shirttail even though he turned around and looked at her, furious, and squirmed and squirmed trying to get loose.

They had a perfect view; in fact they were too exposed to suit Sara Bernice. The baptizing party was upstream, sitting in a cleared-out spot where cows had eaten the grass down. They were sitting on half-rotten logs or leaning against young trees, women holding onto babies' dress-tails. They could even see the flies swarming over something behind the group—chicken bones and bits of bread and watermelon rinds.

They had just finished the preaching part of the service and the people were stirring around, talking, laughing softly. A woman and a little boy walked along the cleared-out place by the creek and climbed up the bank by the bridge. The woman looked at them, her big face shining in the heat, the lines around her throat dark with dirt and sweat. "You go on down," she said to them. "Cooler down by the water out of the sun. You go on down if you want to."

"Best keep the children up here out of the way," Minnie said.

The woman nodded and went over to a pickup and got a fruit jar of water out of the back and handed it to the little boy. John Robert, Lorena, and Patrick simply stared shamelessly as he put his head back and drank, making a little hard *thunk* sound every time he swallowed. Sara Bernice wanted to kick them.

Down by the creek they were getting ready for the baptizing. A boy, his shoes and stockings off, had been crouched down on the bank, his arms on his knees, looking dreamily over toward the other bank where there was a rock ledge sloping out toward the water, a dark shadow under it. Suddenly he got up and started walking slowly out in the water, stooping down every once in a while and cupping his hand in the water and tipping it over on his shoulders, the water running in little streams down his shirt back and front, the cloth sticking to him where he was wet.

"That's our preacher," the woman with the little boy said, right at their feet. She was already down on the creek bank.

"But he's so young," Sara Bernice said.

"He's seventeen. He got the call when he was thirteen. Been preaching ever since."

The boy had reached the middle of the creek and he turned around slowly, the water clear, green, all around him. The floor of the creek was rock, there was no mud to boil up. He stood still, his arms hanging loosely, his hands just touching the water. Sara Bernice could see the red sunburn on his arms where his shirtsleeves were rolled up, and his high cheekbones, his eyes wide apart. She felt something move inside her so that she had to open her mouth to get a long breath. He was so young.

The people on the bank were still, waiting, and he waited out there in the water, moving his fingers a little so that they made a faint splash, like the sound of a tiny frog jumping into deep water. A man stood up on the bank, leaning over and rolling up his overall legs to the knees. His legs were very white, very hairy, with the muscles in hard bunches at the calves. When he stood up Sara Bernice could see his face, red with purplish veins just below the surface, and thin, sunburned hair on the top of his head. He walked quickly out into the water but out in the middle Sara Bernice could see that his mouth was opening and shutting, fast, like a fish just pulled out of the water, and she knew then that the water was cold.

The boy put one hand on the man's back and raised the other so that he seemed to be pointing toward the ledge just above him. He said something, almost in the man's ear, and then, quickly, ducked him down in the creek.

Sara Bernice felt a sudden twitching and twisting under her foot, almost as though Patrick's shirt had suddenly become alive and was trying to get away. "He's going to drown him," Patrick said, horrified, beating his hands against the wooden planks of the bridge. "Make him stop!"

The people on the creek bank stared at them and Sara Bernice felt the blood beating painfully through her face and neck. "No, no," she said. "Be quiet." She wanted to shake him and scream at him, but he didn't get quiet until the man came up out of the water and climbed slowly up on the bank, shaking himself like a dog and sticking his fingers down in his ears. Patrick sat still then, leaning over with his chin in his hand.

A young boy went out, and then two little boys, holding hands, and then another middle-aged man. Sara Bernice was gradually aware of a little stir on the creek bank. There was a young girl, sixteen or seventeen, with long hair down to her shoulders, slowly wringing her hands. "Jesus saveus, Jesus saveus," she said, rhythmically, not in frenzy but as though it were a sort of ritual. Her eyes were half shut as though she were sleepy, or thinking about something very far away. She swayed slowly back and forth. The women, carrying their babies, gathered around her, smiling. "It's all right, honey," they said. "Darling, it's all right." Their voices were soft, caressing. The girl still swayed, not listening to them.

Someone stooped down and took off her shoes.

The men were finished and there was a pause waiting for the women to start. The women stood in a loose little circle around the girl, bouncing their babies up and down on their hipbones. The men stood back, leaning against the trees, waiting.

"Now you go on," someone said to the girl. And the women nudged her toward the water. She stumbled down the bank and on out into the water, not saying anything, but Sara Bernice could still see her lips moving. Her skirt billowed up around her, the water pushing up against it in strange little bulges, like a lily pad, moving in the ripples. She raised her arms out of the water and put them down, slowly, absentmindedly, on the skirt, but still it billowed around her arms.

The boy stopped her in the middle of the creek and they stood together for a few seconds, he cupping one hand down in the water and holding it over her head, the drops sliding between his fingers and gleaming in the sun before they touched her hair, and then they clung there, suspended, like drops of mist on a spider web.

Sara Bernice, watching the boy and girl, thought perhaps they would begin swaying together, starting some kind of ritual dance, but he only slid the girl down in the water, smoothly, gracefully, and it was a bit like a dance, or the sudden swoop of a hawk caught in a current of air. The girl's feet kicked up when she went under, breaking the surface of the creek. Not at all gracefully, but her feet were exposed, cold, for only a split second and then she touched the smooth rocks again and walked toward the bank, her head hanging over as though her wet hair were almost too heavy to hold up.

Sara Bernice could feel how the girl's mood had changed. She was no longer slow, heavy, half asleep, but the cold water had excited her. She laughed at the women holding out their hands to her from the bank. They pulled her up and she stumbled and fell on her knees, still laughing, slightly hysterical. The women smiled indulgently at her, turning with knowing, satisfied smiles to each other. Sara Bernice saw that it was all a part of the game, that the girl was only doing the things expected of her. Everyone would have been disappointed if she hadn't.

The women gathered around the girl, holding up a

blanket, and they undressed her and wrapped the blanket, thin and white, around her. Sara Bernice thought how good it must feel, the warm blanket on her cold, wet skin. The girl shook her hair around her face, running her fingers through it, perfectly calm now. The women still stood around her, holding their babies on their hips, still smiling, but Sara Bernice thought there was something secret about the smiles, something mysterious. They all spoke to the girl or touched her, patting her hair or her arm, leaning over to whisper something in her ear, laughing softly.

Sara Bernice understood it then. The initiation or ritual or whatever it was was over and the girl was wholly accepted, wholly a part of the group; she would always be a part. Unexpectedly Sara Bernice felt tears in her eyes, warm, full—for a second she was the young girl, laughing, protected, shaking her long hair around her head. . . .

She walked to the edge of the bridge and slid down the slope to the creek bank, getting beggar's lice on her dress and starting a tiny landslide in the gravel. "Where are you going?" Minnie asked.

Her answer seemed inevitable to her. "To be baptized," she said. She heard Minnie gasp and even saw her reach out one hand as though to stop her, but she walked on up the bank, feeling sort of vicious pleasure in embarrassing Minnie.

The group on the creek bank didn't notice her until she was almost to them, and then they all looked up, almost at the same second, and stared. She looked around for someone who might be in authority, but there seemed to be only the boy standing out in the water and she felt he was too young. So she simply looked at all of them in general. "I want to be baptized," she said.

They still simply stared at her, no one making any sort of move until the boy out in the creek walked in a little closer, the water splashing around him. He rubbed his hand, embarrassed, over his hair. "Are you making fun of us?" he asked, his head hanging over on one side, grinning. He looked more like fifteen than seventeen.

"No," she said. And she was aware of some flies buzzing just over her head, the sound out of all proportion. It made the whole thing feel unreal.

The boy stood letting one arm swing slowly back and forth in the water, not looking up at her. "You got to be born again," he said. "And you got to join the church."

"I belong to the Presbyterian Church," she said.

He looked up at her. "Well, I couldn't baptize no Presbyterian. You'd have to join our church. You could come next Sunday," he added reluctantly.

Some of the men nodded their heads. The women still just watched. The only one not looking at her was the girl wrapped in the blanket. She had her hair over her face, fanning it out in the sun to dry. No one said anything. "That's all I know," the boy said plaintively.

There was a hostility in all of their eyes. She knew, then, that she was like someone who had come uninvited to a party. She couldn't force her way in. A tree frog sang; they all waited as though they were listening. She knew that they were waiting for her to leave. She turned and walked back up the creek bank. She didn't hurry; it seemed to take her a long time.

Minnie and the children were waiting for her at the top of the bridge. She didn't look at them but simply walked toward the car; they followed her without saying a word. The people on the bank watched, waiting for them to leave.

Sara Bernice drove down the road slowly, and she realized, almost with amazement, that she was crying. The road and the woods on either side looked strangely blurred. John Robert and Lorena were sitting perfectly still in the back seat and even Minnie didn't say anything. Only Patrick seemed angry. He was sitting right behind Sara Bernice and he methodically kicked the back of her seat.

"Silly," he said.

"What?" Minnie asked, relieved to be able to say anything.

"Those people back there." He kicked the seat again, vindictively. "When are we going home?" But nobody answered him. There was only the sound of Sara Bernice's crying, all the way into town.

This story originally appeared in Jordan's Stormy Banks and Other Stories *(New York: Atheneum Publishers, 1971) and is reprinted with permission of the author.*

BEGINNING

Donald Harington

From a porch swing, evening July, 1939, Stay More, Ark.

IT BEGINS WITH THIS SOUND:

the screen door pushed outward in a slow swing, the spring on the screen door stretching vibrantly, one sprung tone and fading overtone high-pitched even against the bug-noises and frog-noises, a plangent twang, WRIRRRAANG, which, more than any other sound, more than cowbells or distant truck motors laboring uphill, more, even, than all those overworked katydids, crickets, tree frogs, etc., seems to evoke the heart of summer, of summer evenings, of summer evenings there in that place, seems to make it easy for me to begin this one. WRENCH! WRUNG! WRINGING!

IT BEGINS WITH THESE PEOPLE:

the girl coming out through that twanging screen door, prettied up fit to kill in her finest frillery, swinging her fine hips once to clear the returning screen door being closed by that pranging, wranging spring. Her name is Sonora. The way these folks say it, it sounds like "Snory" so that is what I shall call her. She does not live here; just visiting, for the summer, with the woman who is presumed to be her aunt, who is at least the sister of the woman who is presumed to be her mother, Mandy

Twichell, of Little Rock, where Sonora lives and goes to school with the rich city kids. She is a very pretty 17, with red hair even, but I am not yet certain that I like her very much. I guess the reason I don't like her too awfully much is that she is inclined to tease me, if she ever notices me at all. One time when nobody was around, she reached down and chucked me right in my generative organ, and twitted, "My, Dawny, for such a little feller I bet you've got a big one!" Imagine. If she weren't essential to the plot, I would be happy to exclude her entirely from this world.

the woman sitting on the porch, the woman presumed to be Sonora's aunt. Her name is Latha, with the first "a" long, and one would conceive that it might be spoken "Lay-thee," in view of the way Sonora's name comes out as "Snory" but there have been only one or two people who have called her that. She is Latha. Miss Latha Bourne, the postmistress of this place—and the heroine, the demigoddess, of this world. I am not certain yet just how old she is, but she's old enough to be Sonora's aunt, or her mother, for that matter, and she's at least three or four years older than my aunt, who is 35. My aunt thinks that Latha Bourne is "crazy as a quilt," but we shall have to see about that.

the boy sitting in the porch swing, trying to make out Latha Bourne's exquisite face in the pale light coming from kerosene lanterns within the house. He is a tousle-haired little whippersnapper, five going on six, who is not related to either one of these females, although he has in common with Sonora that he is just visiting, spending the summer with his aunt, who lives up the road a ways from Latha's place. He comes down here every evening and sits in that porch swing and watches people, until either somebody runs him off or his aunt calls him home. His name is Donald, but the way they say it, all of them, is "Dawny." He likes to come to Latha's place in the evenings because she is a great teller of ghost stories, but mainly he likes to come to Latha's place because he is in love with her, and will always be, even when he is old. Even when he is old, the thought of her will give him twitchings and itchings [and the only way he will ever exorcise her, the only way she will ever give him any peace, is for him to write a book about her, who is, it should be obvious by this time, the Lightning Bug].

189

IT BEGINS WITH THIS SETTING:

the house of Latha, which is also the combined store-post office of Stay More, a community of some 113 souls in the Ozark mountains of Newton County, south of the county seat, Jasper, and the lovely village of Parthenon, west of the village of Spunkwater, north of Demijohn, Hunton and Swain, east of Sidehill and Eden. [One must not attempt to find it on a recent map; one may find Newton County, and one may find Jasper and Parthenon and Swain, but one shall not find Stay More—not because it is some screwball name that I made up in my own head, but because today it is nothing but a ghost town, almost.] *The origin of the name is obscure. Although the expression is common parlance among the natives of that region, as in, "Don't be rushin off, Dawny. Stay more, and eat with us," it is not certain that this connotation was intended by the founders of the town, Jacob and Noah Ingledew, who came from Warren County, Tennessee, in 1837. Some conjecture that these brothers, with prophetic foresight, realized that the village might eventually become a ghost town, and hence the name was meant not as a mere invitation but as a plea, a beseechment. During the last years of its status as a U.S. Post Office, it was resolutely spelled "Staymore" by the postal authorities, over the protests of the postmistress.*

It straddles two green-watered streams of small, good fishing water, Banty Creek (a variant, "Bonny Creek," appears on some maps), the smaller, which empties, near the center of the village, into the larger, Swains Creek, which empties into the Little Buffalo River to the north. In this year, 1939, a crew of W.P.A. men is constructing a cement bridge for Banty Creek where it crosses the main road. There is no bridge on Swains Creek; to reach the schoolhouse one must drive through water over the hubcaps . . . or walk across a precarious foot-log. The roads, all of them, are, of course, only dirt and gravel.

The business census back in 1906–07 listed the following: Ingledew's Commissary-Drugs, Groceries, Hotel, Livery and Notary; Jerram's General Store; two other general stores; three blacksmiths; two physicians, Alonzo Swain and J. M. Plowright; two dentists, Sam Forbes and E. H. Ingledew; William Dill, Wagonmaker [one must remember this one]; Noah Murrison & Son, Sawmill & Gristmill; and the Swains Creek Bank & Trust Company.

Now in 1939 there is only this: Lawlor Coe, Blacksmith; Latha Bourne, General Store and Post Office; Colvin Swain,

Physician; E. H. Ingledew, semi-retired dentist (he pulls but no longer fills); J. M. Plowright, fully retired physician; and what is left of the big Ingledew store, which old Lola Ingledew still runs single-handedly (she lost the other hand in an accident at the sawmill) only for the purpose of providing some slight competition for the store of Latha Bourne, whom she detests with every fiber of her being, or something like that. Last year industry came to Stay More in the form of Oren Duckworth's Cannon Factory, on Swains Creek near the schoolhouse. This opens in June and employs 20 men and women, canning beans during June, and canning tomatoes in July and August; the cans are sent unlabled to Kansas City where a Big Name Food Processor attaches his own label. The factory does not produce cannon; it is simply known as The Cannon Factory.

The post office is at the head of what would be called Main Street were it not just a dirt road with a few buildings on either side, half of them vacated, especially the bank, a stone edifice whose broken glass window stares the post office in the eye all day long. A traveler passing rapidly south on the main road might miss the post office entirely; it is set back in a kind of hollow a hundred feet up the road that goes to Right Prong and Butterchurn Holler, the same road that my Aunt Murrison lives on. At the foot of the main road is the big old half-empty unpainted Ingledew Store. Lola Ingledew, sitting on the front porch of her store, can squint fiercely and count the number of men on the front porch of Latha's store, a quarter of a mile away.

Latha's store is small; the whole building has only five rooms: the large room with the post office boxes and counter at the front end and the merchandise everywhere else; her sitting room, to the left, her bedroom behind it; the spare bedroom, to the right, where Sonora sleeps; and the small kitchen.

A porch runs the whole length of the front. On it, tonight, we are sitting, I in the swing, Snory in the straight-back rush-seated chair, Latha in the rocker, rocking, some.

IT BEGINS WITH THIS MOOD:

[Hell, who has never known a summer evening? But anyway:] from the distance, cowbells are dully clapping thing-thang in dewy fields and shadowy thickets; evening milking is done, and the cows move back to pasture.

From the yard grass, from all around, from everywhere up

191

and down the valley, chirps of bugs scrape crackingly up, and croaks from the creek, and peeps from the trees; you learn to recognize the instruments of this chorus: the tzeek-tzek-tzuk of katydids, the irdle dee irdle of crickets, the tchung of the tree frogs, and that old jug of rum by the bull frogs.

A watermelon seed drops on the porch floor, bounces twice. Sonora smacks her lips and draws the back of her hand across her mouth.

The air is all blue. All the air is blue. The night is hot, more than hot, but blue is cool.

Latha tells Sonora that she looks very pretty tonight.

My dog—Gumper isn't my dog, but he belongs to Uncle Murrison, who is my host, and he follows me around—Gumper comes trotting up and climbs the porch and slobbers on the floor. He is an ordinary hound, and he smells. I am embarrassed for his smell. Sonora kicks at him, and Latha swishes her arms at him and makes a noise in her throat, "Gyow hyar!" which means, "Get out of here" but is the only way the dog would understand that. Gumper puts his tail between his legs and bumps down off the porch; he walks to the great oak in the yard and lifts his leg against it and waters its roots profusely and audibly: another sound for the summer night. Later he sneaks back onto the porch from the side, and curls asleep beneath the swing I'm sitting in.

Latha asks Sonora who does she think she might go out with tonight?

Sonora says we will just have to wait and see.

Other sounds: someone, far off, trying to start a car. Farther off, the bugle-baying of a treeing dog. And more crickets and katydids and tree frogs, faster because of the heat, louder because it's hot.

The blue air carries all the smells of the summer night, which even obliterate the powerful smell of Gumper sleeping below me. The blue air is full of green things, strange wildflowers and magic weeds, and of creekwater, and of some dust and motor oil mixed with the dust and wild dew. Especially of the dew, which is the creekwater and dust and wild green things all liquefied together and essenced and condensed.

Gumper, in his torpid contentment, makes the mistake of striking the floor noisily with his wagging tail. Another thumping sound for the summer night, but because of it he is once again evicted.

"Git home, you smelly dawg!" I holler after him.

*His disappearance brings out the cats. From all over: black
and striped and marmalade, and gray and white and calico. I've
never counted, but I think Latha feeds something like two
dozen cats. They make no sounds to contribute to the summer
night's chorus, but their indolent grace is a decoration, they
festoon the porch rail and the porch and the shrubbery with
their sensuous writhing forms. Some people keep a lot of cats
because they like cats, but Latha keeps cats because she likes to
watch them fuck. I know this for a fact.*

*And now, as the blue of the air darkens, the lightning bugs
come out. At first, as with stars, only one or two (and I would as
soon wish upon a lightning bug as upon a star), but then,
quickly, dozens and hundreds, until the air of the yard, of the
road, of the meadow across the road, of the creek beyond the
meadow, is filled with them. There are at least 35 different
species out there, flashing their cold yellow-green light, and
each species uses a different signal system of flashes. Contrary
to popular belief, the purpose of the flashing light is not
guidance, nor illumination as such, but purely and simply to
make "assignations": the males fly around in the air,
advertising their availability; the females wait immobile on
leaves in bushes and trees, and if they spot a flash coming from
an eligible bachelor of their own species, they return a flash
whose signal has the same intervals.*

[I was disturbed recently to learn from a fellow of my
acquaintance, an intelligent person from Andover,
Massachusetts, that he had never heard of a "lightning bug."
When I described this creature to him, he replied, "We call
those fireflies." This bothered me so much that, at considerable expense to myself, I asked the Thomas Howland
Poll organization of Princeton, New Jersey, to conduct a na-
tionwide survey. The results satisfied me: 87% had
definitely heard of "lightning bugs," 3% had heard of
lightning bugs but thought they were insects who made
thundering noises, 7% had never heard of a lightning bug,
1% thought it was an automobile, and the remaining 2% had
no opinion.]

*What is most uncanny is that the interval of the flash is
dependent not only on the species, but also on the temperature
of any given night. The bugs flash twice as frequently on hot
nights as on cool nights. Thus, the brilliant female must not
only memorize the signal of her own species, but also know
exactly what the temperature is. Otherwise, if she flashes the*

wrong response and attracts a male of a different species, the only thing she can do is eat him.

The male of the species is fickle. As soon as he engages the female in procreative recreation, she obligingly turns off her luring light. But if any other females happen to be flashing their lights in the vicinity, the busy male will quickly disengage himself, as per coitus reservatus, and take off after the competing lady.

Some species of lightning bugs do not eat at all after becoming adults; the adult stage is only for the purpose of procreation; they become adults, they flash, they fuck, they die. This has nothing to do with Latha. She lives.

The lightning bug, or firefly, is neither a bug nor a fly, but a beetle. I like bug because it has a cozy sound, a hugging sound, a snug sound, it fits her, my Bug.

Deep in the dark blue air sing these lives that make the summer night. The lightning bug does not sing. But of all these lives, it alone, the lightning bug alone, is visible. The others are heard but not seen, felt but not seen, smelled but not seen [I have bottled a sample of that air and sent it for analysis to the Meredith Olfactory Laboratories of St. Louis, whose Dr. S. I. Coryell is the leading authority in differentiation analysis, but his report is of little help: "This specimen is broken down as follows: 1.09% glucosides extract from chlorophyll of various field weeds, primarily *Datura stramonium*, or Jimson-weed; 2.03% fragrance of clover-blossom; .08% fragrance of alfalfa; .04% essence of hay, primarily Timothy and Johnson Grass, probably new-mown, but not wholly discrete from residues of same included in .009% bovine excreta; .0085% effluvium of stream water with traces of crayfish, bass and bream, and limestone; .00076% excretion from human sweat glands; .00034% miscellaneous excretions from a canine male animal, possibly a hound; .00026% excretions, mingled, from several diverse feline animals, male and female; .00017% traces of oestrus secretions in various mating reptiles and insects, including .000002% exudations of the insect, *Photinus pyralis* or other species of the Family *Lampyridae*, fireflies. There is also a trace of emanation from the rubber seal on the Mason jar in which you sent the specimen, but apart from this, Mr. Harington, I regret to say that I cannot positively identify the larger proportion of components, and I would be pleased if you would inform me where and when this specimen was taken."]

That air, that blue magical scented balmy air, is the world, the habitat, the home of the lightning bugs. And of my Bug.

IT BEGINS:

one by one, or together in pairs or groups, the boys come. In his dad's car, a '36 Chevy coupe with rumbleseat, is Oren ("Junior") Duckworth, Jr., and his brother Chester. These are the best-looking. On foot, and separately from different directions, arrive the triplet sons of Lawlor Coe the blacksmith, Earl, Burl & Gerald. You should know that the way they say "Gerald," he rhymes with his brothers. Gerald will die a hero with the Marines at Iwo Jima in 1945. These brothers look just alike, which is not much to look at: inclined to pudginess, and over-freckled. Alone on foot comes John Henry ("Hank") Ingledew, Bevis's boy, nephew to dead Raymond Ingledew, who was Latha's beau a long long time ago. Then comes the W.P.A. gang, who are staying with the folks of Merle Kimber, who is a W.P.A. boy himself (and who rhymes with the Coe triplets, though he'd just as soon not); he and Leo Dinsmore are the only ones from this valley; the others are Furriners, which means that they don't come from this valley: Clarence Biggart comes from Madison County and is even a married man, so is J. D. Pruitt, who comes from someplace up north in Newton County, Eddie Churchwell and Dorsey Tharp are from downstate somewhere.

Here are a dozen boys. They have each said, politely, "Howdy, Miss Latha," and they have each said, warmly, "Howdy, Snory, honey," and a few of them have even said, "Howdy, Dawny." One of them, Eddie Churchwell, teases me. "The boogers are sure gonna git you tonight, Dawny boy. I seen one down the road, a-comin this way, and I figgered he was out after me, but he tole me he was comin to grab you." I titter.

They stand around. There are three empty chairs on the porch, but the boys do not sit in these. Some of them sit on the porch rail, brushing the cats aside, but most of them just stand around, some of them in the yard.

Merle Kimber spits. As if on signal, each of the others, in turn, spits. After a while Merle Kimber spits again, and one by one the others do. Clarence Biggart has a reason to spit, because he is chewing tobacco, but the others spit because . . . well, because I guess it makes them look manly, although you'd think that if they keep that up long enough, night after night, we would all of us drown in it by and by. Maybe the spit is a kind of advertisement, maybe a substitute for all the sperm they'd like to get rid of.

It is professional spitting. I have tried to do it but can't. A certain snap of the tongue squirts it out through a crevice between the front teeth, in such a way that it goes in a straight stream and lands intact and compact. When I try to spit, it splatters all over. Any one of these boys could hit a horsefly from five yards away. Naturally, they are spitting only into the yard, not upon the porch. Inside, over the post office boxes is a printed sign, KINDLY DO NOT EXPECTORATE UPON THE FLOOR, but I don't think any of these boys knows what that means, even if they could read; still, they are gentlemen, and know where to spit.

But Chester Duckworth, spitting, is momentarily careless: his blob alights on J. D. Pruitt's shoe. J. D. hauls off with his fist and clobbers Chester a good one; soon they are scuffling in the grass, putting up a scrap not really out of belligerence so much as ostentation: they are showing off for Snory. J. D. is older by several years, nearly 21, but Chester is bigger. They smack each other around all over the landscape; J. D. chases Chester up the road, and after a while he comes back, huffing and puffing and rubbing his wounds. Later, ,Chester too comes back, acting like he was just arriving. "Howdy, Miss Latha," he says, cool as buttermilk. "Howdy, there, Snory, honey. Howdy, boys. Howdy, Dawny, has that 'ere booger man not cotched you yet, tee hee!"

Merle Kimber spits.

J. D. Pruitt says, "Hoo, Lord, ain't it a hot night, though!"

Clarence Biggart says, "Yeah boy."

Junior Duckworth says, "Hotter'n Hades."

Hank Ingledew says, "Might come a rain tomorra."

Earl, Burl & Gerald Coe spit.

Eddie Churchwell says, "Well, now, boys...."

[Now if one has not been reading me carefully, one is anticipating that pretty soon Latha Bourne will start selling tickets and each of the boys will take Sonora into the house. One is not reading me at all.]

Eddie Churchwell says, "Well, now, boys, why don't we just draw straws!"

John Henry "Hank" Ingledew slugs him square on the jaw. Then the big fight begins. Although Merle Kimber and Leo Dinsmore are local boys, they side with the Furriners because

*being a W.P.A. boy is more important than being a local boy. So
it is six against six, our boys against theirs. Knock down, drag
out, clear-to-Hell-and-back-again. Even though they are
serious, and even though they are hurting one another, they are
still essentially showing off for Snory.*

*I have watched this fight so often it no longer interests me. So
I watch Latha and Snory watching it. Snory is feigning alarm,
and even making little screaming noises. But Latha has the
trace of a smile around the edges of her mouth.*

*What does she look like? She is dark, and of very fair skin. She
is taller than average, and neither thick nor thin, but full-
bodied, I suppose what you could call "shapely" though not in
any way to make men whistle.* [I cannot help but think of
Vanessa Redgrave in *Blow-Up*, which of course is ridiculous,
and possibly even an insult to Miss Redgrave, but I have no
doubt that a highly paid make-up technician could take
Latha and after some diligent and thoughtful work
transform her into the spitting image of Miss Redgrave. As a
matter of fact, I have before me—on the wall—a poster
obtained for $1.00 from Famous Faces, Inc., Box 441,
Norristown, Pa. 19404, depicting Miss Redgrave life-size
from the scene in *Blow-Up* when she is about to allow herself
to be laid by David Hemmings in order to "buy" his roll of
incriminating negatives. She is wearing a dark hip-hugging
miniskirt with a wide black leather belt. But she is topless,
and out of modesty has hugged her arms around herself to
cover her lovely breasts. She is staring out of the picture (and
into the eyes of Hemmings?) with large eyes—with the
expression of a very sweet and good girl who has done a bad
thing and is now getting ready to do another bad thing
because of it. (My Aunt Murrison always said, "Two wrongs
never make a right.") Not only have I seen Latha Bourne in
that exact same pose, one afternoon I barged in on her while
she was dressing, but also I have seen Latha Bourne with that
exact same expression . . . and, kindly believe me, that exact
same beauty.] *I love to look at Latha Bourne, which is
something I do more often than anything else, except sleep.
Maybe I disturb her, looking at her so much. The fight goes on,
with grunts and thuds and slams and rips, but I don't watch
it.*

*Here are all of the known facts about her: she was born in
Stay More, in a cabin on the east side of Ledbetter Mountain.
(The post office is at the foot of the south side of the same*

mountain.) Her father, Saultus Bourne, was a subsistence farmer. He died of pneumonia in 1921 and lies buried in the Primitive Baptist Church cemetery on Swains Creek. Her mother, Fannie Swain Bourne, was descended from one of the original settlers of Stay More. She died of apoplexy in 1927 and is interred in the Church of Christ cemetery at Demijohn. Latha has two sisters, Mandy, who married Vaughn Twichell and lives in Little Rock, and Barbara, who lives in California but has not been heard of. Latha attended the Stay More grade school, first through eighth grades, then went to high school at Jasper. She was popular in high school, and at graduation she was unofficially engaged to Raymond Ingledew, a Stay More boy, but he joined the service and was killed in the Argonne— actually, he was only listed as missing, but he never did come back, although some people say that Latha is still waiting for him, which I doubt. Latha had already lost her virginity, at the age of eleven, to some third or fourth cousin of hers. (Well, as they say in this part of the country, a virgin, by definition, is "a five-year-old girl who can outrun her daddy and her brothers," so I guess Latha was a late-developer or else just lucky—or, from another point of view, unlucky.) There was some gossip that as soon as she learned that Raymond Ingledew was reported missing Over There, she began to carry on again with that same third or fourth cousin, but nobody ever caught them at it. In any case, shorly after the death of her father, in 1921, she moved to Little Rock to live with her married sister, Mandy. About nine months after that, in May of 1922, she was committed in the Arkansas State Hospital at Little Rock, where she remained nearly three years. Her escape, in March of 1925, attracted some attention in the Little Rock newspapers. Although escapes from the A Ward, the B Ward, and even the C Ward were relatively routine, Latha was (and today remains) the only patient who ever escaped from E Ward. She was never captured. Some folks insinuate that she lived thereafter as a prostitute in some large city, possibly Memphis or New Orleans or St. Louis, but nobody really knows. In any event, she was never seen again until June of 1932, when suddenly she appeared out of nowhere back in Stay More, with a deed to Bob Cluley's General Store which had recently been foreclosed by the bank in Jasper. Where she got the money nobody knows, though they've had a long lot of fun trying to guess. Two years after establishing herself as proprietress of the store, she applied for and obtained the post of postmistress, after the death of long-time postmaster Willis Ingledew, the father of Lola, who wanted the job and will always hate Latha for taking away what she thought was rightfully hers.

And that is all. Nothing has happened to Latha since. She has received, and rejected, proposals of marriage from the following: Doc Colvin Swain, Tearle ("Tull") Ingledew, our village drunk, and a five-year-old boy euphoniously sobriqueted Dawny.

The fight is over. Our boys, as usual, have emerged victorious, bloody but unbowed. The W.P.A. boys are shuffling off up the road, declaring that they are going to a square dance at Parthenon where the real men are and the real gals are, and that besides you Stay More boys fight dirty.

Junior Duckworth is inspecting his tattered shirt and his dirt-caked abrasions. In front of Snory he holds his arms out as if to display himself, and says to her, "Aw, shoot fire, Snory honey, aint I a sight! I was aimin to take you over to Jasper to the pitcher show, but now it looks like I got to go home and git cleaned up some, don't it!"

Junior and his brother Chester get into their car, and Junior sprays gravel letting out the clutch, and shows off some more turning the car around skiddingly like a maniac.

Earl Coe says to Burl Coe, "You want to see thet pitcher show!"

Burl Coe asks, "Is it Tex Ritter or Hopalong Cass'dy!"

Earl Coe says, "Hit's ole Hopalong."

"Sheeut," says Burl Coe. "Noo, son, let's see what's doing up to thet thar square dance."

"Okey doke," says Earl Coe, then turns to Gerald. "You, Jerl!"

"Fine and dandy," says Gerald Coe.

The Brothers Coe say "See y'all around" to us, and amble off up the road.

That leaves Hank Ingledew. He spits, shuffles his feet, clears his throat. "Snory," he says. "You keer to watch that squar dance, or somethin!"

"Or somethin," she says, echoing, slightly teasing.

She stands up, walks down off the porch, takes Hank's hand.

"See y'all," says Hank.

"Night night," says Snory.

"Be good," speaks Latha. It is a formality; I do not believe she means it. In fact I think she means, "Be bad as you can!"

Hank and Snory walk off up the road, hand in hand.

It is easy enough to surmise that a girl of Sonora's temperament, appearance and popularity might be inclined to promiscuity, but this is not the case. Unless I miss my guess badly, her body, if not her heart wholly, belongs only to John Henry Ingledew. When the other eleven boys are around, he is merely one of them, a rather reserved and inconspicuous member of the gang, but when he is alone with Snory he is her lover. I have watched them make love three times, once in a thicket on the other side of Swains Creek, once in the abandoned tavern up the road from Latha's store, and once in the corn crib behind Latha's place. It is a sight to behold. It is beautiful, and it is awesome, and it is only faintly disturbing to a boy of five whose immature penis can only envy such voluptuous recreation.

I think Latha lives vicariously in Sonora. The younger woman appears, to all intents and purposes, to be the Lightning Bug, but it is the older woman who lives in her and really appreciates it.

Latha and I are alone now. I rock the swing gently, my feet not reaching the floor. Latha holds in one hand a lovely silk handkerchief, which she has been using for the purpose of blotting perspiration from her brow. She stares off up the road in the direction Hank and Snory have disappeared. She raises the handkerchief to her mouth and grips a corner of it between her teeth.

Clouds march past the moon.

The blinking, flashing scintillation of the lightning bugs seems to keep a beat with the music from the grass and trees.

The music runs, and if I listen very carefully I can separate the instruments. They speak to her, my Bug, who does not hear them. Only I can.

The katydids:
Cheer up, cheer up, Bug. Cheap luck, Bug. Sit your seat, Bug. Sweet seat, seat you sit, Bug. Sitting sucking sweaty sweet silk, sighing, Bug. Sweet sullen suffering Bug, sitting swept by swift Swains Creek. Creak your seat, Bug. Swing, swivel, swoop, sway. Switch, Bug, itch, Bug, twitch, Bug, in this tweeting twangling twinkling twilight!

The bullfrogs:
Bug, O come! Bug, a crumb! Drug a mug a some scummy

jug a rum! Hump a stumpy rump! Thrum, you smug dumb Bug! Shrug your chummy bumps! Jump the rug's numb lumps! Bug, Bug, O Bug, *become!* Hum, Bug, hum with your gums, you sluggish bummy Bug! O Bug, O Bug, O hugging, tugging, thumping Bug so mum!

The crickets and cicadas, in chorus:
    Were you to stir your blurry fur and purr, O Bug, I would demur to slur you. Such verse is worse than Satan's curse, but terse as all the universe. Disgust you must such lusty crust, and fussed, and cussed me for it, yet still I trust you will be just, and never bust me for it. Enough rebuff will make me gruff, and puff my cheeks in stuffy huff.
    Sick. sick. sicksicksicksicksicksick.
    Cheap. cheap. cheapcheapcheapcheap dirt-cheap
    Cheer up. cheer up. cheerupcheerupcheerup chirp chirp
    Wish. wish. wishwishwish
    crick critic critter crotch
    O Bug

"Tell me a story."
"Sure, Dawny, but first I have to go out back."
She rises. The screen door WRIRRRAARAANGS. She walks through her sitting room, through her bedroom. There is a faint distant wrirraanngg of the screen on the back door. She walks up the path, she climbs few stone steps, she opens the door of the out-house. It is, for some reason, a two-seater, I don't know why. I doubt that she and Sonora have ever sat there together. I have never found them there together. (Yea, in my watchings I have even spied once there. From behind. From below.)
    Tearle Ingledew comes staggering down the road. A man of 48, he is "The Bad Ingledew," the one out of six brothers who has gone wrong. He has what they call a drinking problem, which means he is never sober. To me he is the Good Ingledew.
    He stops before the porch, spreads wide his arms, and in a thick gravelly voice declaims, "Behold, thou art fair, my love; behold, thou art fair; thou hast dove's eyes within thy locks: thy hair is as a flock of goats, that appear from mount Gilead. Thy teeth are like a flock of sheep that are even shorn, which come up from the washing; whereof every one bear twins, and none is barren among them. Thy lips are like a thread of scarlet, and thy

201

speech is comely: thy temples are like a piece of pomegranate within thy locks. Thy neck is like the tower of David builded for an armoury, whereon there hang a thousand bucklers, all shields of mighty men. Thy two breasts are like—"

I interrupt him, "She's not here just now."

"Who's thet?" he says, dropping his arms and squinting in the dark. "Thet you, Dawny?"

"Yep."

He sits on the bottom step. "Whar's Lathe?"

"She's takin a pee."

"Oh." He puts his elbows on his knees and cradles his chin in his hands. "S'funny," he muses. Soon he rises up. "Wal," he says, "I jest drapped by to give her my love. I'm off up towards Right Prong, to see if Luther Chism's rotgut is done makin yet. Give her my love. You don't let them fool ye, Dawny, about them boogers. They aint no sech thing. I know."

He walks away.

Then—a moment later—what seems to be merely one among a million lightning bugs grows brighter and brighter, coming up the road. It is not a lightning bug but a flashlight. The light comes nearer; soon I can make out the arm holding it and then the figure of a man attached to the arm. The flashlight swings upward and plays for a moment upon the center of the sign attached to Latha's store:

POST OFF
STAY MOR
ARK.

Then the flashlight beam swings along the porch until it comes to rest on me. I raise my arms to shield my face from the glare. I cannot make out the figure behind the flashlight, but something in me senses that he is a stranger, and I am slightly frightened.

"Howdy there, sonny," his voice says, and it is unfamiliar but warm and friendly. "You must be Bob Cluley's boy ... or maybe his grandson."

"Nossir," I reply. "Bob Cluley don't live here no more. He sold out back in 1932."

"Do tell! Why, that was quite a ways back."

"Yessir."

"I notice they've moved the Post Office to here. Is the Ingledew Store gone?"

"Nossir, but it's not the post office no more."

"Who owns this place now?"

"Latha Bourne does."

Silence. Then in a very low voice, as if not talking directly to me at all, he says, "You don't mean it." Then he says, "You don't mean to tell me." Then he says, louder, but tripping on his words, "Are you . . . are you her boy?"

"Nossir. I live up the road at the next place."

"The Murrison place? Then you must be Frank's boy. You kind of favor him."

"He's just my uncle."

"I see. Latha Bourne . . . she don't have any children?"

"She aint married."

"I see. Well, tell me, son, where is she at, right now?"

"I thought she'd just gone to pee but I reckon she must be making hockey too."

He laughs and says, "My, you sure talk brash for such a little spadger." Then he seems to get rather nervous, and says, "I reckon she'll be coming back directly, then?"

"I reckon."

"Well, uh, tell me, is there anybody living on the Dill place?"

"The Dill place?"

"Yes, it's up beyond your Uncle Murrison's, first house on the right up beyond. . . . Or it used to be, anyway."

"You mean where that old blacksmith shop is?"

"That's the one. But it wasn't actually a blacksmith shop, but a wagonmaking shop."

"That house has been empty since that blacksmith died, twenty year or more ago."

"He wasn't a blacksmith. He was a wagonmaker. Well, I guess I'll just mosey up there and take a look around. See you later, sonny."

Quickly he walks away. Very quickly.

Scarcely are he and his flashlight out of sight when Latha returns from her errand of elimination. When she has seated herself again, I tell her,

"There was a man here."

"Who?"

"I don't know. He didn't tell me his name."

"What did he want?"

"Nothing. Just wanted to know who lived here now. I told him. Then he wanted to know if anybody was livin on the Dill *place, so when I said no he headed off in that direction, said he was just gonna look around up there."*

Latha stares in that direction. I detect a quickening of her breathing. *"What did he look like?"* she asks. I have never heard her voice quaver quite like that before.

"I couldn't much tell. He was on the other side of a flashlight. Sort of tall, I guess. Seemed like a nice man."

She is silent a long time.

Finally I have to remind her, you were going to tell me a story.

She comes back from her trance, and smiles, and reaches over and rumples my hair. *"Sure, Dawny,"* she says. Then she asks, *"Would you care to hear a strange tale about a dumb supper? Have you ever heard tell of a 'dumb supper'?"*

"Caint say that I have."

"Well," she says. *"Once upon a time, in a month of May long time ago, a bunch of girls who were just about ready to graduate from high school decided to set themselves a dumb supper, which is an old, old custom that must go all the way back to the days of yore in England."*

"The idea [she, like all others, pronounces this *"idee"*] *is that you take and set out a place at the dinner table, just like you were having company, except you don't set out any food. You put out the plate and the knife and fork and spoon, and the napkin. Then you turn the lamp down very low. A candle is even better. Then you wait. You stand behind the chair and wait to see what happens."*

As in all her tellings of ghost tales, she says these words very somberly, and makes a dramatic pause, and I feel the thrilling chill that makes her ghost stories so much fun.

"Well," she goes on, *"there were six of these girls, and they set out six places, and then the six of them stood behind the six chairs and waited, with only one candle to light the room. They waited and they waited. The idea is that if you wait long enough, the apparition—not a real ghost, Dawny, but a ghost- like image—the apparition of the man you will marry will appear and take his seat before you at the table."*

"Oh, of course it was all a lot of foolishness like all that superstitious going-on, but these girls believed in it, and anyway it would be a lot of fun. So they waited and they waited."

"Sometimes, if a girl was wishing very hard that a particular boy would appear, somebody she was crazy wild about, then

she might get hysterical and really believe that he had come!
Imagine that, Dawny. But the other girls would just laugh at
her."

"Anyway, these girls waited and waited, but of course
nothing happened. Some of them closed their eyes and
mumbled magic words, and some of them prayed, but no boys
showed up, and no apparitions of boys showed up. Until
finally . . ."

I suspend my breathing. It is as near to approaching an
orgasm as a five-year-old boy could ever get.

"Until finally there was this one particular girl who was
wishing very, very hard, and she opened her eyes, and there
coming into the room was a boy! With his hat pulled down over
his eyes, he came right on over to her chair and sat down in it!
And then in the candlelight she saw who it was! It wasn't the
boy she was wishing for at all! It was another boy, the one she
had already turned down twice when he asked for her hand!

"And then she fainted dead away."

I wait. "Well," I say. "Then what happened?"

"Well, after they got her revived, with smelling salts and cold
compresses, one of the girls explained it all to her. Somehow
that boy had found out about the dumb supper. The boys
weren't supposed to know, but somehow he had found out.
And came on purpose. The other girls had thrown him out of
the house, after this poor girl fainted, and told him he ought to
be ashamed of himself. And maybe he was."

"Well," I ask, "did she ever marry him?"

"No."

"Did she ever marry the other one, the one she was wishing
for?"

"No."

"That other one, the one she was wishing for, his name was
Raymond, wasn't it?"

Latha makes a little gasp, and then exclaims, "Why, Dawny, I
didn't know you knew about that!"

"What was the name of the one who came to the dumb
supper?"

She does not answer.

I leave her alone, but I cannot leave her alone for long.
"Latha," I say, sweetly as I can, "what was the name of the one
who came?"

"Won't tell you," she says, and her voice is the voice of a
child.

"Please tell me," I beg.

"No," she says. "You'll have bad dreams, and your Aunt Rosie will come down here and give me a talking-to again for telling you ghost stories."

"I will have bad dreams anyway," I declare.

"No."

"Please."

"No. I won't."

"Pretty please, with sugar and cream on it."

"No. Hush. You stop asking me."

"Was it Tull Ingledew?"

"Law, no!" she laughs. "Back then he didn't even know I existed."

"Was it Doc Swain?"

"He was too old, and besides, he had a wife back at that time."

"Then who was it? Was it anybody I know?"

"No."

"Please, please tell me."

"No."

"If you don't tell me, I'm going to go away and never come back, and I'll never ever love you anymore."

She laughs again. "Or, if not that, you'd be nagging me about it for the rest of my days, wouldn't you?"

"I just might," I say fiercely.

"All right," she says. "His name was Dill. Every Dill. Isn't that a queer name? It wasn't Avery, but Every. He was William Dill's boy, old Billy Dill who used to make wagons."

I break out in a rash of goose bumps. "What . . . whatever . . . what did ever . . . become of him?"

"Nobody knows, child."

"Maybe . . ." I say, pointing up the road toward the Dill place.

"Yes, Dawny, that's what I've been wondering about too."

I suddenly ask, "Can I sleep with you tonight?"

"Whatever for?" she asks, with a big smile.

"To protect you."

She starts to laugh but decides it might hurt my feelings, which it would've. Instead she says, "Your Aunt Rosie wouldn't allow it."

"Aw, sure she would. She don't care where I sleep."

"But I don't have any spare beds, except that one that Sonora sleeps in."

"Why caint I just sleep in your bed?"

She laughs. "My, my," she says. "I haven't ever slept with anybody in my bed."

"Never?"

"Never not all night."

"Well," I promise,"I won't bother you."

She laughs a long gay lilting laugh. "You'd have to let your Aunt Rosie know where you are, and I bet she wouldn't want you spending the night down here."

I stand up. "I'll be right back, fast as I can."

"Good night, Dawny," she says, and waves. "See you in the morning."

"I will be right back," I say.

I run all the way home, which isn't far.

I burst in upon Aunt Murrison, who is reading her Bible by coal-oil light. I have always been a good liar, even then. I tell her that a whole bunch of kids are having a bunking party at Latha's store; they've laid out a lot of pallets and are going to have a real jamboree of ghost-story telling and I will just die of heartbreak if I can't join in.

"Which kids?" she says, eyeing me with leaden lids.

"Well, there's Larry Duckworth, and Vann and Tommy Dismore, and Jack and Tracy and Billy Bob Ingledew, and—"

"I bet them kids don't want a little squirt like you hangin around."

"But Sammy Coe's there too, and I'm older'n him!"

"How come y'all are havin yore bunkin party at Latha's place?"

"Well, she's treatin us to free soda pop."

"Hmm," says Aunt Murrison. She mutters, "That crazy gal . . ." Then she says to me, "Well, you behave yourself, you hear me? Be a good boy and don't bother them other kids."

"Yes ma'am!" I cry, and rushing out, holler back, "See you in the mornin!"

So that is how I came to spend the night with my beloved Bug.

[There remains just another short piece of bug business, and then I am done with these over-long prefatory hemmings and hawings. Another image symbolically related to lightning bugs: that of a book of matches being struck, one by one. It happened like this: with my beard and my pipe and my Harris tweed jacket I was fool enough to think that I could pass for a visiting psychiatrist, but the Keeper of Records at the Arkansas State Hospital said to me politely, "It isn't that we are challenging your authority, Doctor, but our regulations require that we cannot give you access to our records unless we see something in the way of credentials, perhaps only your A.A.P.P. membership card . . ." So I went away and bought a doctor's white smock and came back in the middle of the night and snapped impatiently at the night clerk on duty, "The file on Latha Ann Bourne, please. B-O-U-R-N-E. 1922–25." But the night clerk looked at me and said, albeit pleasantly enough, "Which ward are you from, Doctor? I don't recall seeing you around before. But I suppose you're new. Perhaps your name is on my list here, let's see . . ." One would think that my nerve, which has never been distinguished for its intrepidity, would have failed at this point. But I was extraordinarily dedicated. I went upstairs and walked the corridors and read the names on the doors of doctor's offices, picking one at random. Then I went over to Ward A and read the list of patients, picking one at random. Then I went to a phone booth and called that same night clerk in the Records Office and said, disguising my voice, "This is Doctor Reuben. Please, would you very quickly get the file on Wilson Olmstead and bring it up and slip it under the door of my office? Thank you so much." Then I quickly returned to the Records Office. The clerk was gone. But he had locked the strong wire gate to the Records Room. There was, however, a small opening at chest-level for the purpose of passing documents through, and I managed to squeeze through this. I did not dare turn on a light. I used up three matches finding the 1920's section, and two more matches locating the B's, and one more finding Latha's file. Then I sat on the floor with it in my lap, and opened it, and used up the rest of my matches quickly reading it. It was a thick sheaf of papers, sandwiched between an Admission slip which said, "Committed, under protest, May 12, 1922, by married sister, Mrs. Vaughn Twichell," and a small piece of paper which summarily remarked, "Escaped E Ward, method unknown, March 23, 1925." Several times I burned my fingers because I was so absorbed with what I was reading that I did not watch the match closely. If there is no draft, a book match can be made to burn for a maximum of 36 seconds. This means that I had a total reading time of only about 7 minutes 45 seconds. But I am a relatively fast reader. And the glow of those matches, so help me, was quite uncannily akin to the pulsing flashes of a lightning bug.]

"Dawny, close your eyes."

"Why?"

"You don't want to watch me undressing, do you?"

"But it's pitch dark, I caint see you noway."

"'Close your eyes."

"Okay."

Why is it, I wonder, that all those sounds of the summer night are louder indoors, when you're lying in bed, than they are outdoors, when you're sitting on the porch?

"Well. Now you can open your eyes. But don't look at me."

"Why caint I look at you?"

"Because it's so hot and we'd have to pull the covers up because I don't have anything on."

"You mean you're nekkid?" I begin to turn my head.

Her hand presses the side of my face. "Don't look."

"But it's so dark I caint see nuthin noway."

"Maybe you can. I can see you."

"What's wrong with lookin at you? I like to look at you."

"But I don't have anything on."

"Who cares?"

It is very hot, not a night for covers at all, not even a sheet. I look down at myself, at my undershirt, at my shorts. The faintest breeze comes through the window screen.

"Do you sleep nekkid all the time?"

"Just in the summertime."

"I never knew of anybody sleepin stark nekkid."

"Most people don't."

"I reckon it's a awful lot cooler, that way."

"Oh, it is."

"Can I sleep nekkid too?"

"Dawny, I wish you wouldn't say 'nekkid.' It makes it sound bad."

"Okay, can I sleep undressed too?"

She does not answer for a while. Then she laughs a little and says, "Dawny, you're commencing to make me nervous. If you ever told anybody, your Aunt Rosie or anybody, that me and you slept together, let alone without our clothes, do you know they would cover me with hot tar and feathers and ride me out of town on a rail!"

"Aw, Latha! Do you honestly think I would ever tell anybody? I aint ever gon tell anybody anything about me'n you."

"Maybe," she says, "maybe I better get a quilt and fix you a pallet on the floor in the other room."

I begin to cry.

"Oh, shush, Dawny, a big boy like you!" she coos. "Lie still, and shush."

I keep crying.

She reaches over and grabs me by the undershirt, and at first I think she's going to fling me clean out of the bed, but she just tugs my undershirt over my head, and then pulls my shorts down and off my feet.

"There!" she says. "Now shush."

I shush.

It is hard, from here, to see through the window and watch any lightning bugs. But I don't care. I have my own Bug beside me.

"Close your eyes and go to sleep."

"I'm not much sleepy. Are you?"

"Not much, I guess."

"Tell me a story."

"All right."

She tells me, not just one ghost story, but several, many. Some of these I have heard her tell before, but they are good ones, and the new ones which I have not heard before are very good indeed. They thrill me, they hold me, they seize me, they jolt me, they drain me. It is nearly as good as if I were full-grown and could mount her and ride her, over and over, again and again, till the last drop of my seed were draught off. Often, in the grip of a mighty story's climax, I have to squeeze her hand.

She likes her own stories too, and gets carried off by them, which is why she is such a good teller . . . and which is why she has not noticed that I am staring at her. The moon has shifted from behind a tree, and some of its light comes into the room. She lies staring at the ceiling as she talks, one of her hands gripped by mine, the other hand resting upon her white stomach. All creation does not know a sight lovelier than her breasts. How does Tull Ingledew say it? Yes: "Thy two breasts are like two young roes that are twins, which feed among the lillies." I do not know what a roe is, but it has a lovely sound.

210

"Latha," I say, "I love you."

She turns, and does not seem to mind that I am staring at her, and that there is enough light for us to see one another. "Oh, Dawny," she says. Then she reaches out her hand and rumples my hair and says, "I love you too, and if you were a growed-up man I would marry you right this minute." She pulls me to her and squeezes me and then puts me back where I was. "Now let's try to get some sleep."

We try to get some sleep, but we are both listening.

We listen for a knock, or for footsteps on the porch.

The night passes on. The symphony of the bugs and frogs never stops. The night cools.

Footsteps. My heart thunders. But it is not my heart, it is Latha's. I realize I am in her arms, my ear against her chest.

A voice. A girl's. It is Snory, coming home. Her screen door opens very slowly in a very slow WRIRRAANG, and light footsteps move across a floor, and to a room. She bumps against a table or something.

Then it is silent again, and stays silent a long time.

By and by I ask Latha in a whisper, "Do you think that it might really be him up there? Do you think it's really Every Dill?"

"Oh, I know it," she says, and there is no fear nor alarm nor anxiety of any sort in her voice, but almost a kind of thrilled anticipation. "I know it is."

We sleep.

This material originally appeared in Lightning Bug (New York: Delacorte Press, 1970) and is reprinted with permission of the author.

STORYTELLER

Lewis Nordan

IT WAS WILEY HEARD talking and cooling his coffee at the same time. "You heard about all them grain elevators blowing up in Kansas, didn't you?" Wiley was a short, wiry one-legged man with a red face and white eyebrows. He was retired head coach of the local football team. He stopped blowing across his coffee and took a long, slurping pull, then held up the heavy cup, like evidence, so everybody could see. One or two of those standing around moved in closer to the marble counter and were careful not to overturn a spittoon. They poured cups for themselves and lay their change on the cash register. "See this?" he said. "It's the best cup of coffee in the entire state of Arkansas. Right here in Hassell's Blank Store. Used to be called Hassell's Drug Store, long time ago. Back before any you boys would remember." They tried not to notice Coach Wiley pour a nip of Early Times into his coffee from a flat bottle he slipped out of his jacket pocket. "Yessir," he said, "Gene Hassell sold the wrong drugs to the wrong man. Two men, in fact. Federal agents pretending to work on a truck for two days across the street, out yonder by the railroad tracks, before they come in for pills. On account of which old Gene's pharmacy license got taken away. And so did Gene, come to think of it, down to the Cummins penitentiary. Couldn't get him in Atlanta. It was all full up that year, I think was the trouble. His wife, poor thing, Miss Eva, I swan. She just painted out the word *Drug* on the sign and held a shotgun up under her chin, bless her time. It was that old twelve-gauge of Gene's that kicked so bad, real old gun, belonged to his daddy and ejected shells out the bottom. Remington, I think it was. She pulled the trigger and shot off her face. The whole damn thing from the bottom up, jaw, teeth, nose, and eyes, and broke both her eardrums. Terrible sight to see, even after the skin grafts. No face at all. Can't see, hear, smell, or taste, just keep her alive in a nursing home down in Arkadelphia, feeding her through tubes, and not one pellet touched her brain. It's a sad case, boys. It would break your heart. We been calling it Hassell's Blank Store ever since, and him still in jail, I guess, or dead, but you say you did hear about them grain elevators, didn't you?"

Somebody said he had. Everybody else agreed.

"I know you did," said the coach. "You heard about it on the Walter Cronkite Show, didn't you? They had it on the TV every night for a month, seem like. But I bet you forty dollars you didn't hear what happened the other day over in El Dorado, did you? Just outside El Dorado, I ought to say, over close to Smackover. A dog food factory blew up. That's about like El Dorado, ain't it? Ain't nowhere but El Dorado, and maybe parts of north Mississippi, they going to blow up a dog food factory. But you never will hear that one on the Walter Cronkite Show, nayo-siree, and don't need to. The longer they can keep El Dorado, Arkansas, off the national news, or Smackover either one, the better for everybody, is what I say. Hound Dog dog food factory—and three men are missing, so they tell me. Might of been mule skinners, mightn't they? I think they was, in fact. If any you boys are looking for work they going to need somebody to skin them miserable old horses before they can put them in a can. Over this side of El Dorado actually, up close to Smackover. But that was years ago Gene Hassell went to jail. You boys wouldn't remember him, years ago. Hell, he may not be dead now, all I know. Probably is though. Probably is dead now he can't drink no more of that paregoric. He probably died his second day off that paregoric, didn't he? He'd been drinking it for twenty years. He's been constipated that long. He probably didn't know what to think, did he, down there in Cummins behind them bars, or out on that hot scrabble farm chopping him some prison cotton, when he felt that first urge to go to the bathroom. Hell, he probably died right off, didn't he? Didn't even have to call the dispensary. He probably got him a shit fit and the blind staggers and keeled over with his eyes rolled up. His old crazy paregoric eyes probably looked like the rolled up window shades of Miss Dee's whorehouse on Sunday morning, he was so happy. But not Miss Eva, that's his wife, she's not dead. She's still over to Arkadelphia at the Wee Care Nursing Home, got a married daughter out in California, or is it granddaughter, pays the bills. That little red brick building with the neon sign saying Wee Care out on the old airport road, real nice place, and expensive too. But Jerry Rich down in Prescott, out beyond Prescott really, just this side of Delight, he's the one owns this place now, Hassell's Blank Store. He's owned it for years. Poor old woman had to sell out right away, of course, after she lost so much face here in town trying to kill herself, and her husband in the pokey. The daughter had to sell, I mean. And no face at all, Miss Eva, and never did have much personality to speak of. But old Jerry, he doesn't get up here much any more, long as there's a quail in them cornfields and one old sorry dog in the pen. Not even to change the name on the front of the store. Painting out Gene's name would be a piss-pore way to remember a good man, though now wouldn't it? Lord, but his wife was a boring woman, even back when she had a face. It was three of them missing, though, three skinners, all of them white men, I believe it was, I'm not real sure about that. Dog food factory over in El Dorado, outside El Dorado really, out close to Smackover, Hound Dog dog food factory."

Wiley was still talking. "They used to feed dog food to circus animals. Sounds awful, don't it? But it's true. It'd make them crazy, too. It'd make a trained beast turn on his master, so I hear. Nothing to be done about a bitch elephant once they turn on their keeper. Bull elephant's a different story, trustworthiest old wrinkled buggers you ever want to meet, but not a bitch, you can't trust one with a nickle change once she gets sour on life, might as well save yourself the trouble."

"Why's that, Coach Wiley?" The coffee drinkers turned and looked. It was Hydro, a gawky young man with a broom and a large head.

"Nobody knows," said the coach, "and don't ask no more questions, Hydro. Godamighty. You get on done with that sweeping before you start asking so many questions. But it happened one time over in Pocahontas. One two y'all might be old enough to remember it. Your daddies'd be old enough. Some little off-brand circus or other. Clyde Beatty or something. Naw, not even that good. They had two old scrawny lions that hollered half the night they was so hungry from eating that dried dog food they give them. Probably Hound Dog dog food, when they was looking for meat, like that place blew up over past El Dorado, except that factory wasn't there till ten years ago, so it must have been some other brand the lions had to eat, but nobody ought to feed dog food to a lion and get away with it. King Jesus jump down. It'd take a worthless sumbitch to do that, now wouldn't it? Worthless as a whistle on a plow, as my poor old dead daddy used to say. Daddy he was a funny little quiet man with rusty hair and deep eyes. Housepainter and paperhanger, and a good one too, and a handful of elephants with their nose up each other's ass like a parade and some scrawny old woman in a little white dress and bleached-out hair riding on top of the first elephant, when this baggy old gray African elephant went kind of crazy. *Commercial-Appeal* said she was in heat and real nervous. That's when they dangerous. Some old boy name of Orwell, from West Memphis or Forrest City or somewhere, was quoted as saying that was right. He claimed to know all about elephants, though I can't say I ever knew a family of Arkansas Orwells. Plenty of them in Mississippi, of course, Delta people, but none to my memory in Arkansas. Unless, of course, they come here since the World War, but I think she was just sick of Pocahontas and circus food. That'd be me. Best thing ever happened to Pocahontas was that tornado in 1957, tore down half the town. They just about due another one, if you want my personal opinion. Didn't have many teeth, my daddy, and had fainting spells on top of that, because you notice she didn't bother to pick out her own trainer to step on. That'd be too easy. She had to bring down all hell and her left front foot on another African, one of her own people, you might say. She had to step on some little local boy hired on as a handler. Plez Moore's grandson is who it was, in case some y'all are old enough to remember Plez. Course my daddy always did love his whiskey and had a heart enlarged up the size of a basketball, but the fainting spells commenced long before that come to pass, who I always liked, Plez I'm talking about, and hated to see anything bad come to him in spite of not especially blaming the elephant and never could straighten up his back, Plez, on account of getting syphilis when he was just a boy, stepped right on that poor little child and flattened him out like one them cartoon pictures when a steamroller runs over somebody. He looked like a pitiful little black shadow some child lost. But you couldn't blame the elephant, I couldn't, having to live cooped up in Pocahontas all week and that terrible sawed-off circus. It wouldn't do, though, but they had to kill the elephant, and you can see their point, especially if that Orwell boy from West Memphis knew what he's talking about, though I still think he was from somewhere over in Mississippi.

"Anyhow, that's what the mayor and aldermen said, got to destroy the elephant. They was agreed with by the Colored Ministers Association, which has now got some other name and is joined up with the NAACP. They was quickly agreed with, I might add, which was the first and last time the Pocahontas town officials and the colored ministers ever agreed on anything, except maybe last year when Horace Mayhan—you remember him playing football right here in town and always stunk real bad, before old man Mayhan moved them all to Pocahontas where they'd belonged all along and fit in so good with the paper mill—last year when old Horace won a free trip, so to speak, to Washington, D.C. He had to testify before a senate subcommittee on the subject of who cut them eyeholes into the sheets the FBI found in the trunk of Horace's car, that cream-colored Mustang with the rusted top and STP stickers on the front bumper. That boy gave new meaning to the word *white-trash*, not to mention who sawed the stocks and barrels off all his shotguns and enough dynamite to provide every man, woman, and child in Arkansas fish dinner every night for a week. But the trouble was, of course, that nobody in Pocahontas had a gun big enough to kill an elephant, not even a hungry old scrawny elephant that probably needed killing."

"Shoot him in the eye." The words were totally unexpected, but the minute they were in the air everybody knew it was Hydro again and that he was in trouble. He had forgotten that the coach told him to stay quiet. It was obvious from his enormous face that he thought he had made a good suggestion. The coach stopped talking and looked at him. Everybody else looked at the floor and tried not to breathe. They wanted to become invisible. "Hyrdo, my man," Coach Wiley said, with a chill in his voice that galvanized every gaze upon the floor, "I always kind of liked you, boy. And I know you got your own problems. But listen here. Don't you never interrupt me again. Not now, and not never. Not till you get smart enough to know a whole hell of a lot more about elephants than shoot him in the eye."

"Or," said a voice with an unnatural cherriness, "maybe you could just shoot him up the butt." It was Hydro again, and he had missed the fury underlying the coach's tone. If any of those standing around the coach in the Blank Store had not been too embarrassed to think of it, they might have hated Hydro, and themselves, and they might have hated God for making Hydro so damn dumb. Nobody thought of it. Nobody knew why they depended on Wiley Heard's approval, and dreaded his disapproval. "It's bound to bust something loose up in there," Hydro said, still pleased as he could be to help.

The coach became more deliberate. For everybody but Hydro, breathing was out of the question. Some of this began to dawn on Hydro.

"Hydro," said Coach Wiley Heard, "I am going to say this one more time. Now, boy, I mean for you to listen. Are you listening?" There was no need for Hydro to answer. He had caught on now. "Shoot him in the eye and shoot him up the butt will not do. Not to interrupt me telling a story, nawsir. And neither will anything else do, to interrupt me telling a story. Are you listening, Hydro? Not nothing that you or anybody else that's going to come into Hassell's Blank Store is likely to think up is going to do to interrupt me. So just forget about interrupting me, boy. At any time, or for any reason whatsoever, with shoot him in the eye or shoot him up the butt or anything else. Now do you understand what I am saying?"

Hydro was quiet and miserable. He said, "Yessir," in a tiny whispery voice. He recognized his chastisement. The act of breathing started up again. Throats got cleared, and feet were shifted. Some of the little crowd looked up.

When the coach finally spoke again, it was not to them, not at first, not exactly. His voice was low and deep and coarse

217

and gravelly, and there was a snort of a humorless laugh behind it. "Shoot him up the butt," they heard him say, almost soundless, and they heard the low, snorting laugh. A few of them laughed a little too; they tried it anyway, the laughter, not loud and not self-confident, and when they heard it, they found no pleasure in its sound. For a few more seconds he let the silence continue. He sweetened his coffee again with Early Times, and they made sure they didn't notice.

When he began again, the tone of his story was immeasurably darker. There were no more self-interruptions, there was no more marshaling of irrelevant detail. The story had become deadly serious and even most of the errors of grammar had disappeared from his speech. If the story were told again, or if it had been told without Hydro's interruption, each person in the store could have imagined it as wonderfully comic, the dark, laughing comedy that underlay every tale he told. But it was not comic now. The elephant he said, would have to be killed. It would have to be killed by hanging. Some let out sounds that might have passed for laughs, but none of them were proud to have done so.

"By now the elephant was quiet," he said. "I saw her led to town by her trainer, a dirty man and sad-faced. The bleached-haired woman was with them, too, wearing a maroon suit and low-heeled shoes, the one who rode the elephant in the parade. The railroad crane and log-chain were on a flat car. The chain was made into a noose and put around its neck. The giant gears started creaking, the crane was lifting. I remember a blind fiddler was in the crowd and a little Indian boy with blue short pants and no shirt high up on the top of a locomotive. The elephant's feet were like the feet of a great turtle. The hind feet brushed the air a scant inch above the cinders in the station yard. When she was up, hanging there, choking, she lifted the wrinkled old trunk straight up and trumpeted one time, one blast to heaven, before she was choked dead. Her back feet, her gray old big turtle feet, were just an inch above the cinders, a little inch."

Those who listened stood, silent, and held their coffee cups without drinking. One man, whose son stood beside him, lay an unconscious hand on the boy's arm and pulled him a little closer to his side. No one knew what to say, or do. For a moment, during the silence, they forgot that Coach

Wiley Heard was in charge, in control of the pause. He allowed a few more seconds to pass. They thought of the beast's trumpeting. They did not imagine, even for a second, that the coach's story might be untrue, that he might have made it all up, or adapted it from an older tale, and now maybe even believed it was all true, that it had all really happened on a certain day, to a certain people with bleached hair or sad faces or blind eyes or Indian blood, or any other hair and face and eyes and blood he chose to give them, and that it all happened in a station yard in eastern Arkansas, in a town called Pocahontas. If disbelief crept in, it came like a welcome brother into their company. They poured it a cup of coffee and showed it the sugar bowl and treated it like a friend too familiar to notice. They thought only of the gray feet and the cinders, the little inch between.

Then it was over. The coach released them. With a sudden, unexpected cheeriness, and maybe even a wink, he said, "You not going to forget what I told you, now are you, Hydro?"

"No sir," Hydro said, certain he would not, but still a little uncertain how to act. The coffee drinkers were able to love Hydro again, and pity him and feel superior to him. He shifted his broom and looked at its bristles. Everybody felt confident and happy. Everybody smiled at Hydro's innocence and at his need for forgiveness.

"Shoot him up the butt!" the coach roared suddenly, merry and hilarious and slapping his good leg. "Shoot him up the butt! Great godamighty!" Now they could laugh. They did laugh, uproarious and long. The coach slapped Hydro on the back and called him son and hugged him roughly against him and shook him by the shoulders. "Shoot him up the butt!" he said again. "Got damn, Hydro, I'm going to have to tell that one on you, now ain't I!"

When the laughter was over and the coach had wiped a tear from each eye with a clean handkerchief, he spoke to Hydro in a voice a little different from the one they had been listening to for most of the day. He said, "Let me tell you about my daddy, son. You'd of liked him. He had to walk on crutches all one winter, he had tonsilitis so bad." They knew now that they could stay and hear this story if they wished, but they knew also that it would not be told to them. They envied Hydro. They wished they were Hydro. They wished they were holding his broom and feeling the coach's warm, alcoholic breath on their faces. "Daddy always smelled like turpentine and Fitch's shampoo," they heard the coach say, as if from a distance. "It's the only place I ever smelled the two in combination. It breaks my heart to remember." There was a pause, a silence of a few seconds. "He carried this little nickel pistol with him," the coach said, thoughtful. "I'll show it to you sometime. A little nickel pistol, with walnut handlegrips."

Hydro was happy. Everybody could see that. There was no reason for anybody else to hang around, though. They eased out by ones and twos.

This story originally appeared in Harper's *magazine and is reprinted with permission of the publisher.*

About the Editors

WILLIAM McDOWELL BAKER, after careers in teaching and bookselling, lives in his hometown of Malvern, Arkansas. His essays on Arkansas history have appeared in *Arkansas Libraries*, *Grapevine*, the *Arkansas Gazette* and a book on the governors of Arkansas.

ETHEL C. SIMPSON holds a Ph.D. in Comparative Literature and works with Arkansas collections in the Special Collections Department of the University of Arkansas Library. She has written numerous articles on Arkansas literature and has edited two books in Arkansas studies.